Swimming at Sunset

Dennis J. Gayle

Swimming at Sunset

Printed in the United States of America.

Brilliant Books Literary
137 Forest Park Lane Thomasville
North Carolina 27360 USA

Chapter One

…"We are such things as dreams are made on and
our little life is rounded with a sleep…"
Prospero, in William Shakespeare's The Tempest

Many years later, their descendants remembered and recounted the stories of their families and their first encounters, the occasionally improbable outcomes of the choices they made, and the echoes that subsequently resonated in their lives. At one level, or perhaps layer, of these tales as they begin, David Armstrong and Alessia Amato are working the teller counters in the Marylebone Village, London, England, with long lines of bank customers in heavy, often polyester overcoats, collars usually turned up against this chilly grey Monday morning in December 2009. Light snow dusts the sidewalks outside. The cashiers can easily read currency notes and vouchers in the bank's bright fluorescent lights. He clenches his jaw, tensing from time to time, sitting upright, impeccably dressed in a charcoal-grey suit, a permanently pressed white shirt, and a blue tie with wavy yellow stripes, as he greets each client politely. She smiles shyly at her own patrons, occasionally tossing her long brunette hair, and usually completes transactions meticulously and quickly – but sometimes takes a document to the back office for a manager's signature, her yellow pleated skirt flaring as she walks, showcasing her long honey-colored legs and beige Christian Louboutin shoes. He seems to visit the back office less often. There is a low, but constant buzz of conversation. Each new teller feels ill at ease, on this first day on the job, but also exhilarated by the opportunity to excel in a just encountered environment.

However, where he has a conscious need to exude confidence, she remains more tentative, anxious to avoid mistakes, and self-conscious concerning her accent. On occasion, when an inattentive or limping visitor moves less rapidly, or hesitates to answer a question, one glances at the other, as they both compete to demonstrate efficiency, while extending somewhat reticent gestures of support.

Now and then, David Armstrong mutters well-intentioned, if infrequently accurate, advice to Alessia Amato, who often smiles and nods, evidently, without paying much attention to his *sotto voce* comments. She wonders why her tall, black coworker, who is also a trainee, keeps trying to tell her how to do her job, instead of attending to his own customers. Even so, the morning goes by quickly.

In another approach to the beginning of these stories, a nine-year old Alessia in Reggio Calabria, southern Italy, is standing, eyes wide with fear, outside of her house near the Via Trapezolli Sud, in pink pajamas and a light white robe, on a moonlit night, with her father, mother, and two older brothers. It is cold. They are looking apprehensively at the house next door, which is vividly lit up by flames, and smell acrid smoke, especially when the wind blows towards them. Three firemen from a single firetruck are attempting to prevent the spread of the now roaring blaze, which illuminates the neighborhood, drawing other people out in the street. "*Che terribile inferno*!" cried a distraught neighbor standing nearby, as an elderly woman suddenly rushed from the burning house, screaming, all her clothing on fire, then fell to the street, rolling and screaming in a temporarily unsuccessful effort to extinguish the flames. The girl's father shakes his head, and her mother holds her daughter's little hand even more tightly. The fire seems to blaze ever brighter for an interminable time, as they all stare.

Her brothers are fascinated, drawing closer to the blazing house, despite the sparks flying. It appears to be a losing battle against the noxious, engulfing blaze, and the neighbors increasingly mutter that the raging fire might spread – but then, another fire engine finally arrives, three more firefighters leap out energetically and connect their unfolding black hose to a new fire hydrant, which doesn't seem to open, for a few moments – then as it suddenly does, they train another powerful stream of water on the fire, first flooding the perimeter, then the remnants of ground floor rooms, and slowly, the flames are contained, then put out. As the sky lightens with streaks of pink and hints of daylight, a scene of focused desolation stuns the eye. Residents who can return home do so, eyes somber and thoughtful. While being led away, the little girl keeps looking back.

These stories also begin with a shift in scene to a bright spring day in London, with yellow daffodils blooming on the sidewalks, and black taxicabs, other cars and buses moving in stops and starts through traffic. A dark-brown, thin, and tall twelve-year-old David, with a partially unzipped, white cardigan is walking slowly through a small, crowded Tesco Supermarket in Brixton, accompanied by two shorter friends, each with a green plastic, hand-held shopping basket. When the baskets are filled with canned food, bread, milk, fruit juices, nuts, and flour, they pause near the wines as if looking forward to the time when legal purchases would be practicable for them, then head towards the line waiting for the harried cashier, where the boys remain for a few minutes – and suddenly run out the door, fleeing with their baskets. The overweight, red-faced supermarket manager chases them, shouting angrily "*stop, stop*!" then winded, as they disappear down a nearby side street, calls the police, providing rough descriptions of the boys, who will shelter for far too long in a rather unwilling neighbor's basement, increasingly wishing that they had never robbed the store, even while boasting of their success in escaping.

Their parents take turns to visit, berating them bitterly, but nevertheless, eventually transfer the provisions to their duffel bags or knapsacks, taking them home. For the next few days, police constables, having taken a while to arrive on the scene when called, systematically check each home in the vicinity for the boys, dutifully taking notes on each occasion, without encountering anyone indicating that he or she knows any of them, or can even see clearly, when shown grainy digital photos from the store's cameras. The boys, now sometimes bored, mainly munch nuts and drink orange juice, while hiding, listening anxiously for footsteps on the stairs. Days later, they each return to their homes and families, somewhat chastened. Memories of that time faded only slowly. It was many months afterwards before any of these boys entered such a supermarket again.

Daniel Armstrong and Alessia Amato first encountered each other for lunch in a crowded local Pret-À-Porter. When he ordered a prawn mayonnaise sandwich, she hesitated, then did the same, and they ended up sharing a table, talking about work on the counter. "Where does that accent come from?" he asked. She told him that her hometown of Reggio di Calabria was in southern Italy, near Sicily, but that she had studied in Milan, misunderstanding the persisting puzzlement in his eyes. In turn, she inquired about the scar on his left cheek. "Did you get into a fierce fight in your home island? You sound somewhat Jamaican, and I've heard that such people can be hot-tempered, if excellent in sports," Alessia remarked almost flippantly. In turn. David explained that one day, he either slipped or was pushed and fell in kindergarten school, and that while both his parents were Jamaican natives, he was born in Brixton, in London. He had never seen that Caribbean island that they often talked about wistfully, slipping into an island patois that he could not quite emulate, before his father left. "Someday, I would love to visit Jamaica to see the wide sandy beaches and the blue mountains people talk about." she said pensively. David smiled. "My mother keeps saying that we should all go back for a visit someday - but from what I keep hearing, you might find the reggae music parties, the spicy jerk food, and the Blue Mountain coffee more interesting, since one can find beaches and mountains in so many locations. By the way, neither of my parents was quickly angered." Alessia responded that she enjoyed coffee but had no idea what he meant by reggae parties or jerk food, adding that he might also find some of her local Calabrian dishes such as *pasta arrabbiata* or *ciambotta* - eggplant stew - delicious.

A minute later, Alessia tossed her head, saying that anyway, she was looking forward to travel to many parts of the world, and to experience different cultures, once she'd saved enough money for vacations in locations such as Egypt and India. She emphasized the point with her slender hands. David smiled broadly, in a sweeping rejoinder: "Me too! I would like to visit places such as Robbins Island where Nelson Mandela was imprisoned in South Africa, and the Great Zimbabwe Ruins, as well as the cave paintings at the Matopos Hills in Zimbabwe. Then again, I've always wanted to see Mafia members in your home region, preferably at a safe distance - but you'll probably say you've never come across any." David and Alessia laughed, beginning to enjoy each other. The other restaurant patrons seemed to melt away into the background. After remarking her parents were talking about coming to London to visit, she asked where his father was. David deflected her question about his father, while admiring her elegant gold earrings. By the time they returned to work, they were more relaxed in talking with each other at the counter. For the first time since meeting, they shook hands, somewhat lingeringly, and wished each other "*good evening*," when leaving work for the day, while looking directly at each other. He was struck by her bright, grey eyes, the lightly tanned color of her hands, with such long, delicate fingers, and carried away with him the lingering scent of her recognizable Chanel 5 perfume.

During an eventually agreed Saturday afternoon lunch in Hyde Park, David and Alessia picnicked on the grass under an expansive elm tree, near the sparkling Serpentine lake, and discussed the challenges of dealing with some of their bank's customers, especially the older and evidently often poorer ones, who were always filling out vouchers improperly. The sun shimmered through tree leaves, and sparkled on the nearby Serpentine Lake – like a painting by Claude Monet come to life. A few animated families and couples were enjoying their rowing boats, often splashing each other, and laughing hilariously. They talked about their respective family expectations as to how best to manage their careers – for instance, whether and where each should apply to a university to pursue an advanced degree, such as an MBA, during the next academic year. She wanted to begin graduate studies soon and was concerned that the UK Government proposed to raise tuition fees and to cut funding to universities. Most of the young women in her extended family tended to get married and raise children, after completing high school, instead of pursuing careers.

When David commented that everyone had an inherent purpose, or *physis*, which each person should discover and pursue, Alessia agreed, noting that the classical Greek philosopher Aristotle would have supported this as a *teleological imperative*. She enjoyed the sparkle in his eyes as he talked, the determined jut of his jaw, and his bronzed, often smiling face. "What work does your father do?" David asked. Alessia explained that her father had retired, and used to manage a large vineyard, bringing home succulent black grapes from time to time. In answer to the same question, David said that his father had been a construction worker, then rapidly changed the subject to the picnic at hand. They removed their shoes one after the other, feet almost touching. As they leaned back on their elbows, each picking up another salmon sandwich, their hands brushed against each other for a quietly electrifying moment. To Alessia's inquiry as to what he liked to do in his spare time, David answered that he enjoyed strumming his acoustic guitar, then returned her query. She revealed her continuing interest in painting since childhood, beginning with watercolors and moving on to oil paintings later, mostly of scenery. "I hope someday you will let me see a few of your pictures," he said.

David went on to say that no one in his immediate family had ever been to university, and that his mother had consistently encouraged him to do so. They both paused to admire the purple lilacs blooming nearby in bright sunlight. She felt ever more comfortable, for the first time since arrival in London, as they shared paper cups of Muscadet wine and exchanged descriptions of selected bank customers as well as supervisors. While they were chatting in an increasingly relaxed manner, to her surprise, Alessia's elder brother, Paolo, happened to walk by, stopped, looked absolutely shocked, approached them aggressively, and asked abrasively – "*Just what do you think you are doing there*?"

Alessia attempted to introduce David Armstrong to Paolo, as her co-worker at the bank where she was employed, but her incensed brother ignored the introduction and told her that she should immediately return home with him to help with her usual weekend chores. Alessia apologized profusely to David, who was somewhat stunned, then she got up reluctantly, pulled on her shoes and departed, in a state of obvious distress, lagging behind her brother, who walked rapidly ahead. Each sibling frowned, talking at each other across the distance in between, piquing the interest of others walking nearby. Alessia felt increasingly unhappy as they walked. She had been unusually contented, enjoying her picnic, the scenery in the park, and the conversation with a co-worker and potential friend, who must certainly feel insulted. Meanwhile, David shook his head, muttered to himself that there were always bad apples in any barrel, packed away the remaining sandwiches, wine, paper cups, nuts, and napkins that he'd brought in a covered picnic basket, and slowly headed to the Hyde Park tube station, to take the tube home to Hornsey, where he lived with his younger sister and their mother.

When David and Alessia were next at work, they were uncomfortable, at first restricting conversation to customer requirements. David felt rejected by her brother because of his ethnicity but continued to be drawn to her. Alessia was acutely embarrassed by her brother, who had spent some time questioning her relationship with David and told her parents by telephone how he'd encountered her with a strange black man in Hyde Park, causing them to worry about her. A few days later, because of a customer relations training session organized in the bank's small conference room by the portly, bespectacled branch manager, David and Alessia found themselves on the same competing team, smiling together at the role-playing in which they had been engaged. "*Always remember that we are in the customer confidence game first, and that effective money management is a means to an end,*" intoned their supervisor. Later, David mimicked his comment, *sotto voce* to Alessia, who chuckled, saying "Be careful – someone might hear you!" Next day, they agreed to take a walk on Oxford Street during lunchtime, and to purchase pepperoni pizza slices and apple juice near Bond Street station.

As they walked, Alessia explained further to David that she came from a very traditional family, where parents and elder brothers tended to screen new friends of younger sisters, especially males, carefully, and assumed that such friends would normally come from Reggio Calabria, or the vicinity. David was still curious about Reggio Calabria's exact location in Italy, despite his embarrassed reluctance to ask directly. Sensing this, Alessia explained that her hometown was on its south-west coast, in the vicinity of Palermo, Sicily, leading him to enquire whether this was an area where *mafioso* really were prevalent. She teased him that he was always asking about such criminal gangs, and that his ideas about Italy seemed to have all been taken from sensational movies, such as "*The Godfather.*" By the time that they were walking back towards their bank branch, conversing over the noise of the Oxford Street traffic, while munching hot pizza slices with gusto, and discussing their favorite movies and music, Alessia was again inquiring about Jamaica. She mentioned having heard a haunting yet inspiring record of Bob Marley singing "*No Woman No Cry.*" David reminded her that although his parents were from Montego Bay, Jamaica he'd never been there, but agreed that Bob Marley had been a superb singer, while alive. As they walked, conversing animatedly, Alessia gesturing as usual, he noticed that several people passing by, mainly older men, looked at them askance. But they were soon back at the bank, consciously maintaining a considered professional distance in between.

On the next working day, a dour customer returned to the bank, after debiting his savings account, to complain bitterly to a supervisor that David had undercounted his cash and might have kept the difference. David was interviewed and searched by the manager, then suddenly given notice of termination, under his probationary employment contract, although his pockets contained only clearly personal items. The manager also gave the customer a hundred pounds, against a receipt, the amount claimed as undercounted. Alessia was working next to him on the counter that morning and was absolutely shaken when she was told about her colleague's abrupt termination. "You always count cash out twice and use the note counter for any large sums as we were trained. Why would that customer have had a complaint about you?" she asked him. David smiled wryly. "Maybe he thought I should actually be in a loincloth hunting with a spear in some African jungle, rather than working in a bank in London, handling his transaction."

Later, after completing work for the day, Alessia and David walked out to Oxford Street, found an empty bus stop bench, and talked until dusk fell. David told her that he would immediately begin applying for another job, perhaps at a Marks and Spencer's store near his home. In response, Alessia commented that as he was certainly not going to receive a positive reference letter from his supervisor, if it would help, she would be glad to write a note on bank letterhead at home, having observed him working since the first day they were recruited. Alessia was taken aback at this debacle. She was struck by the precarity of their employment. If such a complaint could be made about David and believed, a young, South Italian woman with good but certainly not native English language, and a definite accent, might well be next in line, since all other counter workers were native British. Then again, the complaining customer might be targeting black people only – an attitude to which she was quite accustomed, although she now thought David had a sturdy, athletic build, attractive, dark brown skin, with expressive brown eyes, a dazzling smile, and was always struck by his very English accent.

Sometimes, she longed for the simplicity of her younger days in Calabria, enjoying *pasta arrabbiata* for lunch, hiking with her brothers in the Sila Greca woods, listening to Tarantella music during festivals, and watching, with mounting excitement, the far too quickly extinguished bonfires leaping on the beach on the night of San Lorenzo – despite her mixed feelings about fires. When her second brother – the youngest - Giancarlo, graduated from the University of Palermo, Paolo had persuaded their parents that, if they looked for work in London, the three siblings would get much better jobs, and be able to send money home to buy a more comfortable house for the family. He repeatedly committed to take good care of their only daughter, Alessia. She was glad for the opportunity to work abroad, and to avoid her mother's all too frequent hints about marriage. However, these days, Paolo sometimes interrogated her about her days at work, much to her displeasure. He treated her as if she were still only sixteen, instead of a very responsible and self-aware, if extremely sensitive and perhaps sensual and partly introverted, woman of over twenty-six years in age. Alessia enjoyed reading and thinking about the characters, stories, and ideas to be found in many kinds of books, which she viewed as windows to the world. She wondered how her life would unfold, and whether she would find new friends in London. Alessia found Paolo overbearing, and Giancarlo was always watching television, or making drawings, or visiting betting shops. David was the only colleague with whom she talked about work, and increasingly life, within the bank. He seemed to be a kindred spirit, who shared many of her attitudes and values, someone who appeared to understand her inner self; sadly, he would now be leaving very soon.

David was seething. He had been with the bank for three months, having begun work on the same day that Alessia had, and he had done his absolute best to learn all of the policies and procedures involved in dealing with debits, credits, checks, money orders, transfers, balance inquiries, and account opening as well as closing. His supervisor had always seemed to appreciate his work before that red- faced and shifty-eyed customer decided to complain about him, and evidently, to make £100 in profit from the bank for his lies. The only person who made his days at work tolerable, and sometimes enjoyable, was Alessia, with her long, wavy, brunette hair, a lovely face in the office's fluorescent lights, her thoughtful grey eyes, always fashionable dresses – and her extremely expressive hands, ever in eloquent motion. At first, she had appeared to be very reserved and to be uninterested in any conversation beyond the minimum required to collaborate in dealing with client data bases and security codes. However, since their impromptu lunch at Pret-À-Porter, their Hyde Park picnic, and a lunchtime walk ending up at the evocative Charles Dickens Memorial at Marylebone Road, they had talked about books they enjoyed, exchanging shared delights in scenes as well as plots from a quite eclectic range of novels, and about their dreams.

David once remarked to her that the best authors provide incandescent lamps, powerfully illuminating human experiences, while building often initially tenuous bridges of understanding between readers and writers. He argued that to see the world through the eyes of others was to develop richer understandings of who we are, and why people do what they do. Alessia snorted suddenly, in a way that surprised him. "Most people don't read to learn about themselves or the world, but for enjoyment or escape, to be transported into other environments and lives, without really facing the perils frequently depicted. This is partly why we all tend to praise fiction by saying that it has the ring of truth, and non-fiction by declaring that it had the feel of a novel." She went on to express surprise at his evident engagement in reading, as he appeared more of a business professional concerned with making as much money as possible than a literary type, generating a hearty guffaw, in turn. It later turned out that Alessia and David also shared interests in mostly classical music, and they sometimes ended up humming bars together from "*The Swan*," or "*Ladies in Lavender*." He enjoyed her descriptions of life in Calabria, as she often called it, her merry laughter, the way that she regularly smiled at him with shining eyes, and her interest in what it was like for him to grow up and go to school in Brixton. She inquired about his business studies at the University of South London, and he wondered how this compared with her experience at the Università Cattolica del Sacro Cuore.

Answering his question, Alessia explained that her studies there were only approved by her parents because her university was a well-known, conservative institution of higher learning, and even then, reluctantly. This was where she lived in a campus residence on her own and met people from far beyond her region and country, for the first time in her life. "At first, I felt so out of place. My freshman year felt so unbearably long, and my sophomore year only somewhat shorter. By the time I felt relatively relaxed at the university, rather than like an isolated, unfashionably dressed country girl with whom no one talked, my senior year was well underway," she said. "I really began to become *me* there, but made very few friends, and unfortunately, have already lost track of most of them now."

"I suppose that you studied business or finance at your university also?" he asked. "Not at all," Alessia responded. "Upon finally leaving home, I wanted to learn more about the ways in which people within a family, community, or team, can support each other, at least in many cases, but instead, all too often, distress and hurt each other, despite their best intentions." David asked impishly, "Would an example be the customer service training that we were given when beginning work at the bank? Do you remember when that trainer said we were each empowered to do all we could to help customers in their '*moments of truth'* with us? He did not bother to explain how supervisors and supervisees should identify and manage dishonest patron complaints." Alessia asserted, "There is certainly no connection between your treatment and best employment practice. Anyway, I ended up studying philosophy and cognitive psychology, where we began with ways of understanding human experience, and the impact of the primordial brain, generating instinctive *fight, flee* or *freeze* reactions. Our cohort then moved on to the paleo-limbic brain, where we learnt a lot about the impact of resonant life experiences, which can lead to guilt accumulation, resentment, and intolerance."

He was intrigued, even though her quietly delivered statements seemed somewhat sententious. "It was actually refreshing to get to the part of the curriculum dealing with the neo-limbic brain. This is the section of our brains that we use to engage in reflection and meditation, applying cognition, memory search, and curiosity to learn new things, including self-management," she added. "So how on Earth did you end up in banking?" asked David. "When I graduated and returned to Reggio, my mother was only too glad to have me help with household chores. The only other work available was in banking or teaching, so I trained as a bank intern, and moved on to customer service, while looking for another opportunity to leave home for more than six months. After this extended wait, it was such a delight to eventually arrive in London!" Alessia answered.

On his final day at work, David invited Alessia to lunch at a local Chinese restaurant, as they also shared an enjoyment of Cantonese-style dumplings or *dim sum*. Alessia hesitated, commenting that her brother Paolo worked in Tottenham Court Road, and would be sure to create additional stress for her at home, if he happened to encounter them. However, when David reminded her that they would no longer see each other at work after that day, and suggested they look for an indoor booth which could not be readily observed by pedestrians outside, she agreed to go. One of the cashiers greeted David by name, upon arrival. They sat together over lunch, on comfortably upholstered vermilion leather seats, munching crunchy shrimp balls and vegetable spring rolls, prawn toast, and black prawn dumplings, while sipping jasmine green tea. Yanni's "*Sensuous Chill*" was playing in the background, and the restaurant became increasingly crammed.

David drew her attention to a couple sitting quite stiffly in their chairs near the window, staring outside and saying little to each other, and imagined them as an unhappily married couple who had decided to go their separate ways. Alessia reflected that no one in her family had ever been divorced. To David's query as to how such couples coped, if they ever found that they could no longer get along together, she responded mischievously that they simply concentrated on having as many children as possible, leaving no time to think about any such concerns, and they laughed merrily for a while. As their lunch was coming to an end, and they were going to the rest rooms, he mentioned his lack of success in getting a job in another bank, without a positive supervisor's reference, then told a quite surprised Alessia that while thinking of applying for a master's degree program at Westminster University in finance, by the next starting date in September. Meanwhile, he had accepted a job as a waiter in the very same restaurant where they sat, so as to maintain at least some level of income.

The next day, Alessia was uncomfortable at work. A new staff member had taken David's place on the counter, a pale young man with a Yorkshire accent who literally kept his head down, when not speaking to customers or supervisors. She decided to take a walk at lunchtime and found herself heading in the direction of the restaurant where her former colleague was now working. A rather flustered David was visible inside, in a white apron with a black and blue branded T-shirt, notebook in hand, attempting to manage orders from a family of six, with a disconsolately sobbing baby girl in a Nordstrom stroller. Alessia walked on by and sat in a little park nearby to munch an apple with walnuts, while sipping Perrier bottled water. She felt lonely and somewhat depressed. At the same time, she found herself recalling some of David's amusing comments during their recent lunch, vividly imagined him clad in a loin cloth, with noticeably powerful, well-developed biceps and triceps – then wondered in surprise at herself for a moment. Light rain began to fall, spattering her grey-trimmed white dress - having no umbrella, she hurried back to the bank. At the end of the day, David sat with his Irish supervisor, who reviewed his work that day, and commented that he would need to move much more quickly between the dining area and the kitchen, as wait times had been unusually long for the customers assigned to him.

On the tube home, David wished he could talk with Alessia, and marveled that he had only known her for a month, and was feeling so out of sorts, having not seen her since yesterday. They had exchanged cellular phone numbers and even addresses, but he knew by now it would not be a good idea to contact her without prior agreement, either at home, or while working. Although summer was approaching, the weather was still quite crisp. At home in Hornsey, when his mother set a dinner of roast beef with rice and red peas on the table and asked him about his first day at his restaurant, he shook his head, saying "It really was a race – as we hand in one set of orders in the kitchen, the drill is to greet new customers at the entrance, seat them quickly, and then take more orders – I was sometimes rushed off my feet, but my manager still told me I was too slow!" His mother smiled indulgently "You enjoyed table tennis in school and often won your games. You will get accustomed to the pace of work there in no time, and if your supervisor is really a reasonable man, as you say, you'll be fine." His sister Danielle, who had just turned nineteen, asked whether he would bring home a few black prawn dumplings, or some shrimp balls for her to taste soon, and David laughed. As the meal ended, he told his mother how much he'd enjoyed it.

Paolo sighed heavily, as he completed work for the day in a basement bookseller's shop which was overflowing with assorted books of all sizes and a range of magazines, and headed for the Tottenham Court Road tube, intending to shop for groceries for the family *en route* home to Camden Town. His brother, Giancarlo, was still looking for work, despite his accounting degree, and was spending too much time in betting shops, after three months in London, while his sister Alessia had settled down to work in a bank and appeared to be doing well – except that she had become far too friendly with a *mente nero.* Sometimes, he wondered whether it had been a mistake to leave home in Reggio di Calabria, despite the opportunities to earn much more income so far from home, in this strange, sprawling, often rainy cosmopolitan city, filled with museums, monuments, ornate homes, shops, businesses, and so many reserved people with strange accents. It was now his duty to maintain the family's honor on behalf of their parents, and to identify a suitable fiancé for his sister, as soon as possible. It was also important to retain an apartment in which they could live decently, and to put proper food on the table, in a country of peculiar meals such as fish and chips, roast beef, or Yorkshire pudding - and to go to mass regularly at an appropriate location, such as St. Peter's Italian Catholic Church at Holborn on Sundays.

While waiting to pay for his purchases at the wearied cashier in the local grocery near home, he heard two young men who were dressed in elegant black suits and black wing-tipped shoes, one looking at a Rolex watch, speaking rapidly in an Italian dialect, and pricked up his ears, realizing that their accents suggested Sicilian or other Southern Italian origins. Paolo was impressed at their suave, confident appearance, and his spirits lifted. He hung back near the crowded canned fruit and vegetables section, until the two men headed towards the cashier, then followed them, so that they all ended up leaving the grocery shop almost simultaneously. "*Sei Italiano*?" he asked them. "*Davvero*," one answered, "Very much so." Paolo walked with them towards the Camden Town tube where they were going and struck up an animated conversation with Benito and Tomassini, as their names turned out to be. They complained about the many lamentable differences between ways of life in London and at home in southern Italy – whether in Reggio Calabria or their own family homes in Campania. He ended up exchanging telephone numbers with his compatriots. The three men promised to be in touch again soon, and to plan an evening at a pub.

Paolo felt elated. He had not had the opportunity to speak with many people from his region of Italy since arrival in London and was already looking forward to finding out more about their families. By the time of his arrival at the creaking wooden staircase leading to the door of their rented apartment, shaking his head, as usual, at the malfunctioning light bulb there, he was already wondering whether one of the young men he'd just met could possibly turn out to be a good match for his sister Alessia. She clearly needed to meet someone suitable, with whom she might be able to settle down soon, and to raise a new branch of the family. Paolo realized that she appeared to be content with her work in London, and evidently wanted to engage in further study, but he was quite impatient to feel less responsible for Alessia and was sure that it was better for his sister to get married instead of working and studying, and perhaps disgracing their family.

A few days later, Benito and Tomassini were looking for the pub in Camden Town where they had agreed to meet Paolo, on this occasion dressed quite casually.

However, they were also engaged in an intense conversation about the information recently received about one of their company's '*safe houses*' in Reading where almost a dozen young women, mainly from Syria and Bulgaria, were undergoing the usual orientation towards supervised life in the United Kingdom, and to their new roles as call girls, while being given a vividly clear understanding as to what would occur if any of them tried to escape. It appeared that one or more local constables had received a tip about that location and might be planning a raid soon. Looking ahead, they agreed upon the importance of identifying police informants in all their major business locations. The immediate question was what the best alternative location for their inventory might be. Benito located the pub first, before they could arrive at a conclusion, and they agreed to return to the topic after having a drink with Paolo, as planned, for the purpose of possibly considering him as a potential network member.

Paolo was already seated at a corner table in the pub, sipping a pint of lager beer with lime, and welcomed them effusively, while offering to get the first round of drinks for his compatriots. As their beer arrived, Paolo raised his glass, saying "*Saluti!*" – enthusiastically echoed by his interlocutors. With pleasantries exchanged, he asked them in what part of London they worked. While cracking his knuckles, Tomassini answered that they were in the olive oil and wine import- export business, and managed warehouses in several locations where their inventories were stored. When Paolo inquired whether their business had been affected by the cloud of volcanic ash from a violent volcano in Iceland – apologizing for forgetting the exact name - that had recently caused the closure of

British airspace, they explained that most of their shipments were made by sea.

By the second round of lagers, an encouraged and duly impressed Paolo began talking about his own publishing business in London, and his family, and ended up inviting his new friends to dinner at his home during the next weekend. Benito accepted, as he drummed his fingers on the table, and after a final round of beer, explained to Paolo that they had to take care of an inventory issue that afternoon, as the three men exchanged friendly goodbyes. Paolo returned home, elated.

Benito and Tomassini traveled to Paddington Station, and purchased tickets to Reading, where they took a taxi to their destination, with some apprehension as to how quickly the reported situation might change. Upon identifying themselves through the intercom at the heavy oak entrance door, with a closed-circuit camera overhead, and a small placard indicating the business premises of "Acerra Import/Export," they were welcomed in, and immediately conducted upstairs to the orientation program's Director, Arkady. He offered them bottled water, and explained that a young woman, recently arrived from Syria, had managed to open the locked casement window of her bedroom, when allowed to rest. She had screamed for help through it, after the first workshop, when the travel documents of new arrivals were confiscated, and working conditions were explained.

The new girl was promptly restrained and given a sedative, and all windows more securely locked. Arkady reported that only two or three people had been passing by in the street below at the time, so it had appeared possible that no one had paid any attention to this event. However, the next day, a police constable had called to inquire whether there had been a domestic disturbance at the address. Although efforts had been made to reassure her, it was likely from her tone that a follow-up visit would occur. After walking through the building, Benito berated Arkady for his ineptitude, and instructed that all residents should be prepared to leave in a leased twelve-seater bus within the next hour, as they could not be safely restrained and kept in the basement or the attic, with no probability of discovery, given the expected search. Once this plan was outlined, it was immediately implemented. A green and white bus was idling outside shortly afterwards. Tomassini escorted the young women to the bus, each wearing fashionable dresses, elegant shoes, dark glasses, and varied wigs, after receiving menacing warnings that family members at home would be killed, without delay, if anyone spoke or tried to flee. Benito became the only person remaining on the premises, poised to address any inquiry, despite an incipient headache.

He did not have to wait long. When Benito answered the doorbell, he encountered two constables, one male and the other female, who introduced themselves and inquired whether he was willing to allow their entry. Within minutes, the visitors were seated in verdigris green living room armchairs, asking rapid fire questions, and concluded the discussion by requesting an opportunity to review the property. The constables, who remained together, were painstaking in examining each room, with Benito bringing up the rear. When asked why there were so many small bedrooms with single beds, he hesitated as to what he should say, and had not formulated a response yet when other questions followed, as to the assortment of women's undergarments as well as sanitary products in dressing table drawers, and in two bathrooms – and as to why there were padlocks on the windows upstairs. Benito finally answered that his company had only recently leased the building as a potential student hostel, and that he had no idea why unwanted property had apparently been improperly discarded, or why windows had been padlocked. From the quizzical looks of both constables, especially when his hands twitched involuntarily, he realized that they remained suspicious, and hastened to explain that he suffered from *tardive dyskinesia*. With their visit completed, after taking digital photographs of the property, including himself, and asking for the registered details of his company, he sighed with a measure of relief, while shaking his head. Benito settled down to the task of cleaning up, removing fingerprints, and belatedly discarding the unwanted items remaining in the building. Within three hours, Tomassini telephoned to say that the merchandise had arrived safely and was stored in South Quay. Benito locked the door of the residence, pulled his Armani coat tight against the chilly, although bright and sunny day, and walked hastily towards the Reading train station.

Next weekend, Benito and Tomassini arrived, as agreed, at the Camden Town address provided by Paolo for dinner, bringing a bottle of Mateus Rosé wine. Paolo welcomed then effusively, introduced them to Giancarlo and to Alessia, and settled them immediately at their old linoleum dining table, covered with a mauve tablecloth for the occasion. He explained to his siblings how he'd met their guests, and they began their meal with toasts to Reggio di Calabria and to Campania. Alessia concentrated upon eating the risotto with baked salmon that she had prepared. In answer to a question from Benito, Paolo explained that the large, gold-framed portrait above the mantelpiece was executed during their parents' wedding. As the conversation continued, the irrepressible Giancarlo engaged the visitors in an animated discussion concerning the respective merits of the Tottenham Hotspur and Manchester teams, who were scheduled to play the next day, as well as the talents of the team strikers on the A S Roma and S.S. Lazio Italian football clubs – having conceded the primacy of Juventus and AC Milan. Giancarlo also displayed his somewhat juvenile sense of humor, asking "*why did the rooster cross the road?*" then answering with a chuckle, without waiting for a response - "*to catch up with all the hens on the other side*!"

When everyone except Alessia laughed encouragingly, he continued: "Did you ever see the sign in the pub down the street? *Those drinking to forget, please pay in advance*! By the way, an angry-looking policeman came up to me near the Camden Town tube yesterday and suddenly demanded '*Give me your name!*' I was surprised into silence for a few seconds, then asked, '*what's wrong with yours*?" Giancarlo also demonstrated his incipient artistic interests, by making credible black and white sketches of everyone at the table, while they were eating their meal. Tomassini, in particular, was startled at how rapidly his likeness had been captured on paper, while musing uneasily that his eyes looked far too calculating for comfort. He glanced at Benito, who also appeared uncomfortable.

In turn, Paolo encouraged his guests, with limited success, to say more about their families and their import-export business. He was pleased to learn that their relatives were mostly olive growers and viticulturalists in Campania and was told again that they traded in related consumer products. Paolo discounted Benito's frequent blinking as an individual idiosyncrasy. Alessia was mostly silent. It was only after a tasty dessert of tiramisu and coffee that Paolo mentioned that his sister had been working so hard in a London bank that she hadn't had time for any social life, although she adored plays and movies. Benito mentioned some of the movies he had most enjoyed, such as "Gangs of New York," and inquired about the kind of motion pictures that she liked best. Alessia demurred, beginning to grow uncomfortable about the nature of this conversation. She became even more apprehensive when Paolo commented that to allow her some recreation, he would gladly invite everyone interested to a forthcoming viewing of "Mission Impossible" near Piccadilly Circus on the following weekend. When Giancarlo and Tomassini indicated that they'd already seen this production, and found it entertaining, Paolo turned to Benito, saying "Well, I can surely count upon you to enjoy a pleasant evening with Alessia and myself." Benito smirked, beginning to have an inkling as to Paolo's intentions, and to wonder whether he might be able to secure a profitable new recruit for one of his safe houses, instead of cultivating Paolo, after appearing to court his sister. She was actually quite attractive, doubtless a virgin, and so quiet as to seem tractable. At the same time, Alessia was becoming increasingly stressed at the direction in which her brother had taken the discussion. She realized that she disliked the attitudes of both guests, who were clearly appraising her, wished she would be left alone to focus upon doing a good job at the bank, where she was still settling in, and decided that she would try to find a way to avoid any such 'chaperoned' movie evening. By the time that dinner concluded, she was suffering from a severe headache.

Alessia ended up calling David from her bathroom that evening once Paolo's guests had departed. He answered after only two rings, but did not recognize her at first, as she spoke very softly. "How is your new job, David?" she asked. At that point, he realized who was calling, and answered "I'm actually missing the bank, except for that supervisor, who is probably very prejudiced against minorities. The restaurant customers all want their orders immediately, and the kitchen staff all need time in which to prepare each meal properly, so waiters such as myself are always caught in the middle." He was thrilled when Alessia responded by telling him that she would go to mass by herself the next day, and would be glad to see him again, if he could meet her outside Westminster Cathedral at midday – and had the presence of mind to inquire whether she could bring any of her oil paintings to share with him. When they met, David approvingly noted her elegant, full-length yellow dress, as well as her pearl necklace, and neat little gold earrings. Alessia was nervous, as she explained that she'd not gone to mass yet, had only a limited time, and asked for his suggestions as to where they could go to talk. He recommended the National Theatre at Southbank, where it would be possible to order coffee and sit comfortably indoors. She agreed. Once seated, Alessia hesitated, took a deep breath, blushed, and proceeded to recount the efforts of her eldest brother to make a match for her. David was incredulous, asking "If, as you say, you get such a very negative feeling about both these guys, why not just tell Paolo?" She reiterated the traditions of her family and region, under which her eldest brother would be expected to assume a parental role, in the absence of their father or mother, and would not willingly take 'no' for an answer, should he decide that an engagement to someone of his choice was in her own interest. He watched her slim, expressive hands, as she illustrated her comments, fascinated, and became even more so, when she recalled having brought a manila folder with some of her paintings.

"Why are some of these depicting cemeteries, graves, and headstones?" he asked, looking through them. "I was always very interested in the shades of light and dark encountered in my family cemetery," she explained, "and sometimes even thought it might be possible to glimpse the residues of departed souls, such as my great grandmother, about whom my mother regularly told me stories." Leafing through other paintings, David's interest was also piqued by her skillful use of chiaroscuro in rendering what she described as the woods near Sila Greca in Reggio di Calabria, with dark tree trunks counterpointing light shining through the many-shaded green leaves, as well as the stark brooding walls of the castle of Caccuri, painted from the memory of a visit with her father.

Alessia felt somewhat relieved, just by talking to David about the situation, while recognizing that her options appeared limited to either claiming illness, seeking family agreement upon her return to Reggio, or pretended willingness to acquiesce to Paolo's plans, for the time being. While looking at her watch and noting that it was almost time to return home, she realized that traveling back to Italy to live with her parents, at this point, would be distressing, partly because of her new friendship with David, and partly since she so much preferred life in London, from what she'd experienced so far. Noticing gathering gray clouds and a drizzle outside, David commented that he had a somewhat battered umbrella they could share. She recalled a proverb from home... "*no relationship is all sunshine, but two people can share an umbrella and survive storms together.*"

Her further reflections led to the conclusion that an attempt to evade the movie visit with Paolo and Benito by pleading a cold or a headache would simply mean a postponement. Also, should she feign serious illness, matters could become quite complicated, leading to a required medical evaluation. Alessia sighed. Perhaps there really was no solution apart from compliance, she thought sadly. When David looked at her in concern, she said "I was just thinking about work at the bank tomorrow." He was inclined to comment upon how much of a relief it would be, if he could return to work there, rather than continuing to wait tables at any restaurant – but thought the better of it, looking at her expression. Instead, he touched her right hand encouragingly. In parting, they shook hands warmly. At David's request, she left her folder of paintings with him, for his further review.

On the next weekend, Alessia found herself in a movie theater seat, in between Paolo and Benito, pretending to watch "*Mission Impossible.*" When the intermission arrived, Paolo offered to purchase pistachio ice cream and bottled water for them, and Benito took the opportunity to try to talk with Alessia, as intended. "How are you finding your work at the bank?" he asked. "Fine." she replied. He followed up with other questions about the movie, what she thought of London, whether she'd ever met a special young man, and when she expected to vacation at her home in Reggio di Calabria, only to receive similar monosyllabic responses, Benito decided to change his approach. Upon Paolo's return, bearing refreshments, Benito thanked him warmly, declaring his deep appreciation for the time provided for him to get to know Alessia a little better, saying that he must be proud of such a pleasant and accomplished younger sister, who looked up to him so much. Paolo smiled, and Benito grew more confident in his approach. Alessia was so astonished that some of her pistachio ice cream fell on her cream skirt.

When the lights dimmed, she tried to wipe it up with her small, decorative linen handkerchief, but Benito noticed, said "Allow me!" to her and taking out his own, firmly wiped the soiled area, just above her knee, while slyly moving her dress up just a little, then held her left hand. Alessia tried hard to extricate her hand, but Benito grasped it tightly, stroking her in a way that felt particularly strange because his hand shook from time to time. When she looked to Paolo for support, he nodded at her, thinking that his plan was beginning to work. It appeared that this pleasant young man from Campania was developing an interest in his sister, that might well lead to an engagement and marriage – although he yet needed more information about Benito's family. Alessia realized in frustration that Paolo was not going to intervene, and Benito was emboldened to caress her hand freely with both of his, for the rest of the movie, to her increasing chagrin.

Once outside the movie theatre, Paolo inquired further about Benito's family, and was encouraged to be told that his father owned fifty hectares of fertile olive groves and vineyards and collaborated with several major companies to export his products, when processed, to other countries, including Britain. Alessia was quiet and pale, looking out at the street during this conversation. How best to manage herself and her life, in such a situation? Benito thanked Paolo again for the invitation, averring that he'd very much enjoyed the movie and the company afforded. He expressed hope that they could see each other again during a small reception planned at his home in Kensal Green the following weekend, to celebrate Tomassini's engagement, and took his leave. Paolo was beaming, and asked Alessia "Isn't he a fine young man?" She responded tersely "I don't like him at all." "Why not?" asked Paolo. "He seems to be very polite, pleasant, and to come from a good family." Alessia attempted to explain that she did not appreciate the way Benito looked at her and behaved, adding that he seemed sleazy to her, then asked "Why did you allow him to hold and stroke my hand, pulling it towards his lap in such a vulgar way, instead of protecting me?"

Paolo responded that handholding was a normal part of courtship, these days, and that she appeared to be exaggerating a lot, given his own presence, concluding with his wish that she would keep an open mind about a well-off young man who appeared to be a good prospect for her, rather than that *mente nero* he'd seen her with in Hyde Park several weeks before. They returned home in silence. On the following day, after Tomassini and Benito met to discuss the security of their leased properties, where inventories of call girls were kept, the fees charged to clients, and the level of protection arranged by their attorneys and security personnel via their networks, they turned to the issue of supply chains. Tomassini had persuaded his sister from Positano to join the company, to help source, transport and manage trafficked women. As part of the process of grooming and introducing five new young acquisitions from Albania to selected clients, she had come up with the idea of a contrived engagement party for her brother. Benito thought this brilliant, saying that if he could get Alessia to come, this could set the stage for him to propose to her. "Are you really thinking of marrying Alessia?" asked Tomassini, startled. "Not at all," answered Benito, "but if I play my cards right with her brother and herself, we will be able to stage a wedding, and afterwards, I can groom her to join our inventory." Chuckling, he retailed for Tomassini the story of how he had managed to hold and stroke her soft little left hand, even pulling it over into his lap against her will, during much of the movie - with the evident tacit support of Paolo - who was clearly looking for a suitor for her. An amused Tomassini cracked his knuckles, as he inquired "And did you manage to enjoy her hand properly?" Benito smiled and said, "Patience is all I need now." His torso jerked sharply as if to emphasize each word,

Tomassini added sympathetically "You have certainly been very patient with your physician, who has yet to explain what underlying medical conditions set off your symptoms, now and then." Benito remarked that it was time to replace him.

Once Benito confirmed the engagement reception invitation for the impending weekend, Paolo was pleased, again telling Alessia that her new friend appeared to be a serious young man, and a likely good catch, given his family and successful import-export business. Alessia frowned. "I'm not looking to catch anyone, but just want to get on with my work and to continue my studies. Besides, why is it so difficult for you to see that he's a shady young man? You're not protecting me as your sister at all, simply trying to push me into an unwanted relationship." Paolo became angry. "You apparently want to destroy the family's honor by living a loose life, rather than settling down to have children with a good husband, as your mother and your grandmother did before you! I'm trying to help you create a future our parents can be proud of. Instead of showing gratitude, you show disrespect!" Alessia felt disheartened and trapped. How to respond? She did not want to distress their parents, aunts, uncles, or other family members, and reasoned that going to the engagement reception with Paolo would placate him, while not committing her to anything further. They eventually settled down to a rather tense dinner, featuring a conversation about an eccentric spinster aunt.

She thought of David's alert, handsome face, looked at her stern elder brother across the newly purchased lime green tablecloth on the dining table, and at her younger brother Giancarlo, who was absorbed with yet another TV football game, asking the latter: "What did you think of Benito?" When Giancarlo answered that he seemed all right for a Juventus fan, Alessia sighed deeply, and told Paolo that she would go to the reception with him on Saturday evening. Paolo was pleased, and came around the table to hug her, telling Alessia that when she was eventually settled down and looking forward to her children, who would certainly be beautiful, she would deeply appreciate his efforts. He felt relieved that she had decided to be sensible and to listen to him. While clearing up the dishes and cutlery after their meal, Paolo mentioned to his brother and sister his increasing concern with the state of their parents' health, especially that of their father.

On the way to work at the bank, the next day, she called David, who was preparing to leave home for his workplace. They arranged to meet for lunch on a bench in the little circular park near the restaurant, where there were marigold hedges, and a carved fountain, with hardly any water playing. David arrived a few minutes late, explaining that his supervisor wanted him to complete service for all his existing guests, and to collect their payments, before going for lunch. She paid little attention to his explanation, instead musing how debonair he seemed. He was taken aback, and angered, when Alessia brought him up to date. "So, your brother actually sat next to you in the cinema and allowed that fellow to maul your hand, instead of protecting you?" he asked, indignantly. Alessia sipped her water and offered him some of the hazel nuts bought for lunch. "Paolo is using his *paleo-limbic* instead of his *neo-limbic* brain," she commented." He feels that the burden of protecting our family's honor is all weighing on his shoulders, and so is viewing everything related to me though an extremely specific set of lenses." She paused. "I shouldn't use such a term, but I had to keep pulling my hand away, since that Benito actually seemed to want to press it over his *manhood* – and all that my brother could say afterwards was that it was a normal part of courtship to hold hands these days." David was thunderstruck. "What a vile person!" he exclaimed – "not your brother, but this Benito." Without conscious intention, he placed his right hand around Alessia's shoulder. She felt understood, as well as comforted, leaning against him, almost automatically. It was only then that both realized that they were seated so closely. Alessia began to sit up, but then relaxed. When David hugged her more tightly, they looked around cautiously, and saw that there was no one else in the park, leaving aside the cooing wood pigeons who were acquisitively exploring around each bench, looking for leftover crumbs and food wrappers. They stared directly into each other's eyes. David leaned forward almost automatically and kissed her soft, smiling lips. When she parted them, after a few hesitant moments, he kissed her more deeply, and they quivered for several minutes. Both were stunned. Neither had arrived expecting such physical contact. They looked at each other, wide eyed. It was Alessia who moved closer again, and David completed their embrace by engaging her in another extended kiss. The sound of a nearby bus out on the street startled them.

When they sat up, breathing heavily, David touched Alessia's lips, telling her that he'd managed to spoil her cherry red lipstick. "I've always wondered about that product name – one puts it on, but it's so readily removed!" she said smiling shyly, as she wiped her lips with a napkin from her handbag. David reached for her hand, then stopped. "I can't forget what that slimy Italian man did to you." Alessia looked at him, still dazed, turned to gaze at a nearby row of red and white amaryllis flowers, bowing gracefully in a light breeze, and then, suddenly glancing at her watch, jumped up. "I'm going to be late getting back to work, and so will you, if we don't return this minute!" she exclaimed. They embraced briefly and hurried back to work, distractedly.

During the afternoon, David repeatedly relived the sensation of their bodies pressed together, tongues dancing in utter delight as they kissed, awareness of the world beyond attenuated. He felt bemused, ended up asking guests to repeat several orders, and even forgot to bring two specifically ordered shrimp balls from the kitchen, despite having his note pad in hand. The restaurant felt somewhat claustrophobic. For her part, having returned to the bank some five minutes late, Alessia felt disoriented, and forced herself to focus upon the completed vouchers at hand. She had experienced her first utterly amazing kisses, with a wonderfully attractive man, who had become her only real friend in London – someone of whom her eldest brother Paolo disapproved, evidently because of his ethnicity and appearance. She had agreed to go to Benito's reception with her brother only to maintain peace between them. But what next? A customer's voice interrupted her reflections – "please give me change in ten rather than twenty-pound notes, Miss Amato," he said, a little sharply, reading her identification tag. Flustered, she apologized and complied.

The following Saturday evening saw Paolo arriving with Alessia at a crowded ground floor flat in Kensal Green, decorated with pink, yellow and red roses. Paolo beamed to hear the strains of Tarantella music, presented a box of nougats that he'd brought as a gift, and exclaimed at the size of the iced, rectangular cake on the dining table, around which guests were toasting the 'engagement' of Tomassini and his sister, Lucia. When she reported that the new Albanian girls were each secured and productively occupied with selected guests upstairs, Benito relaxed, and paid special attention to Paolo and Alessia, offering them limoncello, marzipan cake, apricots, peaches, and chocolates. After several glasses of limoncello, which was redolent of lemon rind, sugar and pure alcohol, Paolo became quite convivial, and settled down to talk in a corner of the parlor with a goateed, bespectacled attorney who had recently arrived from Palermo. Benito took the opportunity to try to steer Alessia aside. But she insisted on remaining near her brother, standing tensely, without any attempt to take part in the conversation, which had turned to the role of media mogul and Prime Minister Silvio Berlusconi in Italian national politics, and did not accept any further refreshment offers. Listening, she reflected upon William Faulkner's remark that "*the past is never dead. It isn't even past.*" More guests arrived, many bearing colorfully wrapped gifts, and the reception became louder. Several began singing and dancing to the music. Paolo's conversation became more animated.

Eventually, Benito appeared to give up his efforts to talk to Alessia and went away. After whispering in her ear, he brought over Lucia, who was a plump platinum blonde in a sheer white evening gown, introduced and left them.

Lucia smiled and engaged an initially inattentive Alessia in a conversation about her engagement and wedding plans. They stood and conversed politely for a while, then Lucia invited Alessia to be seated on a fluffy bisque-colored sofa on the opposite side of the room. They continued talking about Tomassini's wedding and honeymoon plans in Santorini for a while, and Alessia relaxed enough to accept another glass of limoncello from a waiter passing by with a tray. Benito reappeared with an offering of dark chocolates, and took a seat next to Alessia, who turned away from him. When Lucia offered to show her the flat, she agreed. A few minutes later, as they were traversing a damask-carpeted corridor downstairs by themselves, Benito appeared again, and dramatically kneeled before Alessia, grasping her hand, and telling her "*Bellissima* Alessia, I can no longer deny my love for you! Will you marry me?" As Lucia gasped in apparently pleased amazement, and Alessia stood stunned, he took out an emerald engagement ring and pushed it firmly on to her finger before she could react.

Arising, Benito then tried to hug and kiss her. She turned her head, pushing him away. "I'm going to ask your brother, on behalf of your father, for your hand in marriage right now," he declared, "and when we have an agreement, you will learn how to respond to such a good proposal!" Alessia looked around, surprised and shocked, turning to Lucia, who said abruptly that she had to go help in the kitchen, leaving the very distressed, slightly inebriated young woman alone with Benito.

Chapter Two

Melody Armstrong was in her Brixton kitchen, standing before the sink, piled with breakfast dishes and cups, staring out at the little garden outside, without seeing her favorite pink rose bush or the nearby wisteria, as she remembered the day when her husband died. Joseph had left as usual in the morning, setting out with his yellow lunch box in hand, traveling by tube to the construction site in Wembley where he was working. It was almost midday when Melody received a call from someone who identified himself as the site foreman, and she had to ask him to repeat himself twice, after hearing the soul-shocking noun "accident." Joseph had been in an accident with a loaded forklift. When she asked how and where her husband was now, there was silence. As the foreman then told her that he had been rushed to the St. Thomas Hospital, and provided the number to call for further information, her baby daughter, Danielle, began to wail, more and more loudly. Melody did not remember placing the call to the hospital, only that when she eventually got through to the medical resident in attendance, he responded to her inquiry by saying "I'm so sorry, Mrs. Armstrong. Your husband was so terribly mangled that it was quite impossible to revive him. When you can, do call again to arrange the next steps." She put down the phone carefully, warmed a bottle of milk for Danielle, and went slowly upstairs to feed her, with unseeing eyes, while weeping so loudly that her baby stopped sucking to stare.

They had enjoyed swimming on beaches near Montego Bay in Jamaica, where they lived before arriving in London. Joseph was a tall, muscular, and ebullient man, with a merry gleam in his eye, when he looked at her, and a frequently infectious laugh. He worked as a mason on a hotel construction site, while pursuing vocational education at a local college. Melody met him in the public library, where they were both returning borrowed books, most recently, about automobile engines, in his case, and photography in her own. It was hot, and she already had a blue one-piece swimming suit on under her dress, straps showing, holding her beach bag, as she was looking forward to a swim that afternoon. "Good day," he said, nodding to her politely. "If you are heading to the beach, would you take me along too?" Melody smiled shyly. Joseph continued "My home is nearby, so I would just need a minute to collect my swim shorts and towel." When he paused expectantly, and she said, "But I don't know you!" he laughed, introduced himself with confident poise as Joseph Oliver Armstrong, and looked at her admiringly, until she reciprocated. "So now that we know each other, are we going swimming?" he inquired. When Melody hesitated, and eventually nodded, against her better judgment, Joseph told her where to meet him, and departed, all smiles. That afternoon, they swam out to a long coral reef that broke some of the force of the surging cobalt waves, enjoying the exercise, as cirrus clouds scudded above in the bright cerulean sky, and swam back to the reef again, before sitting on a jetty in the breeze, and beginning to talk. Near the horizon, a cruise ship passed a fisherman's boat, bobbing in the sea.

When his eyes swept over her swimsuit, and she reached into her knitted cloth beach bag for her fluffy yellow towel, he told her that she should never hide such an attractive suit, and that it would be more comfortable to continue air-drying, until it was time for another swim, when they would get wet again. Gradually, Melody began to talk to Joseph about her continuing education projects, her increasing interest in landscape photography, and traditional Jamaican cookery classes, and he told her about his part-time work, and the old Studebaker automobile that he was rebuilding at home. She was quite impressed when Joseph explained some of the precepts by which he lived - that the recurrent thoughts of individuals led to actions, which often became habits, in such a way as to define one's character, and eventually, one's destiny. He once commented that people tended to believe what they see, and to see what they believe. When Joseph added an adopted quotation that *'a way of seeing was a way of not seeing,'* Melody was to remember this thought for the rest of her life. He explained his interest in his automobile repair project as a way of focusing upon how to renew and recreate. Joseph told her that when difficulties seemed to block his way, he liked to recall Henry Ford's comment that an airplane takes off against, not with the wind. They bought coconut juice and beef patties for lunch and swam out again. Back on shore, responding to his sympathetic queries, she talked about the trials of her teenage years, as an introspective schoolgirl. It was then that he made another memorable remark, that many people are attracted by novelty, but that relationships can only be sustained by reflected appreciation.

When it was time to leave, as sunset approached, and pelicans soared and darted in search of fishes, just below the waves, and he reached for her hand to walk her home, Melody did not pull away. Later that day, she smiled when Joseph told her that he viewed happiness as the product of continued mutual love, not acquired possessions, although a range of home conveniences could make life easier.

After four months of meeting and talking each day, they had become inseparable, despite meeting their respective parents, who were skeptical to varying degrees, and for different reasons, as to the future of their relationship. One evening, Joseph met Melody at her mother's home for a broiled fish with white rice, okra, and pumpkin dinner. When they had a few moments to themselves on the verandah just outside the dining room, he told her that he'd received an offer of employment as a construction worker from a company called Sir Robert McAlpine Construction Management, in London, in the United Kingdom. Melody was glad for his sake, while saddened by the prospect that they would no longer see each other. As she rocked slowly on her mother's creaking wooden rocking chair, as fireflies or "*peenie-wallies*" flickered in the gathering dusk. Joseph took account of her tone, when she congratulated him. "Aren't you coming with me?" he asked.

In response to her comment that she had no job offer in London, Joseph smiled, held her left hand, knelt on the polished floor, and asked Melody to marry him.

She was stunned. It seemed like yesterday that they had first met, but since then, they had come to know a good deal about each other, most recently developing some familiarity with each other's relatives living in the vicinity of Montego Bay and Falmouth. Melody reflected that he made her laugh, feel wanted and safe, and that her mother, if not necessarily her father, had been encouraging her to consider settling down with him. She tried unsuccessfully to recall the author of a saying found in a recently borrowed, motivational library book..." *what we are is what our ancestors did, and how they survived. We are the memories we don't remember, which live in us...*" Would they look, feel, or behave like their parents, or their grandparents, one day? How would she know what would be a mistake, creating a lifetime of regret, in advance? As Joseph stroked her hand slowly and tenderly, Melody looked at him, asking whether he loved her. In answer, he lifted her from her rocking chair to give her increasingly deep kisses, fondly holding her close as she parted her lips, hugging her gently, until she agreed to marry him.

The next few weeks passed in a dizzying blur. Melody's mother planned for her wedding in a local Anglican church, where her daughter had been baptized, as a baby, twenty-five years before, and undertook the task of embroidering her white wedding gown with blue sequins herself, while planning a reception at their home. Meanwhile, after a long walk with Joseph, Melody's father ordered several cases of Appleton white and red rum, some to make rum punch, other cases to be enjoyed '*on the rocks*' during dinner or toasts. He stored them under all the beds, and bought all the meat needed to create *jerk pork, jerk chicken,* roasted beef, and curried goat on the old grill in the back yard, on the day of the reception.

Joseph's parents and friends brought wedding gifts to his home, wrapped, and unwrapped, and enthusiastically celebrated the forthcoming wedding in a nearby rum shop each evening. He began to wish that the wedding day would arrive quickly, both because he wanted to be with Melody, and because it was increasingly difficult to get any work done, during the days, and he could no longer focus upon his Studebaker repair project. Instead, he invited Melody to take long walks on the public beach with him, or they picked straw baskets of local fruit - avocados and naseberries for the wedding reception, hoping that they would not ripen too soon. Melody was also more and more weary of wedding planning conversations with friends that revolved around the old quatrain of "*something old, something new, something borrowed and something blue.*"

One day, they managed to get completely soaked in a sudden thunderstorm, while returning from the bush with their baskets, and ran to her home, arms laden, perspiring, shrieking with laughter. By the following day, Melody was coughing and sneezing. Her mother prescribed bed rest, giving her ginger tea and a vapor rub poultice, worried that she would not recover in time. However, she did. Now, Melody looked in wonder from the officiating pastor to Joseph, to their family and friends filing into the old wooden pews at the church, with the sun shining through near the alter, where a roof rafter needed repair. She felt proud, fulfilled and extremely nervous. As he prepared to bless their union, the earnest and bespectacled pastor cited Biblical verses from Ecclesiastes in an eloquent cadence that captured the attention of his audience…" *For everything there is a season, and a time for every matter under heaven: a time to be born and a time to dies; a time to plant and a time to reap what was planted…*" Several older members of the rapt audience were moved to cry out "Amen!" As Joseph and Melody gazed at him, contemplating his meaning, he went on to quote Leo Tolstoy, commenting that *when you love someone truly, it is for the person they are, and not the person you would like them to be.* He followed up by remarking that happiness in marriage came from within, not from one's partner. The pastor appeared to reflect personal experience, in earnestly admonishing the couple before him to support each other in enjoyed activities, working as a team, building mutual trust, and making time to enjoy being alone together. Joseph looked amorously at his new wife, awaiting the ceremony's completion, increasingly excited at the prospect of finally taking her to his bed that evening.

The reception at the home of Joseph's parents grew increasingly raucous, as the guests completed dinner, accompanied by rum punch, white rum, and desserts such as potato pudding, and a cornucopia of fruit - papaya, pineapple, soursop, passion fruit and lychee, with more and more couples swaying to dancehall and reggae music, spilling out onto the lawn from the somewhat shaky verandah. The guests repeatedly toasted the bride and groom, while also providing inebriated advice as to how to make each other happy. As the stars came out, and a full moon rose, flickering "*peenie wallies*" danced between the mango trees in a sea breeze, across the road, where *whistling toads* croaked in their own mating ritual.

That evening, the newly married couple arrived at his home extremely late, and quite hot. Joseph took off his cream sports jacket, maroon shirt, and striped, yellow tie, kissed his bride, and invited her to shower with him. Melody became even more nervous but did not resist as he removed her wedding gown, shoes, and underwear, then lifted his naked bride and took her to the shower. As he soaped and caressed Melody under the vigorous spray of water, she became more relaxed and excited. Joseph suckled her hardening nipples, and stroked between her legs, inserting two exploring fingers inside. She panted and swayed on her feet. In response, Joseph turned off the shower, lifted his bride again and hastily threw two beach towels on his neatly made bed, before entering her with his erect member, excitement mounting. It took a few moments before he regained sufficient self-control to slow his thrusting, taking account of her initially mixed pleasure and pain. He stroked her hair, kissed her, and suckled her nipples lovingly. As he massaged her mound, Melody led the way, screaming her first full orgasm. Joseph followed soon after, groaning, then collapsed on top of her.

The next morning, he awakened first to the sound of collared doves cooing in the back yard, and rising on his right elbow, drank in the sight of Melody still asleep, her mahogany hair sweeping across her pillow, mouth partly open, and one of her lovely breasts uncovered, nipple relaxed. Joseph was torn between the impulse to arise and make Blue Mountain coffee for his wife, and the desire to hug her close, once again. He got up, went to the kitchen, activated his small percolator, and returned with two hot cups of coffee, placing one carefully on each bedside table. As the sunlight filtered through the embroidered cream curtains on the bedroom windows, he kissed her face repeatedly. Melody began to awaken, and Joseph licked her now aroused nipples in turn, stroking her vulva until she was again trembling. He threw off the bedclothes, kissed her delightedly down her torso, ended up at her nether lips, and explored her warm, moist folds with his questing fingers, before embedding himself deep inside. The couple attained a steady rhythm which afforded them both growing pleasure, until Joseph shuddered and groaned, emptying himself into his wife, as she cried out in rapture and joined him in coming. When they finally arose, and he lifted her to the shower, Melody smiled. "Are you going to take me to the bathroom in your arms like this every day?" she inquired. Joseph chuckled "I would be glad to do so, if you never get tired of being swept off your feet, soaped, showered, and sexed!" She blushed.

Two months later, Joseph and Melody stepped off their ship from Jamaica at the Southampton docks in England, where they were met by a representative of the Human Resources Department in the Sir Robert

McAlpine Construction Company and taken by train to London. Although travel-weary, they were excited to see the varied greens of the countryside speeding past their train windows, noticing how more and more tall concrete buildings appeared, as they entered London, disembarking at Paddington. The couple ended up in a dingy bed and breakfast hotel in the vicinity for the night. They were taken to look at flats in Battersea, Brixton, and Clapham early the next day, after Joseph signed his employment contract, leaving them even more exhausted. When Melody saw a two-story brick flat in Brixton, steps leading up from the street to a sun-splashed, furnished flat with a small rose garden in the back, two bedrooms above and a basement below, she nodded her head. Joseph ever attentive to her, spoke quietly with the agent, and they were able to move into their new home during the following day.

"Why is it so extremely painful to give birth?" Melody asked herself, remembering conversations with her mother and assorted aunts, while also recalling her readings concerning the gradual narrowing of the female pelvic girdle, as millennial ancestors graduated from climbing to bipedal walking. She told herself that very few mothers died while giving birth, these days. But another series of sharp pains interrupted, then eliminated her thoughts, and as she groaned, Joseph leaned over the hospital bed to wipe her brow, while squeezing her hand. Shortly afterwards, the frequency of her contractions increased, and she wailed, turning her head from side to side. A pleasant nurse arrived to check on her heart rate, contractions, and dilation, smiling supportively at Joseph, who was clearly extremely tense and stressed. "If you feel faint, you should sit in the armchair over there, take a few sips of water, and breathe deeply – otherwise, you won't be able to offer your wife any support at all," she told him. In response, Joseph nodded. "Shouldn't the baby be arriving shortly now?" he asked, "we've been here all day, and she is in a lot of pain." The nurse reassured him that the birth of his son was proceeding normally, and that a gynecologist would be checking on Melody again within the next two hours. Joseph continued to hold her hand, tightening his grip when she moaned especially loudly, and otherwise, looking at the monitors near her bed. He thought about their first weeks and months in their new home. Stray thoughts drifted through his mind.... the unfinished black and chrome Studebaker at his home in Montego Bay that he'd asked his father to sell '*as is,*' the leaking pipe in their master bathroom at home in Brixton – he'd been planning to ask the landlord to arrange for a plumber – the busy worksite in Wembley, where he was normally pouring and molding concrete all day.

Suddenly, Melody's scream snapped him to attention, as the bedside monitors beeped. Joseph grabbed the intercom, shouted into it, and was relieved when a medical doctor arrived almost immediately, saying that she had been making her rounds when she heard the commotion. While checking Melody, she looked at the monitors, muttering that dilation should be sufficient at that stage, positioned her to push, rocking back and forth on her knees, and told Joseph to wait outside.

By the time that David Armstrong was three years old, Joseph often took his son to Clapham Commons in a stroller on weekends, intending to give Melody time to rest, as she was expecting their second child. He would sit on a bench and read from a selection of children's books to David, or tell his son stories of his own, often about Jamaica, or provide running commentaries on the people passing by, sometimes accompanied by their leashed dogs, and even remark on the darting sparrows, blue tits, chaffinches, and speckled starlings in the hedges nearby.

Meanwhile, Melody took the opportunity to complete her household washing and cleaning, systematically moving from room to room, without pausing, and to prepare vegetable beef soup on Saturdays, or rice with kidney beans and vegetables with roast beef on Sundays, for the family's dinner. When he returned home, Joseph always asked her why she had not taken some time to rest, and she regularly but patiently replied that her housework needed to be done.

Although her husband repeatedly offered to help her with such chores, she had long realized that he was much happier sharing in David's care and taking him out for walks. During dinner, they often spoke about their families in Jamaica, the routines of island life, and letters from friends in Montego Bay, some of whom wanted to join them in migrating to London. Once, Melody somewhat shyly asked Joseph whether she had been able to make him happy. He replied, thoughtfully, that for him, happiness came from appreciating fully the available blessings in each person's life, instead of desiring and trying to get what others appeared to have. "You remain my greatest blessing," he told his wife. "When we spend, share time, and exchange love with each other, I am always the happiest man in the world."

On occasion, after dinner, they would sit on the somewhat battered ochre-colored sofa in the living room, before the television set on the mantelpiece, and reminisce about David's birth, recalling how after two increasingly harrowing days of labor, Melody had ended up with a Caesarian section. Joseph would hug her tightly, and trace the uneven abdominal scar that remained, and she would rest her head on his shoulder, marveling how the years since their wedding had flown. On one such occasion, Joseph told her that he had been thinking about what might happen to his family should he become seriously ill or disabled, and unable to work. As a result, he had increased his contribution to the pension fund provided by his employer and ensured that Melody was listed as the prime beneficiary. She enjoyed sitting with him on long summer weekend evenings, after David had gone to sleep. Joseph tended to return home visibly weary from work and travel each weekday, and she tried to ensure that he could relax, eat healthily, and rest in a well-cared-for home, during such evenings; then awaken in time for a quick breakfast – usually toast with ham and cheese, along with coffee - and travel to work by tube the next morning, reading all the way.

When Danielle was born, three years later, Joseph was working on a construction project in Birmingham, and had to get special leave to be with Melody for a week, after she gave birth. Since her sixth month of pregnancy, he had arranged for a Polish neighbor's wife to visit each day, to clean the house, cook, shop at a Tesco in the vicinity, and care for David, after taking him to and from his public primary school nearby. Melody appreciated the assistance but felt unhappy about enduring the last months of her pregnancy mostly alone, the lack of privacy involved in accepting assistance, and the weekly cost for which Joseph had to budget. He arrived at Kings Cross Station only after Danielle's first cries, and held her proudly, somewhat breathlessly, after rushing to be with his wife, who was scheduled to be released to go home that afternoon. Melody urged Joseph to seek a transfer back to a construction project in London, and when he finally ended up back at Wembley, the couple thanked their neighbors, and resumed routines that now included care for both their children. Looking in the bathroom mirror, Melody was disturbed by the weight she had gained, the size of her slightly pendulous light brown breasts, and was concerned that her husband might find her less attractive. However, he enjoyed watching her feed Danielle, and tried to discourage her plan to diet, saying that she was still eating for two. Whenever they were able to put both children to sleep early, and he once again took her in his arms in bed, nuzzling his wife, making her laugh out loud, and entered her, as they rocked with mounting passion, then exploded, Melody felt completely reassured, and relaxed to sleep, awakening in the morning smiling.

Seven years later, Melody sat in her living room, while David and Danielle were at school, and remembered how her world had suddenly turned upside down. She stared at a silver framed wedding picture hung on the pastel walls of the room, recalling her marriage to Joseph in Montego Bay, breathing rapidly as if she had just run a race. He had gone to work as usual only that morning, hugging and kissing her, as she gave him the old yellow lunch box with ham sandwiches and coffee that she'd prepared for him. He had telephoned two hours later, checking in with her from his noisy construction site, for what turned out to be the last time. It had never entered Melody's thoughts that she might end up raising their two children by herself – that she would not ever see or hug Joseph again. When she tried to recall her life as a young woman before her marriage, her memories appeared to be those of an entirely different person, who simply looked similar in the mirror. She now centered her life, hopes and dreams on David and Danielle.

Yet she had continued to borrow and read interesting books from the Brixton Library and remembered Kahlil Gibran's lines…." *Love one another but make not a bond of love…fill each other's cup, but drink not from one cup…. let there be spaces in your togetherness.*" Melody's eyes filled with gathering tears. She reminisced about their delicious dinners and weekend lunches together, realizing once again that she had poured out all of her heart to Joseph, so much so that years after his accidental death at work, the funeral arrangements she made on 'automatic pilot,' her numbed acceptance of a settlement from his employer that augmented the proceeds of the life insurance policy her husband had insisted on buying - as well as information about the annuity to be provided by his pension fund – a wide internal wound remained open in her innermost being. Joseph had been an exhilarating wind that blew Melody away from her earlier years in Montego Bay, depositing her some five thousand miles away, in a city where she would now have to find a way to continue her life as a single parent, as a grieving widow who, throughout their life together, had been contentedly *drinking each day from one cup* with her deceased husband, who still seemed so very exuberant in all of his remaining black-and-white photos. She continued to experience sudden paroxysms of deep sadness and loss, from time to time. But if only for the sake of her children, Melody knew she must move on. As an initial step, she eventually began to discuss options for the purchase of a two-bedroom garden flat with schools nearby, in North London, and considered engaging in volunteer work that would allow sufficient time to manage her home and children.

Chapter Three

Benito was pleased with himself, observing Alessia's distress. He suddenly lifted her up in his arms, and before she could struggle free, walked over to the corner where her brother, Paolo, remained in animated conversation. Immediately upon releasing her to stand, he reached for her left hand, and displaying the ring to everyone present, declared that Alessia had just made him the happiest man in the world, by accepting his engagement ring. As the iridescent blue-green emerald sparkled in the beam from an electric spotlight in the ceiling, Alessia pulled her hand away, and tried to remove the ring, exclaiming in frustration when it turned out to be too tight for her to take off easily. Paolo regarded her, puzzled. "If you didn't accept Benito's proposal, why are you wearing his ring?" Benito broke in, confidently "You know how nervous fiancées and brides can be – happy and loving one moment, anxious and uncertain the next." Alessia squared her shoulders and answered Paolo too loudly "I never accepted this man's proposal nor his ring. He forced it on my finger, and now it won't come off," as she continued twisting and turning it. Benito suavely commented "Feminine nerves, just as I've said, and since Lucia was a witness to my proposal, let's ask her to confirm what occurred." Paolo remained concerned, as he considered his sister's flashing eyes and her angry demeanor. But Benito returned with Lucia and asked her to tell the group what she saw. "Gladly," she answered. "It was all so romantic and sweet. Benito got down on his knees and asked Alessia to be his bride. When she hesitated, he kissed the palms of her hands repeatedly, and declared that his life would be a desert wasteland from that moment on, without her. As she looked at him wonderingly, Benito held out his beautiful engagement ring, and said that if she would accept it, he would immediately ask her brother, on behalf of her parents, for her hand in marriage. When she took a deep breath and finally nodded, he arose, placed the ring on her finger, and since she appeared to be completely overcome with emotion – just the way I felt when Tomassini proposed to me - he very considerately helped her to come over here."

Paolo was now less hesitant, recognizing that Benito not only had a witness, but that he intended to request his blessing. "I agree to the engagement in principle," he said, while indicating the need to discuss it with his sister and their parents on the following day, before saying any more. Benito remained pleased with himself, smiled widely at the group, and thanked Paolo, appearing to be the assured and accepted suitor. When Alessia walked towards the door, still trembling, her brother followed, and both left the reception. Afterwards, Benito and Tomassini thanked Lucia profusely, telling her that she would soon have Alessia to train as a new addition to their inventory, noting that the company's customers would pay a premium for her, as an incredibly attractive virgin. Meanwhile, on the tube home, Alessia and her brother sat in a tense silence, unwilling to continue what had become a quite heated discussion, with so many commuters within earshot. Once at their Camden Town apartment, Paolo took Alessia by the arm, and took her to her bedroom, as Giancarlo was watching television in the living room. "What's *wrong* with you?" he asked his sister, as she sat on her pink-quilted single bed, and he perched on a stool near her mirror. Alessia tried to explain herself calmly, telling Paolo exactly what had happened. He was incredulous. "So, you are saying that both Benito and Lucia are lying, with that very expensive ring still on your finger?" he demanded. Alessia tearfully exclaimed that she would be sure to get the ring off in one way or the other, and to throw it away. "But Benito is clearly a successful businessman, from Campania, and he seems to love you ardently. Perhaps your recollection of events has been affected by your stress, which is indeed entirely normal for a young girl who is contemplating marriage." When Paolo told her that he would discuss the matter with their parents on the telephone, and would talk further to her the next day, asserting that she should on no account throw her beautiful engagement ring away, Alessia felt desolate, as if the walls of her room were closing in on her. After he went downstairs, she overheard him talking with Giancarlo, then much more indistinctly, on the telephone for what seemed to be a long while. Alessia rushed to her bathroom, and eventually managed to twist the ring off, using her lavender bath soap and body lotion, then returned to her bed, where she had recently dreamt of David on more than one occasion, sobbing herself to sleep on her pillow. She awoke several times during the night from unremembered dreams, heart racing.

The next morning, Alessia bathed, dressed, and went downstairs to make coffee and toast, preparing to go to work, as usual. However, as soon as Paolo saw her, he declared decisively: "You will soon be a married woman, with no need to work outside your home. Our parents agree that it is time for you to get used to your new status." Alessia's eyes widened. "What on Earth do you mean?" she asked, "I haven't agreed to marry anyone. In any case, my manager at work is expecting me to arrive by 8:00 am." Paolo answered curtly "Are you still trying to bring dishonor to our family by pretending that you didn't accept Benito's proposal, which has now been blessed by our parents?" Alessia sat down at the dining table in her cream dress, dazed by her elder brother's statements, but determined. "I am not an item of property to be given by you, or even my parents, to anyone against my will, and have no plans for marriage at this time, only for work and study." Paolo became angry. He called Giancarlo, who came hurrying from his room, told him that their sister was determined to dishonor her family, immediately under their parents' wedding portrait, and asked him to help in returning Alessia to her room. Giancarlo was visibly shocked, not at his brother but at his sister. Each of the brothers lifted Alessia by her arms and feet upstairs to her room, despite her vigorous struggles, in the course of which she slapped them both. Her suede high-heeled shoes fell off. They set her on the bed, then Paolo took her room key from the dressing table, told her that when she did not turn up at work, the bank would quickly find someone else, and locked her door from the outside. She heard her brothers talking about her as they descended the stairs, and collapsing on the bed, cried in utter frustration for a while.

After eventually arising, and washing her face in the attached bathroom, where she saw the emerald ring glittering by the wash basin, Alessia took stock of her situation. Paolo, Giancarlo, and now, her parents, were evidently determined that she should marry Benito – a man she hardly knew, and had found somewhat repulsive, even before he evidently collaborated with Lucia to lie outright about his "accepted proposal." She was in a country where women had legal rights and were not obliged to obey the wishes of parents or other family members, regardless. How to get out of her room? She looked out of the old wood-framed window, noting the cracked concrete sidewalk two stories below, and shook the handle of her bedroom door, which remained firmly locked. Hearing her efforts, Paolo came upstairs and told her through the door that he was recommending the earliest practicable wedding to Benito, and that she would have to learn to obey her husband, once married. Alessia looked around her bedroom, which was suddenly now a prison, and was wondering whether she was actually asleep in a nightmare, when her eyes fell on her brown Prada handbag on the floor. She jumped up, took out her new Motorola Razr mobile phone, and called David, who had just left his home for work. She spoke so quietly that it was difficult for him to hear her, particularly as her tale of recent events seemed so bizarre, even to her. When she eventually conveyed her situation to David, he was absolutely shocked. "Should I come to get you now?" he asked. "No," she answered, "you would be late for your restaurant, end up in a fight with my brothers, and would probably lose your job, into the bargain. Why don't you go to work? We will plan a way for us to meet later today, even if you have to catch me jumping from my window!" In response, David commented that fortunately, she clearly did not weigh very much. Alessia was heartened by her discussion with David, while still very confused about her situation. Even if they somehow got together, what next?

Paolo sat in the dining room, reflecting upon the situation. As a young girl, Alessia had appeared shy and tractable, but became increasingly definite about what she wanted to do, when a teenager, after graduation from high school. Their parents had been quite stressed when she took it into her head to apply to a private university far away in Milan, rather than a nearby institution, such as the University of Palermo. Alessia had often preferred reading, playing with her dolls, or watching their mother cook in the kitchen, to games with other girls, and had never learned much of the local dialect spoken on the streets. When at the beach, she would swim by herself, instead of participating in volleyball games with Giancarlo and himself, or simply splashing each other in the water. Paolo recalled how both brothers had resented the way in which their parents had treated their only daughter as the favorite of the family, always preparing or purchasing special treats for her. He remembered accompanying Alessia to her high school graduation dance, and how she frowned when her partner tried to pull her close, looking around and inviting his help. Now he had to assist his sister in an entirely different way, as she remained too stubborn to realize that it was time for her so settle down to raise a new family with a good husband. Both their father and mother agreed that she was in danger of disgracing herself, and the family, if she continued working with all kinds of men at the bank where Alessia had been spending her days. Paolo sighed, and taking out his Samsung Galaxy mobile phone, called the bookseller's shop where he worked, and explained that unfortunately, he was ill that day, but hoped to be better by the next morning. He then called Benito and told him that his family was ready for him to plan a wedding with Alessia as soon as possible, although she was still hesitating as to whether to continue their engagement, because of understandable nervousness about the major change in her life implied. Paolo commented that if Benito treated her kindly and considerately, as her husband, he was sure that their marriage would do well. Benito assured him that he had nothing to worry about, as Alessia would soon come to realize that she had a husband dedicated to her.

After ending the call with Paolo, Benito looked at Tomassini and Lucia, sitting nearby, and laughed, then commented in a gasconade that many people were very easily led by their noses once the right aroma was applied. In response, Tomassini remarked that the Operations Manager in Brighton looked like, and could readily dress as a priest, and could rent a church where the ceremony could be conducted. "Well, what are we waiting for?" asked Benito. I can collect a wedding ring today, and if you will rent a beautiful bridal gown that will fit, Lucia, Tomassini can make the arrangements with Luca for the day after tomorrow."

Tomassini grinned. "This bridegroom is certainly in a hurry!" Benito laughed merrily again. "You can't blame me for wanting to enjoy my bride – and to market her pleasures at a premium soon afterwards. We will need to tell her brothers that I will take Alessia to New York to set up subsidiary warehouses for a while there, immediately after the wedding." When Tomassini asserted that Lucia would have her hands full in training Alessia, and in ensuring that she did not try to escape, or contact the police,

Lucia responded that she expected no difficulties at all. "As soon as Benito has had a chance to fully enjoy himself with her, by the next morning, I will have her first fully paid customers lined up, anxious to take their turns. After a day on the market with little or no food or drink, many young women begin to resign themselves to the situation, while often becoming very depressed." Lucia explained that such young women needed a mother figure, who would take care of them for a few days afterwards, providing meals that were just sufficient for survival, but with generous helpings of sympathy, and then in time, induct them into the business. After a while, most became obedient.

Alessia sat on her bed, having long changed her clothing, and quietly called in sick to the bank, still hoping that Paolo would not remember she had her phone with her. She looked up at the stained white ceiling and the crown molding of her bedroom, and the walls, hands locked behind her head, wondering whether to call the police and report a kidnapping, then concluded that such an inevitably public, investigative visit from uniformed constables would cause extreme embarrassment to her brothers and parents. In the end, Paolo and Giancarlo might well be able to convince the police that what had occurred was really a family disagreement over an accepted suitor that would shortly be settled, notwithstanding her own concerns, caused by an impending bride's usual last- minute nervousness. She had no bruises or cuts to show, just hurt pride, given the way that her brothers had so readily lifted her up the stairs and confined her – and her growing apprehension as to what Paolo, in particular, would do next.

Hearing birds singing on the elm trees outside, wondering idly whether they might be sparrows, Alessia went to the window and looked out wistfully. It was actually a pair of blue jays, with resplendent, black-barred tails, and black collars circling their heads, sitting on a branch, that attracted her gaze. She called David again, and encountering his answering machine, left a message telling him that they might really need to find out how well he could catch her, when he finished work, ending with a sound between a sob and a laugh. She was barely able to put her phone under a pillow, when the key turned in the door, and Paolo entered, with a tray of rice, broiled fish, vegetables, and white wine. "I thought you would need some lunch, since you didn't have breakfast," he said, "I'm sorry that we had such a disagreement about Benito, but he really will do his best to be a good husband to you, and when you get married, our parents will be proud of you." Alessia looked at him, remembering how she had sometimes depended upon her eldest brother for safety away from home, as a child. Once he had courageously faced down a boy whose family was reportedly linked to the *Ndrangheta*, or Mafia, when she found herself taunted almost to tears about her school clothing every afternoon. He was not only taller and more muscular now, but his face was lined, and there were even grey strands in his hair. "Don't you care what your only sister thinks about this man you want to bring into the family?" she asked.

Paolo sighed. "Why is it that you seem so comfortable with strange men, like the one you were sitting with in Hyde Park, a few weeks ago, and so uncomfortable with your own countryman, from Campania in this case, one who is evidently from a well-off family?" Alessia looked into his blue eyes, her stomach growling with hunger. "Why is it that you have been paying no attention to my reactions to Benito, from the very beginning, believing his *proposal story* instead of the truth that I've told you?" she asked in turn. "Aren't you supposed to be protecting me, as my elder brother?" Paolo responded "It is because I wish to safeguard you that your marriage will take place before the end of this week. You have been very confused since meeting Benito. I understand. Many girls don't know what to think, until after settling down. Afterwards, you will be sure to thank me."

Alessia was hungry, not having had breakfast, and after eating her lunch with relish, and drinking the wine, sat at her dressing table to reflect upon the feeling of David's arms about her, and his gentle lips on hers, tongues sweetly caressing each other, while they were ensconced on that bench in the park. "But what kind of future could there be for them?" she asked herself. Just as Paolo had dismissed David as a *mente nero*, so would Giancarlo and her parents. Could her elder brother be right, that she should simply settle for a countryman with a well-off family in Campania, who would be able to take care of her? Should she discard her dreams of working and going on to further studies in London? She remembered Benito sitting beside her in the cinema, holding her left hand in both of her own, pulling her hand towards his lap, and his triumphant smile at the reception, after Lucia had told her story. Alessia felt in her bones that Benito, Tomassini and Lucia were all smarmy, deceitful, and potentially dangerous people, although it was impossible to explain to herself exactly why she felt such a visceral repulsion. By contrast, she longed for an opportunity to kiss David again. Alessia looked at her reflection in the mirror, smiling at the color in her cheeks as she thought of David, then took a sharp breath, as she imagined what marriage to Benito could mean. After looking at the tray brought by Paolo, now with an empty dish, used cutlery, and a little wine in the glass, she had an idea. Her brother was not about to change his mind about Benito, no matter what she said, but at least, he would be sure to bring her another tray with dinner, probably in the vicinity of 5:00 pm when they normally dined. She arose decisively and examined the row of dresses, together with other clothing hanging in her built-in wardrobe, as well as the line of carefully selected casual and formal shoes in the rack beneath.

Alessia chose an elegant azure dress that could be worn at home or outdoors, checked her handbag for space, then fitted in a sweater, shorts, and underwear, alongside her phone, comb, cash, visa credit card, ID, and London Transport season ticket, then found a pair of exercise shoes, slipped them on, and arranged herself in bed with a cover and pillows to re-read an old, favorite novel – Dickens' *David Copperfield.* She settled down to read. Alessia was startled when the key suddenly turned in the lock, her door opened, and Paolo came in, saying pleasantly that he was glad she'd appreciated her lunch, would take the tray back downstairs, and bring her dinner soon. As he turned his back for a moment to collect the tray. Alessia threw off the cover, grabbed her handbag, along with her book, and rushed through the half-opened door downstairs. Paolo dropped the tray on her bed and ran after her, calling upon her to stop. She was at the front door of the apartment as he was coming down the stairs and had a moment of panic wondering whether it was locked. However, this door was normally locked only at night, and opened as usual. Alessia rushed down the rickety outer stairs and into the street, running towards the Camden Town tube station. For a moment, Paolo ran behind her, in an increasingly angry state, and was almost close enough to grab Alessia's shoulder, when he saw two uniformed constables on patrol, and decided to pretend that he was out for a jog. He crossed the street and circling back to the apartment, rather than confronting Alessia in public.

Alessia continued to run as fast as she could and was almost at the Camden Town tube station, panting heavily, before she realized that Paolo was no longer chasing her. She hurried down the staircase into the station, then paused to catch her breath, wondering what to do. It was almost 6:00 pm, she thought, so David should be at home in Hornsey now. Using her season ticket, she walked to the platform towards Euston, planning to change to the Piccadilly line to Turnpike Lane there, almost on autopilot. Where else could she go? It was incredible that she had been locked up in her room by her brothers yet was able to escape twice – from the apartment and again, while running on the street – Alessia had not seen the constables who had inadvertently stopped her brother's determined pursuit, so his decision to turn back was a mystery. Now what? She called David from Turnpike Lane. When he answered, she sobbed in relief. David was aghast. "What's happening?" he asked, thinking that she remained imprisoned in her room, and prepared to go to her family's apartment immediately after dinner. He was both shocked and relieved, when she tersely updated him, telling her "Stay right where you are, at the main station exit. I'm coming to get you now."

David had spoken about Alessia to his mother and his sister, Danielle, who had teased him that even though he had lost his bank job, he now had a girlfriend. He put down his utensils and covered his dinner plate, while explaining what had occurred that day. Mrs. Armstrong was very sympathetic. "How could that poor girl's brothers treat her so badly?" she asked. "If you both would prefer that she come here for the time being, while you decide what to do, Alessia could have the guest room upstairs, and share Danielle's bathroom." For once, Danielle looked concerned, even alarmed, and did not joke about the situation. David got up from the dining table, hugged his mother and sister, then hurried out to the tube station to meet Alessia. When he arrived, she was not immediately visible, and he began to be anxious, thinking that her brothers, or perhaps even that slimy Italian man, Benito, had been able to track and find her somehow. But there she was, in a lovely blue dress with spaghetti straps, as he crossed the street, standing near a news agent, shoulders slumped, her normally well-styled brunette hair in disarray and her eyes red. David folded her into his arms immediately, soothing her and gently stroking her back. Alessia buried her face in the curve of his right shoulder, and shuddered, as she relived the day, hardly believing that they were together, while swept by roiling waves of uncertainties and anxiety as to her future.

Alessia was both glad to see David and incredibly stressed. He led her to a zebra crossing, then across the road, to retrace his steps home, explaining, as they walked past a park with a pond and several graceful willow trees, that his mother was inviting her to stay at their home. Looking at her expression, he hastened to explain, "I mean that she is planning for you to have the guest room, and to share my sister's bathroom." Alessia's eyes filled with tears. Seeing David's alarm, she responded, "How can I meet your family looking bedraggled like this? At the very least, I need to wash my face and comb my hair." As they were just approaching the main park gate, David led her inside, walking with her to a public bathroom with wisterias and bluebells blooming around it, then left her at the entrance to the side reserved for females. While waiting he phoned his mother to tell her that he'd collected Alessia at the tube station, and they were on the way home. He could hear Danielle chanting in the background, "David's got a girlfriend, David's got a girlfriend!" After a while, Alessia emerged, clearly feeling more presentable. As they left the park and returned to the street, she asked him, "Whatever am I going to do? I no longer have a home, nor any clothes or shoes in which to work at the bank." David smiled, hugged her, and gently kissed her lips, then reassured her that she was more than welcome to stay at his mother's home for as long as she wished, and that there was a Marks and Spenser store near the tube station where she could purchase a few dresses and shoes for work, to begin with. She buried her face against his chest once more, then inquired as to why he had never explained the reason for his father's departure. "Did your parents divorce?"

David took her back inside the park, and seated her on a wooden bench, green paint peeling in places. "My father died in an accident at work, after the birth of my sister Danielle," he explained. "We all got into my mother's habit of simply saying that he *left* as she really doesn't want to think of him as dead." Alessia looked at him, wide-eyed, her own problems forgotten for a moment, and inquired as to whether his mother had ever considered remarriage. David told her somberly that he thought that part of Melody's soul had been buried with his father in a Brixton cemetery, and that she had told his sister that when Danielle grew up, if she were fortunate, she would find and marry a man just like him. "You must miss your father a lot," Alessia said gently, holding David's right hand. Nodding, he hugged her again, and then reminded her that dinner was awaiting them at home. They walked back to the quiet street outside once more.

Danielle was delighted to meet Alessia, hugging her and commenting that her brother had been talking about her every day. When Alessia looked at David, Danielle hastened to add that her brother had never praised any lady previously, apart from their mother, who called at that moment from the kitchen to say that their dinners had been warmed up and served. Melody noted Alessia's pallor and still red eyes, so made a special effort to encourage her to relax. However, Melody's kindly intended question as to the wellbeing and location of her parents left Alessia visibly stressed. Noticing her physical response, David remarked that Alessia had very recently experienced extreme communication difficulties with several family members, and that it would probably be more comfortable, for now, to talk about practically any other topic. While beginning to eat, he added that she would need to purchase some clothing for work at the bank tomorrow, and that he was planning to take her to a department store near the Turnpike Lane station after dinner. Alessia told Melody that the beef soup with vegetables provided was absolutely delicious, adding that she did not know how to thank her for accommodating her so considerately in her beautiful home. Melody arose, came over to Alessia, who got up to lean into her warm hug, and began to cry.

David and Danielle also arose, and joined in hugging Alessia, whose tears gradually subsided. "I don't know what came over me," said an embarrassed Alessia. Melody brought her a few napkins for her use, while inviting her to sit and to finish eating her soup while it was still warm. David did likewise. When a drizzle began outside, and a light breeze rattled the bay windows, he commented that while the red, white, and yellow rose bushes in the front garden would be refreshed, they would need an umbrella, and to use the bus, in going to the store.

Later, at the store. Alessia was somewhat shy when purchasing pajamas and underwear, telling David to sit nearby while she shopped. By the time that she was buying two dresses suitable for the bank, however, she repeatedly asked for his opinion, and on several occasions, requested that he zip up the back of her clothing. It took quite a while before she felt satisfied and completed her purchases. As they took an escalator downstairs to the entrance, Alessia sighed and commented that the address on her credit card was the Camden Town apartment where she had been living with her brothers, and she now had quite a balance to be paid off. David took her bags, as well as her left hand, and reminded Alessia that she could sign up for an online, paper-free account, adding that they should go to the post office to complete a change of address form very soon.

After they crossed the street to the bus stop, while waiting for a bus, she asked him, "Are you sure that your mother is truly content for me to be at her home for a while? In any case, I cannot just live there indefinitely, and will need to rent a place of my own." The bus they needed arrived. When they made their way to an unoccupied back corner seat, David put his arm around Alessia, telling her that his mother and sister were extremely glad to have her stay with the family, and that he was worried about the possibility that her brothers, together with their two South Italian friends, might search for and seek to confront her, if an opportunity arose. Alessia paled and looked frightened at the thought. David pulled her closer, kissing her, until she also enfolded him tightly in her arms, breathing more and more rapidly. It was David who suddenly pulled away and rang for the driver to halt the bus, saying in concern that they had just passed the intended bus stop.

It was still drizzling as they walked through the garden, awash with mini ponds of muddy water around the rose bushes, and David opened the door with his key, calling "Mom, we're back!" Both Melody and Danielle came from the living room to greet them. Alessia felt both elated and exhausted. Melody scrutinized her face, then told her daughter to take their guest up to her room to shower and rest, given her plan to go to work the next morning. She led David to the medium smalt sofa in the living room, offering him biscuits and cheese with hot cocoa.

While he munched, Melody told her son that Alessia seemed to be a lovely Italian young lady, asking him whether he was clear as to his plans concerning her. "You are a black man, in a society where mixed-race relationships can be difficult, and from what you've told us, her family has been treating her very badly – but when all is said and done, you surely cannot expect her to be cut off from her brothers and parents for the rest of her life – quite apart from your feelings for each other." David looked at his mother, with those intense brown eyes that reminded her so much of Joseph that she suddenly sighed, and responded quietly, "We are still working out our relationship, where the future is concerned, but are sure we want to be together, Mom. Society is changing around us, and her family will eventually come around." Melody smiled at her son and hugged him. Later, when David went to bed, it was not easy to fall asleep, as he kept thinking of Alessia's kisses, the stresses caused by her eldest brother's plans to marry her to a compatriot regardless of her wishes, and the fact that she should now be asleep in the guest room, a little way down the corridor. Rather than sleeping, however, Alessia was tossing in her new violet pajamas, reliving her day, from the time when Paolo and Giancarlo carried her up to her room, despite all of her strenuous efforts to resist, to the times when David kissed her so deliciously, at the tube station, and later, on the bus. A distantly remembered, ravenous fire came to mind, frightening her again into tears, as she thought of the support of Paolo and even her parents for that repulsive liar Benito's plans to marry her. Alessia sought to gain her moorings, looking at the streetlight shining through the ultramarine curtains of the guest room, with the rain rattling gently on the windowpanes. She took her dog-eared copy of *David Copperfield* from her handbag and tried to read, revisiting Miss Haversham's house once again. However, her body was pleasantly warmed and flushed, as she imagined David gently caressing her soft, responsive breasts, and murmuring in her ears. She eventually drifted off to a deep sleep.

At work in the bank the next day, Alessia was still disoriented. She had dressed that morning, breakfasted with David and his family, then they took a bus to the tube station, traveling south together on the Piccadilly line, parting for the day at Oxford Circus, where they made plans to meet at the end of the day. Alessia had to complete a sick leave request form for her prior day's absence, and had her supervisor approve it. She settled down to the routine of work on the counter, and after a while, began to concentrate fully on her tasks. When it was time for lunch, Alessia reached in her bag for a ham and cheese sandwich with spicy mustard that Melody had provided, purchased a bottle of water from a dispenser in the lobby, then strolled outside until she encountered an empty bench, and ate her lunch. It was a sunny day, and the streets were crowded with shoppers and cars, but her thoughts were gloomy, even morose. When and how could she see her brothers - and eventually her parents – again? Where would or could her relationship with David lead? Meanwhile, for how long should she accept refuge at his mother's home? A pair of chaffinches with their titian and smalt heads, displaying iridescent yellow, white, and black-streaked feathers, chirped in in a nearby beech tree, cheering her up for a moment. She discarded the remainder of her lunch, appetite diminished. Then, noting the time, Alessia sighed heavily and returned to the bank, taking her place at the black marble counter, once again.

David took an order for shrimp balls and white house wine at his restaurant, while hardly listening to the customer, who was also requesting fresh napkins, until he repeated his order, in a querulous tone. Back in the kitchen, while collecting other orders, David was thinking about Alessia, remembering the stress and sorrow in her tearful eyes, and her somewhat disheveled hair, when he met her at Turnpike Lane – but also, the soft sweetness and increasing passion of their kisses in the bus yesterday, causing him to lose focus upon their destination, passing it by several minutes. As he took two bowls of sweet and sour teardrop soup and two cups of jasmine green tea to one of his tables, and the tempo of the background music increased, he thought of his parents' calm, quietly loving relationship – and how, after Joseph had suddenly died, his mother had been wracked by grief, so disconsolate that she had talked of asking a relative to care for her children, so that she could join her husband in his grave. But she would always subsequently regret such remarks, hugging David, and Danielle, telling them how much she loved them. For a few moments he stood at the table serving, staring outside almost sightlessly, while his customers regarded him curiously; then out of the corner of an eye, David noticed a man in a black blazer looking into the restaurant, then glancing away, as their eyes met briefly. David pulled himself together and went to another customer's table to take a pending order, feeling a passing disquiet at the person he'd seen, without being able to explain to himself exactly why. He was both exhilarated and anxious, as he ruminated upon his increasingly intense relationship with Alessia and looked forward eagerly to seeing her again while wondering whether she really felt the same about him.

When they met at Oxford Circus after work as planned, noting the crowd on the platform, he suggested that they walk towards the front of the train, and wait for the next train to arrive. While standing there, David hugged Alessia's shoulders. She turned towards him, her grey eyes warm, affectionate, and trusting. While they were absorbed in a kiss, melting into each other, two trains arrived and departed, without being noticed. Departing and boarding passengers pushed by them impatiently. David stroked her glossy brunette hair and remarked sheepishly that he seemed to be losing himself in her regularly, apologizing for having missed the tubes that had evidently passed. Alessia smiled sweetly, anxieties erased for a few moments, saying that if there was any fault to be found, she also had to confess having lost herself in him. David was thrilled to hear this, and began kissing her again, until an emerging tube passenger irately tapped him on the shoulder, complaining that they were blocking the exit from the train. When David and Alessia eventually boarded, the train was so crowded that she ended up holding on tightly to him, to his pleasure, while he held a roof strap, with the surrounding passengers pressing them further together. David continued to enjoy the sensation of Alessia's body, so close to him that he could smell her lightly sweet Samarra perfume despite the crowd, while seeing her lovely face resting comfortably against his chest. Suddenly he noticed a bearded young man just behind Alessia, with closed eyes, who appeared to be rocking himself against her intrusively, actually causing David to feel his pressure. Holding the young woman in his arms, he swung her away, making the offending passenger lose his balance, and fall against another passenger just before they arrived at their station. As they held hands while walking back to Melody's home, exchanging glances often, David and Alessia wordlessly confirmed their growing affection for each other, along with irremediable anxiety about the gathering future. They also speculated as to why the news had recently been filled with natural disasters, such as an earthquake in Haiti that had killed 250,000 people, another unprecedented earthquake in Chile, 8.8 on the Richter scale, that snuffed out the lives of 500 people in an instant, creating a tsunami, and yet another in Sumatra, leaving thousands of people missing after a destructive tsunami swept ashore.

Beyond the short term, inescapably including questions as to what their lives together might be like, the future of the entire Earth appeared to be in question.

During dinner with Melody and Danielle that evening, David and Alessia were drawn into descriptions of what work was like, at the bank and the restaurant, respectively. Everyone laughed when Alessia recounted the case of a customer who presented a check to be cashed for much more than her account balance, and then apologized, saying that she knew that her forgotten eyeglasses at home would present a problem today – although an eyeglass case was visible in her partly opened handbag. David shared the problem experienced with an overfull customer who ordered an "all you can eat" option called "Lazy Sundays," and who complained at the end of the meal that neither his wife nor himself had had sufficient appetite to justify this selection, so he wanted a reduced, itemized charge. At David's request, his supervisor collected the customer's card, charged the proper amount, then explained to a crestfallen man that selections could not be changed after meal completion - but they were quite welcome to order a few more dim sum rounds, or perhaps, dessert. Another round of chuckles ensued at the dinner table. Afterwards, Melody encouraged her son and their guest to relax in the living room with the television, and to retire to rest when ready, while Danielle and herself took care of the dishes. David and Alessia sat on the living room sofa and held hands. Instead of paying attention to the newscaster who was succeeded by the weather forecaster, they moved closer to each other. David looked at Alessia, and marveled that she was truly beside him, in his home that evening, after all the prior day's stress, and their weeks of working, talking, walking, and eating lunch together, learning to know and to want each other.

When he leaned over to touch her face with his fingertips, she looked at him. They rose silently, headed upstairs to their respective bathrooms, changed for sleep, and then David slipped into the guest room as she sat on the bed.

"Are you sleepy yet?" he asked. She shook her head. Sitting down beside Alessia, he held her face in his hands, kissing her forehead, cheeks, and lips. They settled into a deep kiss, continuing until they were both panting. David was enraptured. Slipping his hand underneath her violet pajama top, he caressed her breasts for the first time, stroking the hardening nubs of her nipples and circling her aureoles, while pulling Alessia in for another kiss. He felt as if he had somehow slipped into a radiant dream, where his most cherished wishes had inexplicably become both real and illusory. As their hearts beat faster and faster, David laid her down on the bed, and placed his left hand between her legs, while continuing to stroke her breasts with his right hand, tongues dancing together. She suddenly begged him to stop, and both sat up, panting. When she asked him in a trembling voice to put on protection, if he had any available, David showed her his condom foil packet, and removed his pajamas. Alessia looked at him, licked her dry lips, and reached out to stroke his turgid member with her soft little hand. In the glow of the bedside lamp, their bodies created a chiaroscuro of light and dark. After he ripped opened the packet, at his request, it was she who shyly rolled the contents onto him.

They heard Danielle showering in her bathroom and held each other in silence until she retired to bed, then resumed their kisses. As he caressed her vulva and clitoris, Alessia whispered, trembling, "You know I've never done this before. Will it hurt?" David reassured her, also whispering, and entered Alessia gently, grateful that the guest bed was a relatively new purchase, so should not creak.

Such thoughts vanished, as she gasped in momentary pain, and he lay still inside her for a few minutes, then resumed, stroking, and kissing her. After initial discomfort, Alessia felt that her entire world had suddenly narrowed to David's hands, roaming her quivering body, tongues tangling, as his mouth swallowed her increasingly urgent moans, and his rampant penis rocked deep inside, ravishing her. "*Ti voglio bene*!" she whispered, "I love you!" once her mouth was free.

David echoed her declaration of love, from deep in his bones. As it rained heavily outside, beating the window like a percussion drum, she wailed, and he groaned their sonorous pleasure.... they dozed tangled in the bedsheets and began making love again. It was almost 5:00 am, when a dazed David slipped back into his room.

Chapter Four

Benito was shocked at the telephone call received from Paolo, telling him that his sister Alessia had escaped from her room in which he'd confined her, pending her marriage. His first impulse was to say angrily that all the arrangements had already been made, based on Paolo's prior assurances. Instead, after taking a few calming, deep breaths, he said, "I am willing to hire a private investigator to find her, if you wish. But have you any idea where she might be?" Paolo explained that she had probably gone back to work at her bank, and had likely booked a hotel room, or even rented an apartment, as she had her own bank account. He paused for a minute, then inquired as to what Benito would do, once Alessia had been located. It was Tomassini, who was listening to the phone's speaker and answered. "Paolo, we can arrange for her return to your home, or to be taken to a convenient hotel, where Lucia can help her to dress, in the absence of your mother or a sister, then immediately afterwards, take her to the church for the wedding ceremony – as you choose." "Are you talking about abducting Alessia?" asked Paolo in consternation. "Not at all," answered Benito calmly. "Once she is located, Lucia will reason with her, until she agrees to fulfill the wishes of her family." Paolo responded that he had tried to persuade her to follow through on her acceptance of Benito's offer of marriage without success, during almost continuous discussion, since the reception. Benito was not deterred. "No need to worry. In our business, we have links with many influential people who can encourage the bank to end her employment there, as necessary, if such work is distracting her from her family obligations," he remarked unctuously.

In the end, Paolo agreed to reflect upon the conversation and to phone again, later that day. He called Giancarlo, and the brothers sat down to a brunch of shrimp fried rice and vegetables at the dining table, which seemed somewhat empty, without their sister. When Paolo commented that Alessia had doubtless gone back to work at the bank, at first, Giancarlo remarked that perhaps she should be left alone to do what she evidently enjoyed. But Paolo gestured to their parents' wedding portrait on the wall and argued that she had already brought dishonor to her family by literally running away from home, adding ruefully that he should have been more careful when taking dinner to her upstairs, while Alessia was locked in her room. While Paolo shared with Giancarlo his conversation with Benito and Tomassini, he felt even more uncomfortable at his impression that the two men might be contemplating the abduction of their sister, despite Benito's too smoothly attempted reassurance. As the brothers completed their brunch with Sicilian red wine, Giancarlo suggested, "Why don't you visit her at the bank where she works now, and wait for her to come outside at lunchtime, so you can talk to her on behalf of our family?" Paolo countered, "Alessia was literally running away from me as fast as she could when we last saw each other. She might do so again. I'm clearly no longer someone she trusts. Why don't you try to talk to her instead? You could explain that Benito is so stressed as a result of his love for her that he might arrange, through his business networks, for her bank to request her resignation, or fire her. Better if she does not wait for that to occur, and if she reconsiders Benito's proposal now." The brothers looked at each other. Giancarlo noted Paolo's weariness, large muscular shoulders slumped, and wondered, not for the first time, why their parents had given him an enigmatic name that literally meant '*a small person,*' then reluctantly agreed. By midday, Giancarlo was standing on the busy street corner near Alessia's workplace, having positioned himself where he could see everyone coming out of the bank. It was somewhat warm, and as time passed, he began to wonder, once again, whether his sister should really be rushed into marriage to safeguard the family honor or should be allowed to work and eventually study further, as she evidently much preferred. He reminisced how she'd admired his drawings, and he'd appreciated her paintings, as young teenagers in Calabria. Now and then, people passing by glanced at him. Giancarlo ruminated that his elder brother was probably right to be always asking why he had yet to secure a steady job, seeking to dissuade him from spending time placing bets on sports teams, making sketches, and meeting friends at the pub. He was growing weary of waiting, and was thinking of turning away when Alessia appeared, searching her handbag for the sandwich wrapped up by Melody. She was startled when Giancarlo walked up to her, and asked him, "What do you want? Why are you here?" Her younger brother explained that their 80-year-old mother, if not both parents, might not survive, if told that she had run away from home, rather than proceed with a marriage that they had approved. Alessia was visibly upset. "I know what is critical to my contentment in life, and what would make me deeply unhappy. Why is my family trying to push me into an unwanted marriage, as if my own feelings and thoughts as a woman don't matter?" Giancarlo felt inclined to agree with her. Even so, he tried to convince her that as Paolo had argued, at her age, a young lady without a husband approved by her family to protect her was courting danger daily. Alessia laughed mirthlessly, telling him that the perils that Paolo worried about would be real only if she allowed herself to be forced into the hands of a man whom she deeply disliked, instead of managing her life as she was doing. Alessia animatedly added that her family should change course and support her life-long dreams and wishes. Giancarlo looked at his sister and told her that she might be right – but he was concerned that at this stage, Benito and Tomassini might attempt to coerce her, if she did not return home willingly.

This comment gave Alessia pause. She felt both angry and afraid. Her thoughts turned to that childhood memory of witnessing a menacing fire that threatened to engulf her family home. This hazy recollection kept recurring, especially during stressful times, but it appeared slightly different on each occasion. Alessia thought of the Dickens novel she was now re-reading, where David Copperfield's memories of his visits to see Estelle presented themselves so distinctively, as he grew up. David had once recommended she read a related work on the recollection of things past by Marcel Proust. She found her ham sandwich and told Giancarlo that she was not afraid of such people and would report any harassment to the police immediately. Her brother smiled. "You were always so quiet and determined. How exactly did you manage to get out of your room when Paolo locked you in?" They walked and conversed for a while. When

Giancarlo asked where she was now living, Alessia looked at her watch and told him that she had to eat lunch and return to work within the next fifteen minutes. Her younger brother hugged her, for the first time in a while, and they told each other to take care of themselves, in parting. Alessia ate her lunch and walking to work thoughtfully, suddenly found herself blushing deeply, recalling last night with David, and realizing that he was now the center of her world. She passed the bank to calm herself for a minute, then hurried back to take her place at the counter.

David kept telling himself to focus upon his customers and their orders all day. He was both exhilarated as he looked forward to seeing Alessia when his workday ended, and worried at the precarity of her family situation, as well as his financial circumstances. For the first time in his life, he found himself thinking about marriage, and recalling his prior facile assumption that his graduate studies would be completed, and a home of his own purchased, south of London – perhaps in Kent – before any such commitment. He recalled a conversation with his father, who was making the point that sometimes, life takes you in a completely unforeseen direction, and it turns out to be the best in which you could ever have gone – a comment that was incompletely understood at the time. While waiting in the hot and congested kitchen for his latest order to be filled, the inviting odor of shrimp dim sum caught his attention, and realizing that he'd not taken a lunch break, David surreptitiously extracted one of Melody's ham sandwiches with mayonnaise from his backpack. He began munching, just as his supervisor looked in with an alert that new customers awaited seating. As he rushed out to greet them, chewing and swallowing quickly, he noted a fair-skinned brunette lady in the queue, who reminded him somewhat of Alessia, and felt a new wave of anxiety concerning their future together. Would she consider marrying him? If they settled down to life together, what would this mean for her relationships with her birth family members? Would they always feel at least scrutinized if not regarded with hostility as a mixed couple? What would their children be like and how would they cope with their own lives in the future? And what would his father, whom he once heard remarking that '*a way of seeing was a way of not seeing*' have thought about Alessia as a daughter in law? He worked on autopilot for much of the afternoon and sighed with relief when the day finally ended.

That evening, at dinner, Melody looked around the table at her children, and at Alessia. While passing a dish of stewed peas and rice with braised beef around, she noted the shy smiles passing between David and Alessia, thinking wistfully about her own early encounters with Joseph. When Danielle joined her in the kitchen as she washed up after their meal, they talked animatedly about the family's guest, who was looking more cheerful and less stressed each passing day. Meanwhile, Alessia somewhat hesitantly told David about her visit from her younger brother, as they sat on the living room sofa, which had seen better days as shown by several sunken areas, before the evening news on the LG television set. It was raining again outside, with occasional gusts of wind rattling the bay windows. He held her hand, and anxiously asked her whether Giancarlo's concerns about their parents, as well as Benito, worried her. She told him she thought her family members would eventually support her wishes, and that she would report any threats to the police.

David turned off the TV set and put on a tape with a recording of his favorite Vivaldi violin concerto, *The Four Seasons*. "Will you marry me?" he asked, with the melodious notes of the joyous spring- themed performance in the background. Alessia looked into David's eyes, her own wide in surprise. Her memory turned to Benito's proposal, as he kneeled on the carpet, with a strange smirk on his face, extending his sparkling ring to her – and the river of lies to her brother Paolo that had followed. After a few minutes, realizing that David was interpreting her thoughtful silence to mean a negative response, she drew close to him, kissing his lips gently. Melody and Danielle returned from the kitchen just in time to see David slipping a slim engagement band with an embedded diamond on to Alessia's *ring* finger, and to warmly congratulate the couple, as the delighted young man hugged his fiancée.

David and Alessia were exhilarated, as they contemplated a future together, with Melody's quiet encouragement and exuberant hugs from Danielle. On weekdays, they established a routine of taking the bus to the tube station after breakfast, and tenderly greeting each other at the Oxford Circus tube station, after long and wearying days at her bank and his restaurant. Upon arrival in Hornsey, they would walk home, hand in hand, taking advantage of the opportunity to talk on the quiet road, traversed by only a few cars, and by a bus every thirty minutes. From time to time, other pedestrians would pass, sometimes looking at the couple in a surprised or even faintly hostile manner. On one such occasion, David and Alessia defiantly held and kissed each other, embracing closely. "*Tesoro Mio*!" she whispered in his ear, "My darling!" They talked about their hopes of finding somewhere to live on their own, while saving enough to enroll in graduate degree programs, although, as David noted one evening, rental payments would make such savings targets harder to reach. Alessia agreed but remarked that it was uncomfortable to take advantage of his mother's hospitality indefinitely, especially as Melody was unwilling to accept her offered contribution to grocery purchases. This discussion remained unresolved. However, when David inquired as to what program Alessia wanted to pursue, she surprised him by indicating an interest in forensic psychology, as it would be increasingly important as part of human resources management, a field in which she wanted to develop a career.

During one of these walks home, David asked whether Alessia would much prefer to get married in a Catholic church ceremony. "But what is the alternative?" she asked, in a measure of bewilderment. He explained that his family had sometimes attended an Anglican church on Sundays, when he was a boy, and had gradually stopped, after his father had left. Alessia became thoughtful. "Do you believe in God?" she asked. "Of course," David replied. "I learnt in biology and astronomy classes about the miracles of design and execution within and all around us – from the human body itself to the incredible wonders of the Earth, and our precise distance from the sun, in what is called the *goldilocks zone* where human life is possible, with all of the incredible reaches of the universe beyond. What are we to make of a cosmos where physicists posit that most of its contents consists of dark energy, with perhaps a fifth constituted of dark matter, and only 5%, such as stars and planets, composed of *normal* matter? In any case, what really is the relationship between the universe's fundamental aspects - matter, energy, space, and time?" He paused to draw her attention to a murmur of starlings in flight across the light blue sky, then continued, "I was amazed to learn recently that cell membranes are continually rebuilt by automatic activities that include the sheath – otherwise, cells die – even so, all humans remain subject to a range of terrible diseases and can be so viciously cruel to each other. It is truly difficult to imagine or picture or understand God, so I'm simply glad to be alive, especially now, with you."

Alessia agreed, "Yes, I remember Shakespeare's character, Hamlet:" What *a piece of work is a man! How noble in reason, how infinite in faculty!"* David smiled, and continued..." *In form and moving, how express and admirable!"* They laughed in mutual recognition. Alessia added "I once read that an average human brain contains more connections between neurons in a single cubic centimeter of tissue than there are stars in the Milky Way." David countered, "Yet human beings cannot understand life before birth, or after death, or God, any more than butterflies and caterpillars can imagine each other." They were silent and pensive. A few minutes later, she asked, "But where do you think we should get married?" David told her that any church of her preference would be fine, as a prelude to the rest of their lives together. They looked at each other and smiled lovingly. On the next weekend, Danielle offered to take a photograph of the young couple in the front garden, where a veritable profusion of red, yellow, pink, and white tea roses bloomed, bobbing in a light evening breeze. David and Alessia hugged each other self-consciously and were embarrassed when Danielle demanded that they kiss each other properly, with her left hand on his shoulder, showing her engagement ring. Alessia was startled into a sudden if suppressed cry, as a thorn scratched her arm. Afterwards, at lunch, Danielle passed the photos around with glee. The couple's contrasting skin tones, their loving, if stiff and self-conscious embrace, combined with the multicolored tea roses lightly dancing in the background made for digital pictures that seemed exotic and truly appealing.

When Giancarlo returned home and recounted his conversation with Alessia to Paolo, his elder brother was angry that his sibling appeared to have eventually agreed with their sister about her freedom to choose her path, regardless of her family's wishes. Paolo paced up and down in the living room as Giancarlo sat uncomfortably at the dining table. Eventually, he declared, "Benito said that his business network could deal with this problem. Given the reaction that you report, perhaps he should." Giancarlo was troubled. "Why don't you try to talk to Alessia directly on her phone?" he asked. Paolo stopped short. "I forgot that she purchased her own cellular phone a few months ago. She must have had her phone with her even while locked in her room, last week and could even have filed a police report!" At this point, he joined Giancarlo at the table, and for a few minutes, contemplated the staircase down which their sister had run, and the front door through which she had escaped, before declaring that it would be a waste of time to attempt such a call, as Alessia appeared unconcerned about her family. Instead, Paolo telephoned Benito and conveyed his conclusions tersely.

At the time of this call, Benito was in Brighton with Tomassini and Lucia, making accommodation arrangements to receive a new consignment of nine young ladies from Slovakia. He adopted Paolo's tone, responding that Tomassini would work with their contacts to locate Alessia and to have her ready for the wedding within the next few days. "But once she is located, how are you going to convince her to change her mind about your proposal?" asked Paolo, in some concern. Benito immediately answered that once Alessia became unemployed, Lucia would help her to see the wisdom of calming down and agreeing to a secure future with him. Benito provided mellifluous responses to Paolo's further inquiries about the church where the marriage would be celebrated, the hotel where his sister would be accommodated until then, and the time when her brothers would be able to see her, to arrange for her wedding gown and to plan their roles in this event.

However, as Giancarlo listened to the conversation from his seat nearby, and the brothers looked askance at each other, Paolo persisted. "Why shouldn't my sister be returned to her home here, where we can prepare her for the wedding, and escort her to the church?" Tomassini took the phone and pointed out that Paolo had reported Alessia's escape from confinement at home, an action that she might well repeat, if allowed. He added that their company would have female security guards discreetly posted at her hotel, where Lucia would keep her company, helping her to see the joys ahead. He remarked that her brothers could come to see her as often as desired until the wedding. As Benito retrieved the phone and stated that their company owned a small hotel in Lancaster Gate that could be used for the purpose at hand, the brothers agreed to the plan, with Paolo's stipulation that Alessia should always be kept safe from any harm.

But Giancarlo was not satisfied. "How can we agree that these two men and a woman whom we just met recently should be allowed to get Alessia fired from work that she enjoys and then take her to a hotel against her will?" Paolo considered the question for a minute, and then replied that Alessia's work was leading her to dishonor the family, and that he'd met Lucia, who seemed to be a pleasant, respectable lady who would soon become Tomassini's wife, and who would be asked to persuade their sister to agree to marriage with Benito.

Giancarlo persisted. "When Alessia has to leave her bank, she will be very distressed. Shouldn't we be there to comfort and encourage her as well, while also accompanying her to this hotel? We don't even have its exact address yet." Paolo clasped his hands behind his back, pacing up and down the living room for a few minutes, then assented. "I will call Benito again tomorrow morning and explain that after '*sleeping*' on the situation, we want to be present as soon as any contact is made with Alessia. This is actually what our parents would expect."

Giancarlo was somewhat comforted by this response, with the memory of his sister's comments as to her wishes for her own life fresh in mind. He remarked that with his recent betting winnings, he could fund Alessia's wedding dress.

Paolo riposted "But have you accounted for past losses yet?" Now in the kitchen, the brothers set out to prepare a dinner of pasta and eggplant, tossed with sardines and spicy chili peppers from Reggio Calabria. Paolo set out three places for dinner, and only realized his error when Giancarlo pointed to the dining table and rolled his eyes at him, before commenting that they both seemed to be missing their only sister. They tuned the TV set to a BBC news channel which was reporting demonstrations against the Government and sat down hungrily to eat.

Benito and Tomassini had already secured a report that Alessia was living at the house of David's family in Hornsey and were even well informed as to their daily weekday routines. Recognizing that another weekend was fast approaching, they arranged to implement their plan to have an Acerra security team collect Alessia immediately, reasoning, as Paolo had done before, that once she did not show up for work, the bank would simply replace her. While David and Alessia were walking home after work, from Turnpike Lane that day, and were passing the park, he told her with a mischievous smile "Why don't we take five minutes to ourselves before getting home?" and led her to an old but serviceable green wooden bench in the park, near a flowerbed with several lovely clumps of wisteria. Once they were seated, Alessia looked at the ring he had given her admiringly, and asked "what was that music that you played when asking me to marry you?" When David explained his composition choice at that time, she commented smilingly that his sparkling Vivaldi piece might have expressed their feelings even better after her acceptance of his proposal. In response, he took her in his arms and kissed her passionately. Alessia clung to him, and the world faded away as they held each other, David gently stroking one of her long bare legs as she stretched it across his lap. A team of three security men in black suits with "Acerra Import/Export" lapel pins and red ties suddenly arrived, accompanied by a driver in a silver Jaguar, parked just outside the park gate. Realizing that the couple were intensely engaged with each other, the men quickly entered, and arrived behind their bench. Once it was evident that no one else was in the immediate vicinity, the person closest to David took out his Luger revolver, checked that the security was on, and motioning to the others, hit David so hard on his head with the butt that he fell unconscious, away from a terrified Alessia, who opened her mouth to scream. However, after one more quick check on the surroundings, another team member placed a damp chloroformed cloth over her nose and mouth tightly, cutting off her incipient scream. As she also lost consciousness completely, the three men swiftly lifted her by her arms and legs to the waiting Jaguar, leaving her handbag behind in their haste. Within a minute after the attack on the couple, the team members were driving away, with the driver carefully observing the speed limit and with Alessia slumped, still fully unconscious, mouth partly open, between two of her captors in the plush grey leather back seat of their car. The driver gave them a jubilant '*thumbs up*' sign.

Chapter Five

David groaned as he came to his senses, lying on the grass near the park bench where they had been seated. His head hurt and as his recollection returned, he looked wildly around for Alessia, exclaiming in deep alarm upon seeing only her handbag. Pulling his Apple iPhone out, David placed an emergency call, telling the dispatcher who answered that his fiancée had been abducted after he'd been knocked unconscious in the park. When asked for a description of the attackers, and how they had arrived, he was pulled up short with the realization that he had no idea as to the answers. David attempted to explain that the attack occurred while the couple had been preoccupied with each other, only to hear the dispatcher suppress a snort, before undertaking to send a police team to interview him on location. His next call was to Melody, who was sitting awaiting Alessia and himself at the dining table. She was absolutely shocked – even more so when he explained that he had not seen their attackers at all. Melody and Danielle took turns talking with David, eventually eliciting the fact that his scalp was actually bleeding, and then telling him that they would be coming to the park as quickly as possible. David picked up Alessia's handbag and looked at the contents in increasing distress, noting her phone, office keys, comb, purse with cash and a credit card, a make-up kit, and her London Transport card. He was realizing that the contents might help in searching for her when a police car arrived with two constables, followed shortly afterwards by Melody and Danielle.

The constables took his signed statement, including the anxiety repeatedly expressed by his fiancée about the behavior of her brothers, and that of Benito – although he was unable to state the latter's surname or address - one telling David that he should not have touched Alessia's handbag, as the other used gloves to place it carefully in a plastic bag. The older policeman photographed the site of the attack and remarked that a set of closed-circuit surveillance cameras should be located on lamp posts within three blocks away, in both directions, before also taking a photo of David's still bleeding scalp injury. They promised to contact him as soon as any information became available, giving the young man a number to call as well, with any additional information that subsequently occurred to him. As they were going, David thought to look up Alessia's former address on his phone and added this to his statement. Upon their departure, Melody ascertained that the bathrooms nearby were unoccupied, and took David into the cleanest area to wash the abrasion on his head with water, then wipe it as far as possible, telling her son that it might be best to take him to the nearest clinic so his scalp could be properly checked. David was distraught, his head pounding, and did not argue.

Melody and Danielle took him to a clinic by taxi for emergency care. After an extended wait, which was followed by careful hair removal around his cut and abrasion, treatment with tetracycline, and the application of a bandage, they all left for home somberly. Melody was both grateful to yet have her son, and alarmed.

Alessia regained consciousness slowly, in a very disoriented state. She found herself on a bed in a strange room, realizing first that her hands and feet were secured to the corners of the bed, and subsequently, to her horror, that she was dressed in her underwear only. She groggily remembered embracing and kissing David, their excitement mounting on a park bench near his family's home – and then, feeling stunned, seeing him suddenly fall to the walkway, followed by a strange darkness. Alessia felt increasingly frightened. What had happened to David? Where was she? She pulled on her bonds, twisting on the bed, and moaned in frustration, having recognized that it was impossible to free herself.

Alessia looked around the windowless room at the vermilion-patterned wallpaper, the brass lamps on either side of the bed, and the mahogany dressing table. She could almost smell the smoke of a deadly fire blazing in the distance. Seeking to calm herself, Alessia recalled the afternoon when, during a family visit to the Pallino National Park near the small town of Civita, where only residents understood the Ambereshe dialect, her mother taught her "*box breathing*" as a means of releasing stress. Unable to sit up, she closed her eyes, inhaled for a count of four, held her breath for a count of seven time, exhaled for another count of eight, and repeated the process for a few minutes. Time passed. She idly looked at her fingers and toes, wondering why her longest digits were differently positioned, while shivering slightly as she looked around for her clothing.

When the door suddenly opened and Benito entered, closing it behind him, her increasing anxiety combined with anger. "What am I doing here? Free me at once!" she demanded. Benito smiled. "I'm sure your parents taught you to greet your future spouse more politely and forgive you only because we had to take special measures to address your disrespect for your family's wishes." As Alessia looked at him, wide-eyed, Benito came closer and held her left hand up as far as it would go, for her to see that in the place of David's discreetly diamond-studded engagement ring, the ostentatious emerald that she had left near her bathroom sink in Camden Town was once again firmly on her finger. Benito added, "Your brother Paolo was happy to help return your ring to its rightful place. When we get married tomorrow, in the presence of both your brothers, you will have a magnificent wedding band to accompany it." Alessia looked at Benito, thinking that he must be insane and told him "You already know that I have no wish to marry or to see you at all. Let me go!" As his eyes traversed her body, she tried to jerk her hand away from his, and pulled on the ropes once again, without success. Benito sat on the bed, telling her that she needed to learn to respect her family, including her future husband. She gasped as he massaged her sensitive breasts through her scalloped lace bra, and then exposed her, to her complete chagrin, squeezing her nipples. "Your aureoles are even lovelier than imagined. I can tell that it will be a pleasure to take and to tame you!" he declared, leering, as he bent menacingly towards her. "Your choice: obedience or discipline?" Benito said, alternately twisting, and pulling at her taut nipples and slapping her delicate breasts again and again, harder, and harder, until she moaned loudly with unbearable pain and shock. Alessia saw stars as Benito tormented her cruelly.

"Which will it be?" he asked, his eyes roaming down her body to her delicate matching pink lace underwear. "Please stop!" she cried out, tears gathering in her eyes. "That's better – as long as you intend to be respectful and obedient from now on" he asserted. Benito stroked her smarting breasts playfully, for a long time, repeatedly circling her aureoles, as she turned her head away and sobbed into the pillow. "You are probably thirsty. Lucia, whom you must remember, will come with a drink for you. I will return to play with you some more later." Benito left the room, leaving Alessia sobbing more loudly in distress. She eventually calmed down and considered her situation. If David had been left alive, he would have reported her sudden abduction to the police and would be sure to try to find her himself. Benito had mentioned a wedding tomorrow with her brothers present – her bared, defenseless breasts were still painful - she would surely have an opportunity to let Paolo know just how completely wrong he had been about the man he wanted her to marry regardless of her wishes. Alessia wiped her tear- streaked face on the pillow and realized that she was indeed feeling thirsty. How long would it before she could have that drink? Would it be safe? Was Benito planning to rape her when he returned? If so, what could she do to resist? As she was trying to come to grips with her situation, the door opened again, and Lucia came in with a glass on a tray. "Hello dear," she said cheerfully "I suppose that Benito has begun training you. I will take over when he's finished, but in the meanwhile, here is a nice, refreshing drink for you. Let me pull you up on the pillow and then I'll let you sip." Alessia drank from the glass of cold water awkwardly, registering a slightly bitter aftertaste. Lucia commented that her breasts looked very pink and sore, went outside briefly, then returned with a soothing ointment which she applied gently, massaging her in a series of practiced circular motions, after removing her bra completely, and placing it under her pillow. It was not too long afterwards that Alessia felt drowsy again.

David was sitting alone on the sofa in the living room. It was extremely late. Melody and Danielle had long gone sadly to bed, but he had been unable to sleep. A stray memory of running away from a supermarket somewhere came to mind - his heart was beating faster and faster. His abraded scalp hurt, as he wondered where Alessia might be, what was happening to her, and what he could do to help her now. Pacing up and down quietly, he alternated between a sense of shame that he hadn't been able to protect his fiancée, and grim determination to find her as soon as possible, with or without police assistance. Once he had made up his mind to locate the address where Alessia's brothers lived early in the morning, and to confront them regardless of whatever racial prejudices they might have, David went upstairs to sleep. By 6:00 a.m., he had left a message calling in sick for his supervisor, as well as a note for his mother on the dining table, where he had cereal with milk and coffee, before traveling from Turnpike Lane to Camden Town. Once there, he found a bus stop map that to his elation, included the street sought. Upon arrival at the entrance, he climbed the exterior staircase, recalling Alessia recounting how she ran out of the flat a week ago, and rang the bell.

It was Paolo who came to the door in his crimson cotton dressing gown, not quite awake. He frowned to see David and demanded "What do you want?" "I realize that you are surprised to see me here, but your sister is my fiancée," David replied in a rush. "We were attacked in a park yesterday. I was knocked out from behind and she was abducted. The police are investigating. May I come in?" Paolo's frown had deepened at his first words, but his face changed with alarm as David continued. Wordlessly, he stood aside for the entirely unexpected visitor to enter. Once David was seated in the living room, Paolo demanded the details. As David spoke, Giancarlo came downstairs, joining the conversation. By the time that he concluded, both brothers were aghast. "Are you sure that our sister was taken away by force?" Giancarlo asked. David explained how her Prada handbag had been left behind in haste and showed them his bandaged scalp. "It is likely that the police will visit you today to ask questions about Benito and Tomassini," he added. Paolo was deeply conflicted and perturbed. On the one hand, he remained opposed to what was evidently now a relationship between Alessia and David. On the other hand, he was deeply distressed at the thought that his sister had been apparently abducted, likely by countrymen whom he had trusted too much.

Paolo recalled Benito's sudden visit two days before, to request the betrothal ring he'd given his sister, saying that she would want it upon agreement to their marriage. He felt betrayed and chagrined as to Alessia's current circumstances.

Giancarlo looked at him. In answer to the unspoken question asked, Paolo said that he would call Benito right away, and demand to see their sister. He paused. "But suppose he denies any knowledge of this attack? Could it possibly be someone else?" Giancarlo added that Benito would probably adopt that approach anyway. David said that it might be a good idea to avoid alerting Benito that the brothers were aware of what had happened, as this could make Alessia's situation even worse. Paolo paled. David went on to suggest that he call the police right away and provide any additional information they could, including the address where Tomassini's wedding reception had taken place. Meanwhile, he offered to reconnoiter the location for any sign of Alessia. Paolo agreed, and David left in haste for Kensal Green. But once at the address provided, he looked around in puzzlement. It appeared to be quiet, unlit, and deserted. No one was there.

Alessia dozed and dreamed about another visit with her family to the orange groves and palm trees of Santa Severina. She could taste the sweetness of an orange eaten in one of the groves there, and revel in its bright citrus smell. In a liminal state between dreaming and waking, Alessia recalled a line from Antonio Machado, one of her favorite classical Spanish poets…" *Los ninos corriendo y los naranjos encendidos*," or "*the children running with blazing bright oranges.*" She jerked awake when the door opened again and was instantly shocked anew to find herself spreadeagled almost naked on the bed, with Benito approaching her once more. He sat down next to her, admiring his handiwork in the yellow electric lamp light, and placed what appeared to be a Leica camera on the bedside table. She looked away from him, scared. "You had better get used to me," Benito said quietly. "You will belong to me completely after our wedding tomorrow and will never see that David again." Alessia tried not to show how much his words distressed her and continued to avoid his eyes. "Do you remember how you tried to pull your hand away from me in the cinema, while we sat with that foolish elder brother of yours?" he asked. "You will never refuse me anything again." Benito produced a pair of scissors, and casually cut away her remaining underwear, throwing the remnants to the ground. He pushed his fingers roughly inside her, warning that she should neither move an inch nor utter the slightest sound, unless it entailed enjoyed submission. She felt profoundly embarrassed, and her face rapidly flushed bright red – no one, including her family physician at home in Italy, had ever seen, or touched her in such a manner. But Alessia remained still as ordered and wrapped herself in further memories of her life growing up in Reggio Calabria. She remembered the enticing smell of the baked bread and fresh cheese that they had all relished in Sano and Precacore, almost tasting it as they explored the old, deserted part of the twin towns. Her memories took her to another day's outing with her parents and brothers to the brooding hilltop castle of Caccuri where they enjoyed goat milk with olives, as they wandered through the groves. Then there was the resplendent summer day when her father took his nine- or ten-year-old girl to the vineyard where he worked and lifted her up high on his sturdy shoulder to the treillage to touch hanging bunches of luscious black grapes. Benito had four fingers exploring inside her now while rolling his trembling thumb over her clitoris in an effort to excite her in spite of herself. He paused, picked up the camera, took a few full-length and close-up photos of her, then resumed his efforts. Alessia felt sore, excruciatingly stretched but emotionally numb. Her absent response annoyed Benito, who was now jerking spasmodically. Eventually he said "You are as dry as an old dishcloth now, but I will make you scream in ecstasy after our wedding. You will beg for my time and attention. Then I have friends who will also enjoy taking you, perhaps together. You will learn to do exactly as you are told and to respond as required." Benito rose angrily and stalked out, leaving the door wide open, to her alarm.

Meanwhile, at Kensal Green, David called the number given him by the officers who had taken his report and asked for an update. He thought that it was probably too soon to expect any developments. It was a surprise to be told that an expanded print from a closed-circuit surveillance camera near the park, taken three minutes after the attack, had captured both a person appearing to be Alessia in the back seat in between two men, and the automobile license plate. He had to ask for this information to be repeated, as the traffic noise on the street was interfering with comprehension, and exhaled slowly, not having realized that he had been holding his breath. David was also advised that one set of officers was on the way to interview Paolo and Giancarlo at their home, while another team was speaking with the owner of the silver Jaguar in the print at a residential hotel in Lancaster Gate. The officer told David, who was now both very anxious and somewhat hopeful, that he was welcome to request an update later. The young man considered returning home to wait, or even going to work after all – then decided that even without a specific address, for which his request was declined, he would travel to Lancaster Gate immediately, to see whether he could help in any way to find his fiancée. Perhaps he would be able to identify the address if he were in time to see the expected police cars. At that very moment, Alessia was feeling more exposed and stressed than she had ever been in her life. Nevertheless, she attempted to calm down, renewing her breathing exercises, and focusing upon memories of her times together with David. She became increasingly hungry, chilled, wanted to visit a bathroom, and grew more tense, hearing voices from time to time in the corridor outside. No one came in, however, and telling herself that Benito wanted her to be scared into submission, Alessia resolved to relax as much as she could, ignoring her surroundings.

Tomassini was taken aback to receive a call from an informant that the police had been able to trace the Jaguar in which Alessia had been abducted and were on their way to interview him as the registered owner, at the Lancaster Gate address of record. Stuttering his gratitude, he ran to locate Benito, who was sitting in his office with Lucia, and shared the news. Benito considered the situation quickly. "Lucia, why don't you ask our corporate attorney to join me now? Tomassini, would you be willing to take Alessia and the three Albanian girls that Lucia has been training to the South Quay warehouse on the Thames immediately?" Tomassini assented, commenting that he would leave the Jaguar and take the Rover instead, as well as Lucia, who had already left on her errand, and use the side entrance rather than the main street. Within the next few minutes, the residential hotel became a beehive of focused activity. Lucia had her charges in the back seat of the Rover, by the time that Tomassini arrived with Alessia wrapped in a sheet in his arms, with a blindfold over her eyes and a gag on her mouth, her arms tied behind her. He opened the trunk and placed her inside, told her to be still during the coming drive, which would take about thirty minutes, then closed the trunk and drove off in haste. When three police constables eventually arrived, they were invited into a quiet residential hotel to meet with Benito and an Acerra Import/Export LLC attorney, who assisted in the former's courteous responses to questions. The constables were told that the Jaguar at issue was indeed registered in the company's name but was used by a number of senior staff members with no specific sign-out procedures; that neither Benito nor anyone else at hand had seen Ms. Amato since the day he proposed to her, given her brothers' report that she had literally run away from their home; and that he was still deeply distressed by the sudden disappearance of a lady he very much wanted to marry. When Benito took the constables on a tour of the property, it was evident that he'd learned from the experience that had occurred in Reading. The hotel rooms and related public spaces were tidy, with few occupants, and the offices appeared to be in normal use. In the course of successive interviews, the few hotel residents at hand politely indicated an inability to assist with the inquiry at issue. The police officers ended up with photographs of the property, photocopies of personnel files, and Benito's commitment to advise staff members who might have used the Jaguar the day before to visit the local station to provide statements, as soon as possible.

After the team left, in answer to Benito's question "Were they convinced?" his attorney answered with a decided negative and advised him that his company should send the security team involved in abducting Alessia across the Atlantic, as well as the young lady herself, immediately, while changing the company's actual inventory and sales to olive oil and wine imports as soon as possible, to match Acerra's articles of incorporation. He added that as an interim measure, his stock of young women could be moved to Ireland or to France. In response, Benito remarked that he would also advance his plans to open a branch in New York and charter a flight to travel abroad with Alessia and the team by the following night. Meanwhile, Tomassini and Lucia arrived at South Quay, turning directly into the underground garage, and closing the door. Lucia led her three passengers to the elevator, and Tomassini followed, with Alessia wrapped up in his arms once again. He removed the sheet covering her but not her blindfold or gag, until she was once again spreadeagled and tied up in a bed as before. On this occasion, he paused, eyes and hands roaming over her body. Alessia stiffened and turned her face away, as he commented "Benito is going to enjoy you first, but I will take my turn before anyone else. You will soon learn to relax and obey, like all the other young ladies." Soon after he left the room, Lucia arrived with a small green bowl of warm pasta and vegetables, accompanied by water. She pulled Alessia up, using a second pillow, and fed her with a fork, then took her, hands tied behind, to the mini bathroom, in answer to her captive's request. As Lucia was leaving with the emptied bowl and glass, Alessia asked her where they were now, and whether she could have a little more to eat. Lucia shook her head. "I'm sorry, my dear. You are on a special diet just now and are welcome to ask Benito any other questions when he arrives." Once she had turned the door and gone, Alessia sobbed once again for a while, before calming herself, thinking wistfully of her last experience with David. Surely if he were still alive, he would have found her by now, or reported the attack on them to the police, she thought, despairingly. What would become of her? Alessia looked around her new location, noticing a window with leafy birch trees outside swaying gracefully in the breeze, grey clouds scudding past in the sky, a small brass chandelier in the ceiling, and two bedside tables, shadows on the wall. Her stomach growled. She longed for a good meal, her limbs to be freed and her body dressed, shuddering involuntarily with the memory of Benito then Tomassini, pawing her and saying that they and other men would each be enjoying her - her last conscious thought before dozing again.

David was momentarily elated to locate a hotel at Lancaster Gate with two police cars parked outside, and waited anxiously, only to shake his head in confusion when the constables emerged and left, with documents in hand, but no sign of Alessia. What should he do now? He paced up and down on the opposite side of the road, and soon regretted his lack of a vehicle to drive when a tall man in a grey overcoat hurried out, entered a parked silver Jaguar, and drove off. David looked around for a taxi, hoping to follow, but had no luck until several minutes afterwards. By that time, his intended quarry had long since gone. David was caught between the impulsion to enter the building, and the sense that it would be more important to find out where the car had gone, at such speed. When a middle-aged couple came out of the residential hotel, holding hands, he was emboldened to enter, looking for the reception desk. There was no one there, so he glanced at the open guest registration book and the shelving with room numbers. In a corner of the reception desk, David was startled to see a recognized ring that quietly sparkled, and reaching for it, confirmed that it was the one he'd presented to Alessia, noting their first names inscribed inside. The young man looked around, still astonished. Hearing voices coming from the interior passageway, he rapidly placed the ring in his pocket, went outside, and once on the other side of the street, called the police station to report what he had found.

It took a while to find anyone who was able to access his report of the attack. Once he did, David was reprimanded for going inside the residential hotel alone – but also advised that if he were confident that this was the engagement ring he'd given Alessia, it would be entered into evidence, and other company offices raided. It was during this conversation that David learnt the results of the Lancaster Gate hotel police visit, and first heard the name Acerra Import/Export LLC. He agreed to visit the station with the gold ring at issue and set out to find an internet café where he could institute a full online search. Within an hour, he was engaged in the planned search. Finding that Acerra had its main warehouse at South Quay, David decided to take the Jubilee Line down to the dock area, after pausing for a quick hamburger lunch, and to call his mother. Melody was deeply concerned about his efforts to locate Alessia and tried to encourage him to leave the investigation in the hands of the police. She tensed, remembering the terrible day that Joseph died. However, when David told her that he could not relax or rest for constantly imagining what might be happening to his fiancée, Melody understood and begged him to be extremely careful, saying that she could not cope if he were to be seriously injured or even killed as a result of his efforts.

Benito frowned as he drove to South Quay. He regretted not having reversed roles with Tomassini, and taking Alessia there himself, remembering her appearance and attitude on the afternoon that he met her at home, then their visit to the cinema along with Paolo. His thoughts lingered on the pleasure of suddenly lifting her up at the "reception," Alessia's expression as he maneuvered Paolo into initial acceptance of their "engagement," with Lucia's assistance, and her attractive curves as she was tied down, fully unclothed, to the bed at the Lancaster Gate Hotel. Even when powerless to move, or to resist his hands roaming over her at will, she seemed to possess an indefinable spirit that he found alluring. Benito berated himself for wool-gathering like a teenager while driving, as he had to brake suddenly to avoid an overtaking taxi, but soon resumed his ruminations. Perhaps he would consider keeping Alessia for himself, once they arrived safely in New York. As he drove through Bermondsey, Benito resolved to talk with Alessia, try to win her over gradually, and to keep Tomassini – or any other male – away from her, at least for now. A few moments later, as he turned on the wipers in response to a shower, Benito pulled himself up short, reflecting that he had to pay full attention to his company and the safety of his team, including himself, and could not allow himself to daydream. Instead, he should continue making his family in Campania proud. The traffic was now lighter, so he put on a news station, listening out for any information that might impact his company, while reaffirming that it was time to convert Acerra Import/Export PLC into a legitimate olive oil and wine business in the United Kingdom, and to identify other locations for his much more lucrative, if illegal, business lines.

As Benito was driving into the underground garage at the South Quay building where the Acerra warehouse and offices were located, David was riding the escalator up from the platforms of the nearby tube station. He had no clear idea as to what to do, apart from wanting to find and release Alessia, and was thinking that his mother might have been right, in encouraging him to leave such actions to the police, once it was clear that officers were on the job. But where were they now? And what had become of Alessia – had her ring been forcibly removed after she was abducted – and if so, why? David was tempted to call the police station again, but realized that at this rate, he would soon be disregarded as a nuisance. Taking a deep breath of the Thames-infused river air, he made his way to a six-storey building that clearly displayed the name, Acerra Import/Export PLC. How had what seemed to be a well-established company become involved in attacking a young couple in a quiet North London park? he wondered. Answering his own question, David recalled Alessia's descriptions of Benito and Tomassini, and was convinced that the person he had seen hurrying to the silver Jaguar at Lancaster Gate had been one of them. It began to rain again, so he took shelter near the entrance to the building, glancing inside from time to time. There was no one visible in the entrance hall. From his location outside, David could see an elevator as well as a staircase, with green marble steps and gleaming steel rails. A pizza delivery man approached, holding several large flat cardboard boxes precariously, and asked him whether this was the Acerra address. David nodded, then had an idea. "If you are running late on other deliveries, I would be glad to take them upstairs for you." In response to the hesitant look of his interlocutor, David added: "I was waiting for the scheduled time and was just about to go in for an appointment." The delivery man asked him to sign a crumpled receipt and handed over his boxes with an almost inaudible sigh of relief. David stepped inside with an assurance he did not feel and began climbing the staircase. At the first three floors, only quiet corridors were visible, so he continued climbing.

However, while approaching the fourth floor, David heard the sound of two men conversing, then suddenly shouting in some sort of dialect through a partly opened door, and unexpectedly heard the name "*Alessia*." He froze, then decided to walk down the corridor away from the continuing argument. Towards the end, he noticed a partly opened door, and was shocked to his core to see Alessia totally unclothed, each limb tied to a bed corner, breasts bruised, and eyes closed. David almost cried out in anguish. Pulling himself together, he noticed a key in the outer lock, took it out silently, entered the room, placed his pizza boxes hurriedly on the floor and locked the door again quietly from the inside.

Alessia opened her eyes, and was sure she was dreaming again, upon seeing David, and smelling one of her favorite foods. Her stomach growled once more. She shook her head, becoming convinced that David was no dream, when he knelt and untied the rope holding her right foot to the bed, with tears spilling down his face. Alessia tried to call his name, her mouth dry from the coarse cloth of the gag used. In an odd way, she felt even more ashamed for her fiancé to look at her now, than she had felt when Benito and Tomassini had manhandled her.

David put his finger to his mouth, signifying silence, and continued removing her ropes. When she was finally free, he tried to help Alessia up, but her legs gave way. Sitting awkwardly on the bed, she pointed to the pizza boxes. Realizing that she was hungry, he opened a cardboard box beside her, watching Alessia for a moment as she began to eat, flexing her hands and feet to improve circulation – then he looked around the room, searching for her clothing and finding none.

After eating several slices of hot pizza, Alessia began to feel alive again, and very thirsty. She motioned to the wash basin in in a bedroom corner, and he found a little drinking glass, cleaned it as much as he could, and helped her sip, making several trips. It was only then that Alessia looked at David, saying his name rather hoarsely, placing her head on his shoulder. "Did anyone…. attack you?" he asked, deeply pained, looking closely at her thighs, quite unready for a positive answer. She shook her head, wanting to speak, but unable to just then. Only then did he notice Benito's ring shimmering on her left hand. Eyes narrowing, David pulled it off, tossing it to the floor. Then he kissed her lightly, looking at her still bruised but beautiful breasts, telling her that they had to get out of the building quickly, so she needed some sort of clothing. She pointed to the two white unfitted cotton bed sheets on which she had been lying, and helping her up, he pulled them off rapidly and wrapped each fully around her, tying rather insecure knots under her slim arms. He adjusted the sheets to cover her legs as much as possible. David felt as if they were in an adventure movie, such as "Raiders of the Lost Ark," but realized that whether or not the men who had shouted were armed, Alessia and himself could easily be overpowered, especially since she was clearly feeling weak. It might have been foolhardy to arrive without advising the police, after all.

He went to the window, and looking out, was pleased to see a sturdy-looking red fire escape, then became suddenly alarmed to hear voices approaching. Opening the window, he lifted Alessia up, her bare feet swinging, pushed her through the window and as she stood on the narrow ledge waiting for him, climbed through, closing the window from the outside – then berated himself for wasting time.

David willed himself to avoid looking down, slung Alessia over his shoulder, with a moment's sense of gratitude that she was slender and light, then hurriedly began his descent. There was an increasingly loud pounding on the door of the room they'd just left, accompanied by imprecations. David picked up speed, his fiancée swaying on his shoulder, attained the second-floor level by the time that a tremendous crash signified that the door had been broken down, and managed to leap to the pavement as Tomassini looked through the opened window above.

David thought he heard a gun fire but did not pause to confirm his impression.

He had no time to look for a taxi, and thought public transport safer, in any case. Heart pounding, he ran towards the tube station, Alessia's arms and legs swaying. As they neared the entrance, he had just enough presence of mind to ask whether she could walk, then hugged her shoulders, holding her wrapped sheets to ensure their retention in place. Alessia nodded and they began their journey down the escalator, David's legs trembling from his exertion. They attained the northbound platform, tacitly agreeing to ignore the curious glances of other passengers. She winced when stepping on a discarded bottle cap. When a train finally arrived, after changing at

Canary Wharf and at Green Park, David found a semi-secluded seat for two, and Alessia curled up, with her head in his lap. She was sound asleep when the couple arrived at Turnpike Lane, and groggily responded to a query as to whether he should purchase a dress and shoes for her to avoid any more stares by saying, "please just take me home." David called a taxi, and they completed their extraordinary journey in relative comfort. The roses in Melody's front garden had never looked more welcoming, as they stepped through the gate.

Danielle was first through the door, as David entered through the front gate, once again lifting Alessia in his arms. Melody followed, letting out a breath she had not known had been held, upon seeing her son, who had not been in contact with her for several hours. Turning her eyes to the young woman he held, Melody exclaimed to see how pale and utterly weary she appeared, while noting the sheets in which he'd wrapped her and Alessia's dirtied and bruised bare feet. "Are you alright? Was she hurt?" Melody asked David anxiously, in rapid fire fashion. Danielle held the door for them to enter and David placed his precious armful on the sofa, her eyes closed, before answering affirmatively to both his mother's questions. His sister followed up with a query as to whether Alessia needed medical attention. "I doubt it, but we'll know for sure once she has bathed, eaten and rested," he responded. It was still difficult to believe that they were all together once again. Melody offered to give Alessia a bath, an offer that her son would previously have accepted. But David shook his head, saying that he would take care of his fiancée, and that he hoped she would be able to enjoy dinner after a shower. Taking this cue, his mother and sister hastened to the kitchen to prepare dinner, while he took Alessia upstairs to his bathroom, where he filled the tub and helped her in. She opened her eyes and looked at David, still somewhat dazed. "Do you think that they will come to attack us all here?" she asked – then exclaimed, noticing the discolored bandage on David's head for the first time. "Relax and enjoy your bath," he told her lovingly. I will let the police know that you are back with us shortly. They will take care of those criminals.

Why don't we catch each other up with what happened, starting with you?" So Alessia relaxed in her bath, inhaling the scent of lilac foam, while David scrubbed her gently and tenderly but thoroughly, and told him what had happened to her.

He was stressed throughout her haltingly provided story, particularly when learning how Benito and Tomassini had treated her. In turn, while holding and stroking her left hand, the young man explained how he had ended up in the room where she had been held at South Quay. Alessia pulled him closer and examined his bandaged scalp anxiously. "I remember screaming when you suddenly fell out of my arms on that park bench," she said. "And I will never forget coming through the door and finding you tied up on that bed, five or six boxes of pizza in my arms," he responded. "I hope they are caught and sentenced to prison for the rest of their lives." When Alessia reminded him that he needed to update his police report, he helped to complete her soak with a shower, and then took her, wrapped in a towel, to her room to dress. While she did so, David placed a call to the police number provided, and waited until a constable was available to take his details and look for the related file. The polite routine responses provided on the line were interrupted the moment David reported the rescue of his fiancée and gave a status report. He was told somewhat sharply that instead of going into the building at South Quay himself, it would have been much safer to let the police complete their investigations and apprehend the culprits.

David retorted "If your wife or partner were in the hands of such criminals, would you have waited? As it was, Alessia was beaten and tortured." His interlocutor cleared his throat and demanded that they both come to the station tomorrow.

When they went downstairs, Melody and Danielle seated them at the dining table and brought a hot dinner of baked snapper with rice and green peas out from the kitchen, promising an apple pie dessert afterwards. It now fell to David to tell the absorbing story of the attack and abduction of Alessia to the rapt audience of his mother and sister, who kept looking from one to the other protagonist. As he ended, Melody poured chilled white Spanish wine for each, toasting their safe return. Danielle asked Alessia, now in a recently purchased green muslin dress, with low-heeled light brown shoes, how she was feeling. "So much better! I wondered whether it would be possible for me to see any of you again and wasn't even sure that David was alive," she answered. Melody bent her head in a silent prayer of gratitude, then inquired what time they planned to go to the police station in the morning. As dusk fell, David ensured that the entrances to the house were carefully locked and placed a large kitchen knife in its cover next to his plate. Alessia was now nodding off to sleep at the table, so David lifted her up once again and took her upstairs to her room. "Are you planning to lift me to bed every night after dinner?" she inquired, smiling. David leaned forward, kissed her lips, and stroked her hair. However, as he attempted to get into bed beside her, she hesitantly demurred, asking him for a little time in which to first bury her dark memories of the past two days. Telling her gently that he understood, the young man replaced his discarded clothing, wished her a good night, and went quietly down the corridor to his own room, with the selected kitchen knife still in his belt.

Chapter Six

Benito looked around the room where Alessia had been held – the now bare mattrass on the bed, with an opened, partly consumed box of pizza, the unlocked window where Tomassini stood staring at the escaping couple and noticed the emerald engagement band he'd placed on the young girl's '*ring*' finger lying on the titian carpet, along with other haphazardly tumbled pizza boxes. Picking up the ring, he quietly asked Tomassini where he has placed his pizza order, to be told that it had been at "the usual place near Canary Wharf." Benito frowned. "How did the order end up here? Where were the reception staff and the security guards?" When his companion looked at him blankly, Benito took up the pizza boxes from the floor, and finding the contents still pleasingly warm, invited Tomassini back to his office. After placing a call to the company's Human Resources Manager and demanding an immediate report on the ground floor staffing at South Quay that afternoon, he asked Tomassini to join him in a few slices of pepperoni pizza with steaming coffee from the percolator in his office. Benito was deeply chagrined. Police officers had already been investigating Acerra Import/Export PLC in connection with an unexpected Reading facility visit; had also searched the Lancaster Gate residential hotel after somehow tracing Alessia's abduction to the company, and the young man who had been attracting her had inexplicably managed to walk into the main office and warehouse complex a short while ago, escaping with her successfully. The two men consumed the contents of a pizza box – Tomassini declined the coffee, in favor of Peroni Italian beer. After a burp he sneered "Such a pity that your intended bride got away! We were all looking forward to an opportunity to intimately enjoy her alluring body. Instead, we may have police officers visiting here soon." Benito tensed his lips but agreed with the latter statement and told him to ask Arkady to arrange transport for all the young women accommodated at all properties in England to be transferred by the following day to the company's main residential hotel in Paris, France. He also told him to ensure that their olive oil and wine inventories were prominently positioned in the storeroom downstairs. Once Tomassini left, Benito called his attorney to consult with him about the risk arising from David's escape with Alessia that day. This conversation left him grimly determined to stop his losses.

When his HR Manager arrived with the requested report, Benito berated her furiously, shouting that all he could see were excuses for reception staff taking lunch, making restroom visits or in one case, feeling unwell at the same time. Veins bulged in his forehead and his hands shook, making her all the more frightened of him. Once she departed in distress, he called the company's Security Director and gave terse instructions for the Armstrong home where Alessia was staying to be burnt to the ground by the next night, preferably with all occupants – but with no means by which the perpetrators could be traced. Benito then confirmed his chartered flight to New York that night, accompanied by Lucia, three security guards, and selected young women from Bulgaria and Albania, all customer favorites, making a mental note to discuss with Tomassini the techniques he should use in refocusing the UK branches of their company to wines and olive oil. He still felt furious with himself for allowing the current situation to unfold and took an aspirin in an effort to relieve a headache.

Meanwhile, Paolo and Giancarlo were sitting in their living room, explaining to an earnest, bespectacled policeman and a taller, athletic-appearing female colleague with penetrating blue eyes exactly how they had met Benito and Tomassini, and the way in which the former's engagement to their sister Alessia had come about. Paolo was extremely uncomfortable. If all that David had said was true – and he now had no reason to doubt it – he'd managed to put Alessia in serious danger by bringing their compatriots from Campania into their lives and in forcing her to proceed with the engagement to Benito. Paolo recalled Alessia's complaint after their cinema visit with Benito and swallowed hard. Just as he was reflecting upon the situation, Giancarlo responded to a query by providing detailed descriptions of each man, even finding some of his rough drawings from the occasion when they came to dinner. At that point, the officers asked to see the location upstairs where Alessia had been confined. They all ended up in her bedroom, where the female officer took photographs and made notes, then inquired: "So you were both unaware that these men intended to kidnap your sister – and also that your own prior involuntary confinement of an adult woman in an effort to force her into marriage was illegal?" Paolo stammered that he had had his sister's best interests at heart, acting in place of their parent. He went on to explain that Benito had given every impression that he really wanted to marry Alessia and was truly committed to making her happy.

As they all went back downstairs, he was forced to respond to a quick follow-up question about the family names of their Italian compatriots that he had never received that information. After the officers left with their detailed notes and the drawings provided, Paolo and Giancarlo returned to their seats in the living room in distress. The gathering night outside seemed much darker than usual, with streetlamps and the noise of traffic obliterated by the bleak tenor of their thoughts. Each wondered in what state and where their sister might be at that time, and how the situation could ever be explained to their parents, who were awaiting news of Alessia's marriage with anticipation. When the telephone rang with a wrong number, both jumped.

Meanwhile, Alessia tossed and turned in her bed. She was experiencing what her mind recognized as post-traumatic stress syndrome and remembering the displacement activities in which she had engaged in order to cope, but this realization made no difference to her emotions. Alessia was flooded by vivid recreations of her abduction – Benito's taunting and torture, leaving her breasts still feeling bruised, Tomassini's hands all over her body, while making comments about himself and others enjoying her, Lucia's involvement in managing her imprisonment in both locations. The re-created experience of hunger, thirst, and chill air on her bare skin – whatever happened to her clothing, shoes, and handbag? – led her to pull the blanket up to her chin. It occurred to her that Lucia had been carefully limiting her access to food and water – had this continued, she would likely have lost the will to resist whatever was done to her, eventually. Was this a standard technique? Could these men really be involved in human trafficking? As it was, Alessia felt extremely violated and shivered anew, with the recollection of strange male hands manipulating her vulva at will. She thought of David, remembering sadly how pained he had appeared when she refused his offer to hold her, and perhaps make soothing love to her, earlier that night, as he slowly dressed and left the room. She loved and was deeply grateful to him for rescuing her, all by himself, and recognized how readily his efforts might have been countered. At the same time, Alessia felt as if she might never want to have any man look at her nude body or touch her again – despite telling herself that it was critical to consciously manage her feelings, and to recognize David as her beloved fiancé. She was almost drowning in unwanted memories that swirled around her like a kaleidoscope of a malign landscape, in which she herself was irremediably caught. Eventually, she fell into a troubled sleep, tossing and turning. David was also restless throughout the night, reliving his regaining of consciousness in the park, to find Alessia vanished, with only her handbag left behind; then his mother gently cleaning that now bandaged scalp wound; his first police report; and the meeting with her two brothers at their home, which would once have had an entirely different resonance. Scenes tumbled through memory, in no particular order, but kept returning to the moment when, after so tentatively climbing the stairs in that South Quay building, he ended up opening a door off that upstairs corridor.

David had been absolutely shocked, almost to the point of vomiting, to find Alessia tied to the bed as she was, completely naked, in a position that had left him certain that she'd been raped, perhaps repeatedly – until she shook her head in answer to his question. At the same time, her behavior earlier when he wanted to comfort her and renew their love in her bed made him think that she'd been assaulted and hurt in some way – apart from the obvious bruising suffered. David clenched his hands, savagely wishing it were possible to attack and even kill Benito and Tomassini. He had to force himself to calm down, breathing deeply, to avoid thoughts that, even were they practical, could only generate new, very serious problems. Recalling his undertaking to arrive at the police station with Alessia later in the morning, he wondered about the best route, what he should tell his manager at the restaurant about the additional time away from work now required – and whether the bank had determined Alessia's job to have been abandoned, after three days without any word from her. It began to rain outside, and he opened the window a little, in the hope of enjoying the freshened air, and the scent of the wet roses in the front garden. David heard someone visit the bathroom down the corridor, looked at his bedside clock, tossed off his blanket, and huddled against one of his pillows in an effort to invite still elusive sleep. It seemed a long while before he relaxed to rest.

At breakfast the next morning, Melody looked at her son, then Alessia, in turn, noting their stressed body language and apparent sleepiness. "Did you both rest well last night?" she asked. Everyone laughed for a moment, when David replied "Yes" and Alessia answered "No." As Melody poured coffee, adding cream without sugar, and Danielle brought scrambled eggs with cheese and toast from the kitchen, David mentioned that he was required to visit a police station in the City that morning, together with Alessia. To his sister's inquiry about work, he indicated that he would call his supervisor at the restaurant once it was open. In an effort to show appreciation, he told his mother that their breakfast was tasty, but Alessia ate only some of her toast, morosely moving the rest of her meal around with a fork.

While sipping coffee, David fervently wished that her abduction had never occurred; and that if it had to happen, that they could return to the stage of demonstrably loving and supporting each other. He realized that although she'd recounted what had happened to her after regaining consciousness, Alessia had not said very much about how she felt during her captivity. He recalled the recurring questions raised during his own university philosophy class, as to why terrible things often happened to good people, and as to exactly what was present in the universe at its point of origin in an infinitely small, dense singularity. No time for such ruminations now – Alessia and David looked at each other, and wordlessly agreeing that it was time to dress for their police station visit, got up from the table. Before going upstairs, David went to Melody, who was still seated, hugging her from behind. She closed her eyes for a moment, remembering the way his father used to give her similar hugs, after breakfast or sometimes dinner, then smiled a bit too brightly at her son. Melody was grateful for the couple's return and reflected that Joseph had remained a blessing to her – his life insurance proceeds had enabled her to purchase her only recently insured flat. She sat for a while with Danielle in silence, remembering.

Within the next hour, David and Alessia were approaching the police station. Despite his efforts to engage her in conversation, she answered pleasantly but said very little, making the young man more worried about her state of mind. Once inside, the couple was directed to an officer who introduced himself as Detective Inspector Jeffries, and after seating them in his office, pulled out a file and turned on a tape recorder, having perfunctorily confirmed their agreement. He first requested a recapitulation of David's prior report. It was at this time that Alessia heard additional details concerning David's experiences after they were attacked in the park. She listened attentively as he recounted the prior day's events, including his conversation with her brothers, and his visits to the Lancaster Gate residential hotel, followed by the research that led him to South Quay. When he was explaining how he entered the building, and eventually found Alessia, Detective Inspector Jeffries commented that they were both very lucky to be alive and asked several detailed questions as to exactly when he did, upon finding her, and why.

One question gave the young man pause: "How did you feel when you found your fiancée, and what was the first thing that you did?" David held the arms of his polished wooden chair tightly, bent his head, and attempted to stifle a sob. He was told to take his time and to pause until he was ready to proceed. Alessia's grey eyes widened, focusing upon David as he answered the questions posed, step by step. Her own hands trembled slightly in her lap, and she breathed rapidly.

When the police officer was satisfied that he had a full accounting from David, he turned to Alessia, asking her to recall her experience after regaining consciousness in as much detail as possible. She tried to maintain as much composure as possible, remembering her mostly successful efforts to manage the fears and pain experienced at the hands of Benito, Tomassini and to some extent, Lucia. For a while, the officer allowed Alessia to tell her story at her own pace. Eventually, he began to drill down. His first question was whether she would not find it easier to deny having been raped, rather than to provide such information. Alessia paled and stood her ground. "Everyone who knows me is aware that I'm always truthful," she said shakily. A few moments afterwards, the officer focused his questioning upon the torture she had experienced, and inquired as to exactly where, by whom, and for how long digital penetration had occurred, and the comments made by her attackers meanwhile. David placed his head in his hands, when Alessia answered haltingly, before bursting into tears.

David felt desolate, while his fiancée was led away by a female officer for further questioning and a required medical examination. Detective Inspector Jeffries offered him a glass of water, then explained that there had been several prior complaints recorded about the company run by Benito and Tomassini. Acerra Import/Export was properly registered and appeared to be engaged in trade in wines and olives from Southern Italy. However, there were increasingly strong if so far unproven suspicions that the company was also involved in human trafficking, importing young women mainly from Eastern Europe. David looked at the officer, as he went on to comment that Alessia's abduction appeared to fit into that pattern of activity and repeated that they had both been very fortunate so far. When he casually remarked that it would be best to have a police security detail posted outside their home for the next few nights, David thought for a moment that he was in a continuing nightmare. Alessia returned, and the policewoman accompanying her presented a signed medical report for addition to their file. Once she had left, David asked the detective whether he had been joking, or at least exaggerating, when indicating the need for a security detail outside their home at nights. Alessia looked frightened at the response that everyone present was dealing with what increasingly appeared to be a criminal gang, that needed to be prosecuted to the fullest extent of the law. The couple finally took their leave, after signing their reports, receiving warnings to be very careful, at least until investigations into the company had ended with arrests, and the reiterated assurance that a security detail would be in place at their home that night. David and Alessia sighed heavily upon returning to the bright sunlight, light blue skies, and the slow-moving traffic outside, and smiled tentatively at each other. She was pale, and walked with a slight limp, but accepted his suggestion that they should have lunch in Green Park, where they ended up by tube, after purchasing prawn sandwiches and chilled white wine.

Alessia was not yet hungry, and still very stressed. When David drew her head against his chest and stroked her hair, she sighed again, this time, in a more relaxed manner. A few minutes later, her head was in his lap, and she was sleeping soundly. David looked around at the multivariate shades of green presented by the manicured lawns and the tree leaves waving in the light breeze, especially enjoying the violets, petunias and red roses framing several of the nearby walkways. Most of all, he felt a sense of gratitude that they appeared to be emerging from a terrible storm that had pushed them brusquely apart. As he stroked Alessia's back, she shifted, breathing deeply. When she eventually awoke, they looked at each other, and finding the encouragement sought in her eyes, David bent to kiss her. Sometime later, they noticed the nearby food, began to munch, and laughed, if somewhat tentatively, when he observed that these were much like the wholewheat sandwiches they'd first eaten together at Pret-À- Porter. After they had each enjoyed a paper cup of wine, David asked Alessia how she had really managed during her abduction. Glancing around the park, she paused to listen to a pair of starlings, with striking blue feathers and yellow breasts, then looked directly at him. "I prayed for you to come rescue me, and you did, although not before I'd begun to give up all hope," she said, then explained how she had used her childhood memories and meditation to remove herself from her physical situation. In turn, she asked him the same question, wanting particularly to know how he would have reacted, had their worst fears been realized. It was then that David told her how empty he had felt, when she disappeared from his side that afternoon, and how desperate he was, until it was possible to have her home safely again – while repeating the security warning received at the police station. "I'm so sorry, David," Alessia said suddenly. He looked at her intently, still stroking her hair. "I shouldn't have shut you out last night," she explained. David bent and held her close. "It was painful," he confessed, "but I understood," adding that he was proud that she had been able to implement the stoic thinking of the Roman philosopher emperor, Marcus Aurelius, that the quality of her thoughts was truly central to her experience.

That night at home, after a somber dinner of Melody's rice risotto, stir-fried vegetables and baked salmon, everyone took turns looking anxiously outside through the bay windows in the living room, after David had relayed the warning given by Detective Inspector Jeffries. Danielle was excited when she spotted two uniformed officers in a car across the road, and sometime later, identified two more police officers standing guard behind the flat, through the kitchen window. Melody encouraged everyone to get some rest, given the security detail at hand, pointing out that they would all be better placed to cope with the following day after a proper night's sleep. On this occasion, when David accompanied Alessia to her room, they sat, talked, and kissed tenderly for a while. He stroked her hand, brought out the ring retrieved in Lancaster Gate, and looking into her eyes, replaced it on her finger. Both smiled and hugged each other closely, recalling the deep distress of the prior two days, and ended up under the white silk sheets together, clothing tumbled on the floor. Alessia was deep in a nightmare that clung to her consciousness, despite her effort to shake off the images of Benito and Tomassini surrounding her. It was only when she heard a loud splintering sound, followed succeeded by a series of other such noises, that she awoke to the realization that David was beside her, and thought a whiff of smoke was in the air. Sitting up, she shook her fiancé awake. As the smell of smoke intensified, they scrambled into their discarded clothes, and had just put on their shoes when Melody's voice came through the door, telling them that the house was on fire.

"Grab whatever belongings you can," she cried, "we all need to get out now!"

Danielle was still in her pajamas, sleepy-eyed but shocked, when they all ran down the stairs, arms laden as instructed. The living room carpet and curtains were in flames, which were flickering intensely and rapidly spreading. There was a loud knock on the front door. Melody hesitated to open it for a few seconds until shouts identified the persons at the door as police officers. She grabbed a blanket that was beginning to smolder from the sofa, tamped the sparks out, threw it around Danielle and opened the door. Four officers shouted at them simultaneously to come outside at once. As they did so, the flames inside arrived at the staircase, climbing rapidly upstairs. Melody looked at her home, adrenaline flowing, as intense leaping flames began to engulf it further; then they followed the officers to their cars. A policewoman who identified herself as Constable Jameson apologized that despite the presence of the security detail, the house had been attacked, in a way that might have been deadly for all occupants. As a fire engine alarm howled in the distance, Alessia found herself caught between present and past, watching the angry red flames billow and swell through the roof. The gritty black smoke made everyone present cough. It took three fire engine crews to subdue the fire, eliminating the alarming potential for it to spread to the houses next door. Melody felt desolate at the loss of her carefully selected and decorated home, exhilarated that everyone was safe, and grateful that she had remembered to stuff her home insurance policy into the little brown suitcase on her lap, thinking of Joseph, who had always urged insurance policy use.

Benito was still fuming at the loss of Alessia while flying across the Atlantic in his chartered Learjet, in between email exchanges with Tomassini in London and his advance party lead in New York. He paced up and down the narrow passageway, collected snacks from the galley, paused to greet other team members who were awake, then returned to work on the business plan for Acerra Inc. in the USA. When a message reporting that Mrs. Melody Armstrong's house had been burnt almost to the ground, he was elated, until further information followed that while the operation had been implemented without a hitch, the occupants had all escaped. Benito had developed his business, over time, by applying his understanding as to what customers most wanted with imagination and patience, drawing upon his experience during his early efforts in Campania. Now he resolved to ask Tomassini to remain informed about Alessia's whereabouts, with the goal of abducting her again when she least expected it, regardless of her circumstances, and bringing her immediately afterwards to join him in New York, or wherever his main residence might be at that time.

Opening his briefcase, Benito extracted a folder containing several enlarged glossy photographs of Alessia on the bed where he had begun to tame her. He leafed through the pictures, pausing at each one, inhaling and exhaling in appreciation. Feeling somewhat better, he chuckled, recalling his cinema visit with Alessia and Paolo, then invited Lucia to sit with him, and to discuss the initial arrangements to house the young women accompanying them in New York, and the marketing strategies that might be most productive. When Benito eventually dozed off, he awoke with a start from a vivid dream about his first apprenticeship in Acerra, where he combined roles such as messenger and security guard and looked so longingly at one particular young lady from Palermo who worked directly with his boss that he was thoroughly beaten for his incautious glances one hot and sunny afternoon.

By the morning after the fire, Melody and Danielle, together with David and Alessia, found themselves in a small Finsbury Park hotel, sharing the only accommodation available – a bedroom and bathroom. Melody insisted that the couple sleep on the bed, after persuading a housekeeper to provide extra blankets so she could make sleeping spaces available on a sofa for Danielle, and on the bisque carpet for herself. They all went to bed late, slept in the outdoor clothing snatched up when leaving home, and awoke early, in their unfamiliar surroundings. David and Alessia restrained themselves from talking with or touching each other, while quietly blowing a few "air kisses." Danielle curled up on the somewhat lumpy sofa, which appeared to have a musty odor, and awoke several times, wondering where she was for a few moments, then peeking over at her brother and his fiancée, smiling on one occasion to see how their feet stuck out from under the sheets and touched – while observing the similarly in the color of their soles. Melody found the carpet to be quite thin, and turned frequently, reliving the sight of her home in flames, missing Joseph more than usual, and feeling grateful that none of her family members – a grouping in which she was now beginning to include Alessia – had been injured or worse. She made tentative plans to contact her insurance company and a real estate agent in the morning, then realized that although the sky outside was pearl grey, it was already time to arise. Looking around and recalling the need to share a single small bathroom, Melody became the first to get up, moving as quietly as she could, while stretching, feeling the aches in her back caused by sleeping on the carpet.

Danielle was next to shower. Realizing that only a small soap was available, she tried to be considerate in lathering herself. Her thoughts drifted to the afternoon when David called to report the assault in the park, and the abduction of Alessia, about whom she continued to have mixed feelings. Alessia was so very pale compared to her brother, and her accent was clearly foreign. So were her mannerisms, such as frequent hand gestures. The water from the shower suddenly cooled, causing Danielle to gasp and to turn up the heat, hoping for more warmth. A few moments later, while drying with part of a somewhat tattered towel, she looked at herself in the mirror. The way in which David often looked at Alessia reminded her of Trevor, who had been inviting her out since their senior school year – except that he wore glasses constantly. It had been months since they'd had an opportunity to exchange kisses in an empty classroom, and Danielle was beginning to feel ready for further attention. And then there was Ahmet, whom she'd encountered at a music concert, leaving her in a daze simply after holding her hand and gazing into her eyes. She was still in a reverie when someone knocked briskly on the door. After rapidly dressing, and opening the door, she found the "*lovebirds*" as she called them waiting outside and heard their mother commenting that breakfast downstairs would soon be over. As David and Alessia replaced Danielle in the bathroom, she overhead the hesitancy with which her potential sister-in-law accepted her brother's invitation to shower together and decided to watch the local morning news on the television while waiting for them. Much to her surprise, the first images that greeted her included searing images of their home in Hornsey engulfed in flames last night. Melody joined her on the sofa to watch, first holding her daughter's hand, then hugging her, as they each relived the events that had occurred.

Danielle told her mother that she felt as if they were living in a dream. It took some time for David and Alessia to emerge from the bathroom, with the latter blushing timidly in a way that made the observant Danielle sure they'd taken the opportunity of some privacy in the limited space available to enjoy each other.

During a breakfast of baked beans, tomato, fried egg, and toast in the restaurant downstairs, they settled down to discuss the situation. Melody explained her plans to visit her insurance broker and an estate agent, suggesting that they also shop for clothing and try to identify a more comfortable if yet affordable hotel.

David added that he needed to meet with his supervisor at his workplace, and that Alessia, who nodded as he spoke, should probably meet with her supervisor by appointment at her bank. Over steaming coffee after their meal, it was agreed that Melody and Danielle would deal with the issue of accommodation; David and Alessia would travel to central London and meet each other at Oxford Circus after settling matters with their respective managers. When Alessia commented that her manager might not believe her reason for being out of touch for almost a week, and David suggested she take the police report along with her, she colored and looked stricken. He hastened to add that perhaps such a document, with all its personal details, should remain private. As a group of customers entered the hotel restaurant, with a gust of air following, they all realized that it was windy and rather chilly outside and agreed to include warm clothing purchases in the day's itinerary without fail, then to meet at the hotel by 3:00 pm, or to connect by phone beforehand. As they left to walk to the Finsbury Park tube station, it began to rain, so all four picked up speed. David and Alessia traveled south, holding hands on the escalator. Melody and Danielle north to her insurance broker's office. On Oxford Street, the young couple browsed for clothing in a number of stores, before finding two dresses and sweaters for Alessia, one set of which she changed into immediately, and a sufficiently comfortable change of wear for David, who was reluctant to release his fiancée's hand, as they approached her bank in time for her appointment. Kissing her lips in a passionate goodbye, he turned away in the direction of his workplace, after they agreed to meet in an hour in the Oxford Circus tube station. Even so, he ran back to hug her, saying "Let's not be fooled by the idea that lightening cannot strike the same person twice – please be alert for anyone who seems too interested in you. In fact, I will stay here until you return from the bank, and we can go to the eatery together!"

When Alessia emerged from the bank, she looked thoughtful. In answer to David's question "How did the discussion go?" she responded, "They are willing for me to return tomorrow – a temp has been taking care of my counter station." As they walked towards the restaurant, trying to continue their conversation over the noise of double decker bus engines, black taxis, assorted automobiles, cyclists, and the distracted crowds on the sidewalks, Alessia explained that her supervisor had attempted to call her mobile phone, the day after she'd called in sick, and when she didn't respond, had concluded that she had either abandoned her job, or had been involved in a serious accident. He had been startled to learn that she had been attacked and abducted, and peppered her with questions, which could indeed have been answered by a copy of the police report. However, Alessia remained glad she had decided to avoid sharing it. Nevertheless, the discussion had taken her into a swirl of very recent memories that she preferred to bury. As they were arriving at the park near the restaurant, and they sat on their usual bench, enjoying the cooing collared doves with their black-circled necks, and several newly planted, pale pink dahlias, accompanied by yellow calendula flowers, for a few moments,

Alessia told David that it might well be a long time before she was able to forget her experiences at the hands of Benito, Tomassini and Lucia, and asked him, in advance, to forgive her if she sometimes appeared less ardent than before in their physical relationship. She haltingly and shyly added that it was occasionally still uncomfortable for her to be touched intimately by anyone, even while loving him. David reassured her of his ready understanding, telling her that he would not easily forget how he felt, after finding her tied up on the bed at South Quay either, hugged her closely, took a deep breath, and went into his restaurant, which was full of intently conversing customers. For a while, he couldn't find the person he needed to speak with.

David eventually talked with his supervisor in the restaurant, in between the latter's continuing directions to staff. He found it difficult to explain clearly what had happened to him and to his fiancée, during the prior week, given repeated interruptions. Both became somewhat frustrated. In the end, he was asked, "Do you want to resume working here with your probation clock reset to zero?" Upon answering affirmatively, David was told to begin work immediately on a shift that would end at 6:00 pm. He was now very uncomfortable, wanting to work, but wishing to ensure Alessia's safety that afternoon. In the end, with permission, he went out to talk with her, and the couple agreed that she would browse in Oxford Street stores, after updating Melody by phone, lunch at Selfridge's, and return to meet in the nearby park when he was leaving the restaurant. With time on her hands, Alessia made her way from make-up products to handbags and back to clothing during her first stop. She could not but recall her recent experiences, like a repeatedly rewound movie, returning again and again to her feelings as she lay bound to successive beds. Alessia attempted to control her thoughts, again recalling Marcus Aurelius' comment in his *Meditations* that the happiness of one's life depends upon the quality of one's thoughts. Nevertheless, she realized anew that experiences such as hers, including assault, abduction, imprisonment, and torture, could not be waved away, and remembered Locke's assertion that all human knowledge was derived from ideas presented to the mind by events, including those she had endured.

She deliberately focused upon David's bravery in coming to her rescue by himself, and against all odds, managing to extricate her from people whom she now categorized as criminals. Later, Alessia found herself thinking of Paolo and Giancarlo. After explaining the afternoon's plans to Melody, who indicated that together with Danielle, she would be looking for more convenient accommodation meanwhile, Alessia decided to call her brother Giancarlo. The line dropped shortly after they greeted each other tentatively, and he inquired where she was. Giancarlo answered on the first ring of her renewed call, asking about her location, safety, and health in a strained voice. As nearby customers were seeking sales assistance, at least one somewhat angrily, it was sometimes difficult to hear each other. However, she managed to answer her brother's alarmed questions, and to explain that she was staying with David's family. Alessia was relieved that Giancarlo was evidently unaware of the prior night's fire but was caught off guard by his indication that Paolo wanted to speak with her. In introducing her to Benito and Tomassini, her elder brother had set a chain of very unfortunate and painful consequences in motion and had refused to listen to her concerns. She cried out, startled, as a passing male customer accidentally stepped on her left foot, then hastily apologized. Giancarlo, who heard what sounded like a scream without following the brief conversation that ensued, was extremely worried, and Alessia had to explain what had occurred twice before he calmed down.

At that point Paolo took over the phone. He immediately apologized profusely for his actions and took full responsibility for ignoring her assessments of their compatriots. Alessia relented and found herself explaining what had happened to her, once again editing the details of her imprisonment while making the implications clear. "I now realize that my efforts to take care of you and to arrange for you to be married, without taking sufficient account of your own preferences, were wrong," said Paolo, by way of underscoring his prior contrition. Alessia could hardly believe her ears. Her conversation with Paolo in particular, but also with Giancarlo, made her feel as if she were exhaling, letting go of a measure of family-related stress, for the first time in a long while. When her elder brother invited her to visit with David, if he remained the person she really wanted to marry, Alessia assured him, in an almost ebullient manner, that they would be sure to accept. After Paolo again sought reassurance that Benito and Tomassini had not violated her and told her of his understanding from the police officers with whom he had been talking that they had fled the country, they ended the conversation. Alessia felt truly encouraged that it would be possible to interact with her brothers again, and that they might accept David as her fiancé. Looking at her watch, she suddenly realized that it was getting late in the day.

When David stepped out of the restaurant where he worked and entered the nearby park, he did not see Alessia, only a few other seated persons. Anxiously, he rounded the fountain with a cluster of marigolds in the center and finally saw her holding a bag, looking pensively at the blue jays nearby. David came up behind Alessia and was about to surprise her with a hug when he reconsidered his plan and greeted her instead. Turning, she smiled happily, invited him to sit, and opening her bag, held out a container of warm lasagna with plastic spoons. David joined her, smiling. "I did not see you at first and began worrying immediately," he commented, taking the container. "How about a penny for your thoughts?" Alessia affectionately stroked his head and taking a spoon, joined David in enjoying their very late lunch. After eating and drinking bottled water, they talked for a few minutes about their afternoons, and her recent hopes to visit with her brothers soon, then walked towards the Oxford Circus tube station. It was after 7:00 pm before they rejoined Melody and Danielle in the hotel lobby. Melody had completed a constructive discussion with her insurance company and an estate agent but had not made any headway on securing a more comfortable hotel for the night. They ended up with shrimp chop suey takeout food from a local Chinese restaurant and retired to the very same small room which they had shared during the previous night. Danielle claimed the first shower, as soon as supper was complete, containers discarded, while Melody talked with the couple.

A week later, they were still in their small, somewhat claustrophobic Finsbury Park hotel room, awaiting the results of an offer made by Melody, using her home insurance policy proceeds, on a garden apartment near Alexandra Park. They had each purchased a few more items of clothing, including fluffy felt slippers and comfortable silk dressing robes for sleeping and wearing when in the room.

Danielle often awoke at night, sitting up to look around, listening to her mother, David and his fiancée breathing. She was fascinated by the relationship between them, carefully observing how they tentatively hugged each other lightly at night, with legs occasionally uncovered and rested on each other while tossing, or the way in which Alessia regularly appeared flushed, and her brother relaxed, when they emerged from the shower, whether morning or evening. Danielle's thoughts kept turning to Trevor and Ahmet, wondering what it would be like to kiss and hug either of them now. While waiting for David and Alessia to complete their ablutions, Melody took the opportunity to talk with her daughter about her next educational step and encouraged her to decide at which universities to apply, to begin her baccalaureate degree next September. On the most recent such occasion, Melody ended up suggesting that Danielle talk with Alessia about the factors that influenced her in selecting a university for her first degree. The following Saturday, while Melody and David went with the estate agent to execute the title to their new home with a banker's check, Alessia and Danielle talked on a hillside bench in the nearby Alexandra Park, enjoying the view.

Danielle was conscientious in beginning their conversation with questions about university choice, as they listened to sparrows chirping in the white-barked birch trees, under a cerulean sky, where a murmur of starlings soared, with brown squirrels darting across the grass. Alessia talked about her interest in exploring the disciplines of psychology and philosophy at a well-regarded university which was some distance away from her home in Reggio Calabria, but with an environment that gave her parents every confidence that she would be safe.

Danielle nodded in understanding, and Alessia went on to talk about some of her freshman year experiences. When she mentioned meeting some of the young men in her class at co-curricular events, such as class debates, always with staff members nearby as chaperones and organizers, Danielle asked, "So you never had an opportunity to talk with any of these classmates alone?" Alessia chuckled and explained that she had not really talked with any man alone, apart from her family members, until she met David at work. Danielle was incredulous. "You don't need to say that because I'm his sister, you know. I won't betray your confidence if you share with me before getting around to talking with him!" Alessia looked uncomfortable for a moment, then placed a hand gently on Danielle's shoulder. "I'm afraid that you will think me quite boring; families are so protective about their daughters' honor in my culture that men have been known to fight viciously and kill each other, when even unintended untoward remarks are made," she told her. "When I worked in a bank near home as an intern, all of the young ladies on staff spoke with male colleagues only when dealing with business requirements, in the presence of other ladies. We avoided looking them in the eyes when speaking. One memory from those days is of sitting with a co-worker at my supervisor's desk, and observing his hands, with long, manicured fingers and the gold cuff links on his monogrammed shirtsleeves." Alessia then asked, "And you, how many handsome boyfriends did you have in school?"

Danielle snorted in response. "I actually had opportunities to meet very few boys, only one or two, and was almost always far too shy." Changing tack, she asked directly, "How did you know when you fall in love, and what was it really like?"

Alessia paused to consider the question, looking serious. "Love is like a tentative, initially tenuous stream in the soul that magically links you and another person, without warning. It gathers force into a river with sparkling, sunlit bubbles that refract and reflect through the eyes of both, when seeing each other, until neither wants to look away" she said musingly. "In the end, love is mutual acceptance, understanding, and appreciation." Danielle looked at her in silence for a while.

Then she asked, "And what is lovemaking actually like?" Alessia closed her eyes, took a deep breath, and responded "I suppose it's different for each person, gender, and age. For me, it is as if that river suddenly encountered a succession of rapids, and ultimately overflowed into a sonorous waterfall full of iridescent, shooting stars, at the same time as extremely violent earthquakes rock the riverbanks, creating eddies of electromagnetic currents that ripple through your body, soul, and mind, until you entirely lose yourself in utter ecstasy." Danielle tentatively hugged Alessia, noticing her moist eyes. She returned the hug for a few moments. When they once again sat up, Alessia blinked her eyes and asked, "How did we get from the factors involved in university choice to an intense talk about love and extreme ecstasy? Let's go to meet your mother and David. They must be ready to talk about furniture purchase and other arrangements for moving in." They walked out of the park in a companionable silence, crossed the road after waiting for a few cars to pass by, and entered the latched green gate of Melody's newly purchased home after a few more minutes, pausing to enjoy the untrimmed grass of its garden with lilacs, peonies, hollyhocks, and daffodils, and the cozy patio just before the entrance, already furnished with four rattan chairs and a table, attained after climbing three sturdy wooden steps.

Melody and David were inside busily taking measurements and calling furniture stores. As they entered the living room area, David swept Alessia into a hug, lifting her up, while Melody wondered aloud whether the new arrivals were not anxious to move out of the hotel that very evening, if at all possible. David set his fiancé down and commented that once the kitchen appliances and the beds were in place, they could add other needed items afterwards. The afternoon was spent in a blur of activity - calling distributors, arranging deliveries, double-checking measurements and eventually, supervising the installation of a four-burner electric stove with an oven, a refrigerator, two beds and a velvet red sofa with cream cushions. It was getting quite late when Danielle inquired how they would manage to sleep without sheets for the beds. In response, Melody suggested that they leave immediately, stop near Turnpike Lane to purchase linen, towels, dishes, and soap, as well as a few groceries, travel back to Finsbury Park to their hotel, check out, then return to their new home. They were all caught up in the spirit of this "*moving in*" project, exchanging ideas as to what to purchase for the house, and by way of food items in rapid fire fashion. Eventually, the four arrived with their parcels, shopping bags, and suitcases back at their new home via taxi, still talking animatedly. It was getting late. Danielle and Melody set out to "*christen*" the kitchen by baking cod with lemon and cilantro, together with jasmine rice and green peas while David and Alessia went to shower. He inquired as to how her visit to the park with Danielle had gone while soaping her back.

Alessia retailed the first part of their conversation with confidence in a well- completed assignment but hesitated when turning to the young ladies' discussion of love. David turned Alessia around, enjoying the feel of his soapy hands gliding all across the curves of her body and her immediate responsiveness, although she tensed for a minute, before relaxing. It was only after the excitement and loving exertions of their shower had come to an end in mutual completion that Alessia felt able to share with a somewhat amused David more of the day's earlier discussion with Danielle. He kissed her neck repeatedly, as he dried her with a fluffy new bath towel and commented that for him, making love with her was also like the combination of two rivers merging with an intense, rippling earthquake, made even more powerful by an abiding sense of wonder and deep gratitude that they were actually together, and planning to remain so for the rest of their lives.

A weekend later, Alessia and David were ascending the steps to visit Paolo and Giancarlo at their home in Camden Town. Her brothers met her at the door, embracing her and kissing her cheeks in turn, then shook David's hand and invited them in for a coffee. Everyone present was nervous for different reasons. Once everybody was seated, Paolo told Alessia that he wanted to apologize to her again, this time in person, for his prior rejection of her repeated assessments as to the character and intentions of Benito and Tomassini, and for his own treatment of David when she was attempting to introduce them in Hyde Park, as well as his subsequent related comments. "I was trying to protect you in the only way that elder brothers learn how to do in Reggio Calabria, acting on behalf of our parents, so did not listen to you sufficiently, or pay attention to your preferences, and hope you will not only say but mean that you forgive me." Paolo added. Giancarlo smilingly interjected that he had no idea that his sister was so strong and energetic until the day that they both lifted her, twisting, and turning like an eel, up the stairs to her room. "I tried to hold your feet and you kicked me quite hard!" he recalled. Alessia smiled in return "Of course, I forgive you both, although it likely will be a long while before my sleep is no longer punctuated by memories of my abduction." David, who was seated next to her, squeezed her hand, and Giancarlo asked the couple when and where they planned to get married. This question once again lightened the mood in the living room.

When Alessia responded that it was their hope to decide some of the details with her brothers, Paolo rose and offered to get marzipan from the kitchen to accompany their coffee while they continued to talk. "I also brought your favorite pistachio ice cream," he said to Alessia upon returning, "together with some of the nuts themselves." His sister laughed, commenting that she'd had no idea he had remembered her snack preferences, and began to eat her treats. When Giancarlo inquired how his sister had actually been rescued, Alessia said proudly that her fiancé had arrived at the hotel where she was held and had saved her, all by himself. Ending the poignant silence that followed, David mentioned that they had been contemplating a wedding at St. Peter's Italian Catholic Church in Holborn, to approving nods from the brothers. Alessia showed off her diamond- studded engagement ring as they munched and drank espresso coffee. Paolo looked thoughtful, and asked "should you have children, in what religion will you bring them up?" Without missing a beat, David responded that they would naturally be introduced to the Catholic faith of their mother. Giancarlo offered to be David's best man and Paolo declared, not to be outdone, that he would be glad to give Alessia away on behalf of their father, who was still not well enough to travel to London. Later, as Alessia went upstairs to her former room to reminisce, and to collect much needed clothing, as well as shoes, the men sat and talked about the couple's honeymoon options. Giancarlo made one of his trademark jokes, as they continued to discuss wedding logistics, saying "Take my advice – I don't use it anyway" – then asked, "what is your best definition of a jury?" When David responded that in the UK, a jury was a body of legally selected persons who were sworn to inquire into any matter of fact, and to arrive at a measured verdict based on the evidence presented, Giancarlo laughed. "No, my friend: a jury consists of twelve people who determine which client has the better attorney!"

Chapter Seven

Tomassini sat in Benito's former large wood-paneled office at South Quay and explained to his visitor once again, as calmly as he could, that Acerra Import/Export dealt only in premium wines and olive oil. He stated that the company had now identified and immediately fired several 'rogue' senior staff members who had independently and secretly engaged in illegal activities such as trafficking young women into the United Kingdom for prostitution. His interlocutor, Detective Inspector Dutton, leaned back in his chair, 'steepled' his hands and inquired "So you have the usual Human Resources records concerning these staff members ready to hand over now?" Tomassini had been briefed to respond, as he now did, "We will of course hand over all available documentation that you might require." His visitor expressed satisfaction, and went on to inquire about Alessia's abductors, with a pointed question. "Were you either involved in Miss Amato's kidnapping or the assaults that she experienced afterwards?" Tomassini felt his own temperature rise suddenly but answered smoothly that her abductors were among the staff members who had been fired for illegal initiatives that compromised the company. He went on to comment that while Ms. Amato had evidently been held at the company's premises for a short while, based on exit interviews provided by departing staff, he had not seen her himself since meeting the young lady at her home, when invited by her brother, and again at a reception in Kensal Green that they had both attended. "Are you saying that you did not molest or assault her while she was held by company staff?" persisted Detector Inspector Dutton. Tomassini felt very grateful that Alessia had been blindfolded when brought to the Lancaster Gate hotel and transferred to South Quay, fully sedated before, and at least partially tranquilized during her stay, and that the issue now came down to his word against her recollection while in a traumatized state. "I have no idea what statements Ms. Amato might have made," he responded. "My understanding from the reports provided by the departed staff members involved was that she may have been sedated during her abduction. In any case, I must reiterate my earlier remark as to the extent of my acquaintance with this unfortunate young lady." When asked about the location of Benito, Tomassini responded that he had returned to Italy to deal with urgent family matters. After a series of follow-up questions and answers, the conversation concluded when Tomassini telephoned the Human Resources Director, requested the records of the recently fired staff members, and provided them all to Detective Inspector Dutton, together with his own signed statement.

The police officer warned Tomassini that he would be called upon to testify, and that his passport should be handed in to the Metropolitan Police Office, then left.

Tomassini shrugged his shoulders, when alone at last, and reflected that there were really no mistakes in life, only lessons either learned or ignored. He had spent as many hours as possible in preparing for the just completed visit with the company's legal advisors and HR specialists, and in related encrypted telephone discussions with Benito. As a result, the men identified in the documents so 'reluctantly' provided to his police force visitor were no longer in the country, and the last addresses indicated represented safe "dead ends." Alessia herself was another matter. However, there were no third-party witnesses to his interactions with her – or to Benito's evidently rough initial training, for that matter – and given her undisputed sedation, any untoward recollections could readily be contested. Now to confirm that all of the young women managed by Acerra were indeed abroad, more or less safely, and that additional contracts for premium wine and cold-pressed, virgin olive oil were executed in Campania then backdated. In a sense, Tomassini was actually glad to have Benito far away at work in New York, instead of providing continuing direct instructions in person as his senior partner. Arising from the desk, he looked out of the double-glazed window over the swirling grey Thames and recalled once more the scene below when that young man, David Armstrong, had somehow managed to escape with Miss Amato, and the only shot he'd been able to fire from his Luger had missed.

Tomassini's memory wandered to his time with Alessia at the Lancaster Gate hotel, where he wrapped her up in a sheet after placing her in a gag, a blindfold, and tying her hands behind her, then threw her over his shoulder; and the enjoyment experienced when he settled her in the bed down the corridor there at South Quay, tied her limbs once again to the bedposts, freed her otherwise, and fondled her at will for a while. His mind wandered further, to his adolescent days in Campania, where most young men who were not working legitimately or studying at universities had ended up in local gangs, or even in the Mafia, engaged in financial extortion or drug running. He had come a long way since those early networking days. Tomassini hoped that his new role as Acerra Import/Export UK CEO would provide a launching pad from which he could build his personal wealth significantly while remaining free from legal complications of any kind and allowed himself to daydream for a few minutes about the new multi-storey garden home he would begin to construct, perhaps in Wales, once the story of Ms. Amato's kidnapping was no longer in the newspapers.

Several weeks later, Melody was experiencing a mixture of intense feelings, as she sat with Danielle in a front pew at St. Peter's Italian Catholic Church, listening to the entrance song, greeting and Act of Penitence of the Mass where her son would wed her daughter in law to be. The sun transformed the magnificent stained-glass windows into a dramatic, glowing triptych as it became warmer within the Church. She listened to the liturgies and observed the Communion, joining silently in deeply felt prayer. Melody then watched Paolo, whom she'd recently met, walk with Alessia down the aisle to meet David, standing near the altar with the officiating priest, who had agreed to say Mass for the wedding because Paolo had been among his most devoted parishioners. Melody recalled her own marriage with Joseph in Montego Bay – in some ways, seemingly only yesterday, eyes filling with tears as past and present images blurred in her mind, bridging thousands of miles across the restless, cobalt-green Atlantic Ocean. David who had been such a happy baby in his perambulator, often smiling at his parents - it seemed only a short while ago - was now suddenly a man standing so tall and proud with Giancarlo next to him, as Paolo placed Alessia's hand in his, then turned to take his seat. She recalled a remark made by Graham Greene that time travels out of the future, which doesn't exist yet, into the present, which has no duration, and into the past, which has ceased to exist. Looking intently at the couple, Danielle recalled her afternoon in the park with Alessia when they explored the meaning behind the demonstration of love before her, and followed their responses to the priest, noticing the expectant stillness in between. Alessia breathed in the scent of incense and wondered for a moment whether she was awake or dreaming, then having grounded herself in the reality of the moment, grappled with recurring anxieties. Spirits lifting when she saw David smiling through her veil, Alessia stood next to her husband-to-be and they turned again to the priest, who continued the ceremony. As they stood at the altar, a photographer began taking a series of wedding photos, as prearranged.

Afterwards, walking back down the aisle to the door with David, who had somewhat tentatively kissed his bride in public, as if '*fixing*' their new relationship in a photo darkroom, Alessia was startled to see someone who resembled Tomassini sitting and conversing at the back of the church. As the couple continued to the door, she convinced herself that her imagination had been tricking her and concentrated on the firm grasp of David's hand. On the way to the wedding reception, which had been arranged at the home of her brothers in Camden Town, Alessia and David talked about their weekend honeymoon plans at a guesthouse in the Isle of Wight. She asked David to take his acoustic guitar along, never having heard him play. The couple also warmly praised Melody's thoughtfulness in not only meeting most of their vacation travel and accommodation costs, despite her modest finances after purchasing and furnishing her new home near Alexandra Park, but also in insisting that her son and new daughter-in-law remain there, until they could accumulate sufficient savings to consider purchasing or at least renting their own abode.

Upon arrival at their weekend honeymoon guesthouse, Alessia and David encountered the plump receptionist and owner, Mrs. Portia Harrison, who welcomed them warmly, introduced herself, and invited them to call her 'Portia,' but then sought somewhat hesitantly to confirm that they were Mr. and Mrs. Armstrong, who had been married the previous day. David responded dryly, "Yes we are," and offered to provide their certificate. No need at all, said Mrs. Harrison. "Did you have any trouble with your families, since you are evidently so different in background?" she asked. Alessia was embarrassed and stressed by the question, but David lightheartedly said "what's the point of getting married to someone who looks and behaves exactly as one does? Don't you think that marriage should always be a wonderful lifelong adventure of discovery?" Mrs. Harrison beamed, disarmed, and led the couple up to their bedroom, where a welcome snack of wheat biscuits, Gouda cheese and cashew nuts with beer and wine awaited them on a table. "The bathroom tub includes a jacuzzi, and dinner will be served downstairs at 7:00 pm," she told them with a smile. "Do enjoy your afternoon!" When they were alone, David and Alessia embraced and kissed each other, then fed each other snacks, and sipped cabernet wine, before changing from their travel clothing and setting out eagerly to take a walk. It was an absolutely beautiful day with smalt skies, and cirrus clouds scudding under a light breeze from the west. Chaffinches chirped in some of the beech trees, their delicate light green leaves still heavy with dew. They walked along narrow lanes with hedged grass verges and tantalizing views of the seascape in the distance from time to time. "So, what does it feel like to be married?" asked David, smiling, "did my response to Mrs. Harrison exaggerate?" Alessia squeezed his hand. "It will take a while for me to become used to having you as my husband," she answered, returning his smile, "but it helps a lot that you have been my best friend for months, and more recently, my very own expert teacher where all the wonders of love are concerned!" As they rounded a corner and paused to enjoy another view of the now cobalt sea, David told her that the shimmering seascape beyond the beach reminded him of a fractal, and that in his senior year at university, he'd been very interested, for some reason, in such fractals, as well as in Fibonacci series. "I recall that fractals are diverse geometric shapes that create mesmerizing patterns, presenting smaller and smaller copies of themselves - snowflakes, river deltas, honeycombs, blood vessels, flowers, trees, nautilus shells and spiral galaxies." commented Alessia. "Can you remind me how Fibonacci series are constructed?" David grinned. "I will not only remind you that in such a series, each term after the first two represents the sum of the two prior terms but will be glad to illustrate loosely by means of a small poem, then in person! This is how the poem goes:

Kiss
me
again
tongue and lips
like Fibonacci's
sequence, each movement a
spiral
enfold, unfold, a working through
and against, again."

David followed up by hugging Alessia lovingly, and then kissing her repeatedly, in line with the poem's instructions, until as she hugged him in turn more tightly, both were breathing heavily, and decided to retrace their steps up the hill to the guesthouse, where Mrs Harrison invited them into the dining room smilingly.

After dinner, David and Alessia enjoyed their jacuzzi for a while, soaking in the warm bubbly water, and teasing each other. When she noticed his guitar case in a corner of the room while relaxing in the jacuzzi, Alessia reminded him that she was looking forward to hearing him play, as promised. "I'll be glad to play you a few tunes, after we get up and dry off," he replied, "upon the condition that we remain nude as we are!" They sat on the bed, cross-legged, and he strummed a few tentative notes, then launched into a vibrant rendition of "*Guantanamera*," followed shortly afterwards by a haunting version of "*Cancion de Aranjuez*."

Alessia was stunned. "I had no idea that you could play so beautifully," she observed, as his last sonorous notes died out. Smiling broadly, he hugged and kissed her again. David spread her legs and stroked her vulva lovingly. "You are so exquisitely delicate and so absolutely beautiful," he murmured, "my garden of delight, making me think of passion flowers and pink roses." She responded teasingly, "You may have an appropriate analogy, to the extent that pollinated flowers bear other flowers – but then, flowers include both male anthers and female stamen!" As they relaxed together in the radiant afterglow of lovemaking, Alessia remarked that when they first met, she had been such an innocent and shy young girl, who had never been looked at or touched intimately by any man – she could hardly believe they were now married, and so completely comfortable without clothing in each other's presence. David particularly liked to suckle her nipples frequently, and to admire her breasts. On one such occasion, after he tried to remember the source of an extravagant quotation declaring such mammary glands to be '*heavenly globes of delight*,' Alessia tartly remarked upon having read that such anatomical features were unique to human beings among other primates, inflating during puberty and remaining so for life – whereas in female apes or monkeys such swelling occurred only during lactation, although in all primates, their primary purpose was to feed the young - then held him close.

The couple's honeymoon weekend flew by, and it appeared to be only a few kaleidoscopic moments until they were saying warm farewells to Mrs. Harrison and found themselves once again on the tube to their workplaces in the vicinity of Oxford Circus. During such journeys, Alessia was becoming accustomed to interpreting the distinctive looks some fellow passenger gave David and herself: some wistfully observing the adoring way in which they often looked at each other; others appearing visibly angered at the sight of Alessia's hand enfolded in David's, wedding rings displayed, emphatically demonstrating the contrast in their complexions; and others, usually young men, who mainly ignored her husband and leered at her suggestively, evidently concluding that she must be *'easy.'* In turn, David felt so proud to think of Alessia as his wife and to continue accumulating eidetic memories of their exchanged love that he usually ignored the passengers around them. He still could hardly believe that they now belonged to each other completely. At the same time, he was preoccupied by the challenge of saving sufficient funds for a home rental, repeatedly calculating the sum of first and last month in deposits as well as a month's rental for a one-bedroom flat, and other related living costs, in relation to his quite limited monthly salary.

David regularly reminded himself, and sometimes also Alessia, that the difference between dream and achievement was self-discipline, and resolved to identify a more rewarding job as soon as possible. Once, following a discussion about accommodation plans, Alessia had offered to contribute towards the required savings, leading to their first disagreement, although ended as swiftly as it begun, with David accepting her observation that his neo-limbic brain had yet to "*get in gear*" where this subject was concerned. He reflected that this comment probably also applied to his continuing concern for her safety, underpinning his insistence upon meeting her outside her bank, so that she would never be unaccompanied in public, despite her repeated assertion that there was no need for him to *mollycoddle* a strong young woman. At the same time, Alessia continued to experience disorienting flashbacks to her time in the hands of her abductors, so vividly, now, and then, that she had to share these unwanted memories with her ardent husband just as they were engaged in the throes of passion, as she abruptly became rigid, shuddering with fear in his arms. David would then hold her gently, stroking her back using a level of therapeutic pressure and a rhythm she'd taught him, which regularly reminded her that human skins and eyes are the primary vehicles through which we navigate our entire worlds.

Danielle had begun to attend the London Metropolitan University in Holloway Road, having chosen to register for a baccalaureate degree program in architecture. As most of her classes were in the mornings, she often left home with David and Alessia. At first, she hesitated to accept their invitation to travel with them, since they shared the same tube line down to the Holloway Road Station, thinking that she would be in their way. However, the trio often found themselves engaged in vivacious conversations, one of which led to a decision by the young couple to also register for part-time graduate studies at London Metropolitan – Cognitive Behavioural Therapy in the case of Alessia, while David selected a program in Economics, Finance, and International Business. During an orientation meeting, he struck up a conversation with a classmate from Brixton, who turned out to be a human resources manager at an Oxford Street store. A few classes and discussions later, David was recruited as a floor manager, at a net salary level that reinforced his delight at being able to provide his restaurant with the expected notice of departure. Meanwhile, the annuity provided by Joseph's pension allowed Melody to manage her household expenses, and to volunteer with a non-governmental organization program that engaged her in reading to senior citizens in the neighborhood – motivated by recalling one of Joseph's comments concerning contentment – *"Be selfish and help someone."* She was glad to get out of the house on a regular basis, and usually delighted in the wide- ranging conversations that continued each evening at her dinner table. During one such evening, the TV news concerning the arrival of Pope Benedict XVI on a state visit to Britain led Danielle to inquire why neither David nor Alessia had been to a church of any kind since their marriage. Both looked at each other and smiled, while Melody gently scolded her daughter for her inquisitive question.

When David commented that his sister seemed to have more time on her hands than they did, between work and study, the latter including weekends, she somewhat morosely retorted that architecture had turned out to be a much more demanding taskmaster than initially realized. David teased her that she might eventually become famous for building new cathedrals, following the footsteps of the twelfth century Tom Builder in Ken Follett's book "*Pillars of the Earth.*" Danielle jauntily responded that she hoped to learn how to create unique and spectacular, environmentally friendly residential architecture in a style that no architect had ever dreamt of before. Melody brought out a custard with nutmeg for dessert, along with a Jamaican rum liqueur, as the television announcer was reporting on a major new wind farm project that had just opened. To Alessia's question as to whether the next generation of the family would benefit sufficiently from sustainable energy investments to survive, David remarked that so much depended on the relative cost-benefit of such new energy sources, and Danielle immediately added each such source seemed to generate its own problems – for instance, in the case of the wind farm just launched, the turbines were expensive and spoiled the landscape. Melody looked on smiling at the banter between her children at the table, and the gusto with which everyone in her family appeared to be tackling their dessert. She remembered how much Joseph had enjoyed her custards, sighed quietly, then commented gently that human life was most enjoyable when taken one day at a time, in a spirit of consistent gratitude for each person's blessings and hopes for the future. Danielle quietly reflected that perhaps one such blessing for her might turn out to be Trevor's decision to transfer from his current institution to London Metropolitan University, joining her there, as she looked forward to an opportunity to learn more about him.

Danielle was enjoying her classes, readings, and projects, while continuing to be fascinated by her brother's relationship with Alessia. They usually appeared to be so comfortable with each other, especially in the mornings, that their occasional disagreements or evident if silently felt stresses seemed remarkable. Now, meeting Trevor at the student cafeteria for lunch, she was recalling Alessia's definition of love, while looking into his animated brown eyes, glancing at his labile lips, and listening to his description of an intense childhood argument at home between an unimaginable seven siblings about the respective responsibilities for household chores. She pushed her fish and chips meal distractedly around her plate, dividing her attention between her former school friend, sudden memories of her brother's bleeding head, after being attacked in the park while sitting with Alessia, the frantic yet determined look in his eyes when telling Melody and herself that he was going to try to find his then fiancée, and the textbooks on architectural history that she needed to review for a class assignment. Trevor finished his lunch of beef burger and fries with ketchup, drank his now tepid coffee, and hurriedly departed for his next Management class, leaving Danielle reading at her table. Glancing up at his receding figure in shorts and a T-shirt, she wondered whether to accept his invitation to a student union party that weekend, then decided to defer that decision until later.

One evening, David, Alessia and Danielle agreed to remain late at London Metropolitan University to listen to a special presentation by a visiting Professor of Mathematics and Physics from the Sorbonne University in Paris, France, concerning the intriguing topic of time. An audience of over one hundred students and invited external visitors had crowded into a lecture theatre, with the lectern on the stage lit by a spotlight, and with the screen behind displaying a projected view of the Earth from space. She began her lecture in accented English, speaking in an energetic contralto. "Time is an attribute of matter and energy, as with length, width, and depth. It changes its nature and impact with our unit of measurement. How many of you have paused to contemplate the varied ways in which human languages and cultures depict time, as *walking, running, freezing, flowing, fleeing, and expiring*, for example? We all try to manage time each day, by the use of alarm clocks and synchronized watches, without readily remembering that time is inevitably subjective, with multiple internal individual answers to common questions such as *how much time do we have left?*" She continued by positing that the case for a single, stable reality remained unproven, and that there might well be an infinite number of realities, then posed two rhetorical questions: *don't we all experience time as variable, so that an hour can seem like a minute or a day, depending upon our circumstances and mood?* For instance, how much time do blissful lovers spend in a first rapturous kiss, compared to the same individuals separately in a dentist's chair?

The presenter mentioned Einstein's unified field theory, together with the continuous stochastic processes of Brownian motion, commenting that from a relativity theory perspective, events may be simultaneous or sequential, consequent upon the location of the observer, and contending, for example, that within a black hole in space, time ceases to exist. She added that every imaginable notion of time is linked with specific physical events, such as the swing of a pendulum, the earth's orbit, or the vibrations of a quartz crystal, and noted that since the Earth had long been gradually slowing down in its daily rotation, days grow slightly longer as a result. The lecturer remarked that as one objective measurement of time, every 5,700 years, exactly 50% of any given cluster of carbon 14 nuclei would decay into nitrogen 14 nuclei. Most audience members were fascinated, including David, Alessia and Danielle, although some shrugged or smiled, thinking to humor the presenter, and several simply appeared puzzled. As the lecture ended, she speculated that at some future point, mathematical models outlining different kinds of time might well be developed, demonstrating that linear sequences constituted only one variant of human experience.

The presenter concluded that this would make it possible to understand much more clearly common events such as human dreamscapes, or any given child's variable description of time, whether spent in joyous play or in stressful situations, or mystical accounts of meditation and prayer. When questions were invited, Danielle was the first to raise her hand, and inquired as to the implications of her argument for recorded human history, and for projections as to the fate of life on Earth. After thanking her for this question, the professor remarked that contrasting accounts of the Earth's creation from various religious perspectives constituted a good starting point, then noting that most historical accounts tended to be written from the viewpoints of conquerors or elites, argued that recorded internal timelines of critical events such as the pillage of Rome by the Visigoth tribes in 410 AD, or the Battle of Hastings in 1066 AD would be sure to differ, depending upon the writer. After quoting from Julius Caesar's *De Bello Gallico* (The Gallic Wars), she then continued by contrasting the varied public comments reported in the media about the validity and reliability of climate change projections then ended with the observation that everything really was relative. Other questions and answers followed, leading to several lively exchanges, and then the lecture ended with a warm vote of thanks.

Alessia had settled into the work routines at her bank and was on good speaking terms by now with most co-workers and all the managers, who perceived her as a dedicated and generally pleasant employee. She usually had her lunch in the small lunchroom at the back of the bank, then regularly called David, sometimes also Paolo or Giancarlo, who were unfailingly curious as to whether she continued to enjoy her marriage, when they would travel to Reggio Calabria to meet her parents, and when the couple expected to begin having children themselves. She usually fended off questions about travel and children with the somewhat tart answer "as soon as their savings after expenses permitted." During one of her conversations with Giancarlo, Alessia was startled to learn that he finally had secured a job, as an olive oil sales manager for Acerra Import/Export PLC. "Isn't that the same company where Benito Esposito used to work before he disappeared?" she asked, startled, drawing on information provided to David by Detective Inspector Jeffries after their visit to his office. Giancarlo responded, "I didn't know that was his surname – in any event, he has long left the company, which, I understand, is now run by Tomassini Rossi." Alessia gasped audibly, then composing herself, commented that Giancarlo might have forgotten that Mr. Rossi had also been involved in assaulting her after her abduction six months ago.

"I understand that it may be a while yet before you are able to put that experience behind you," replied Giancarlo, "but found no active police inquiries into any company executives or complaints about Acerra's staff when I checked it out, before signing on, and I have nothing to do with the company's senior executives. If you can tell me about any current issues that I should be aware of, I will hand in my notice and begin looking for employment elsewhere." Alessia felt an uncomfortable sensation at the pit of her stomach but told Giancarlo in a consciously composed tone that she had no new negative information about Acerra and recalled that Paolo had long been urging him to get a proper job. That afternoon at work, Alessia had to retrieve several errors at the counter, fortunately made and corrected before any customers or supervisors were aware of her distraction. When she told David about the conversation with Giancarlo later, he commented, "Incredible! That's the guy who was shooting at us while we were escaping from South Quay!" In the end, David understood her reluctance to press her brother to leave his first full-time job since arrival in London. But that rainy night, tossing on the turquoise satin sheets of their bed, Alessia found herself vividly repeatedly reliving her assault and torture while abducted, and her husband tried in vain to comfort her.

David found it difficult to balance his business studies at London Met with his full- time store floor manager role, as he was anxious to excel in both, while also trying to provide all the emotional support needed by Alessia and to manage their relationship well. On some days, she literally sparkled with the joy of being alive and together with him, sometimes impulsively hugging and kissing him, or humming while preparing special Italian dishes for the family in the kitchen, such as *pasta arrabbiata.* On such occasions he would often tease her, saying that she was on a mission to fatten Melody, Danielle, and himself with carbohydrates and starch, while she munched only a little of these exotic meals, despite their delightful odors, so that she could remain in shape, should she ever want another husband. On other days, Alessia was quiet and pale, even when smiling, and her grey eyes appeared to be tinged with a deep, indefinable sadness, notwithstanding his efforts to tell a few jokes about therapists, bankers and artists that always seemed to fall flat. David was anxious to build a marriage that was as durable as the relationship between his father and his mother, with, he hoped, a much happier dénouement. He was also still learning the ropes as floor manager at the store, trying to balance between often imperious customer demands for products that had yet to arrive, or for otherwise unavailable designs or styles, and staff expectations that he would at least mediate between unreasonable customers and employees who were doing their best to placate them. Meanwhile, his business studies classes required very careful scheduling, and independent study was almost impossible, except at nights and during some weekends. Alessia always appeared to understand this continuing dilemma. One evening, as Joseph's grandfather clock ticked on the wall, David asked while they were alone at the dining table for a few moments "How do you manage your own work at the bank and your studies so effortlessly?" "I try to keep priorities in mind," she answered. When David's hurt expression betrayed his thoughts, she hastened to add that he would always remain her first priority, and she knew that her work at the bank counter had to be done. When it was possible, she completed her cognitive psychology projects, and otherwise, put them off. David was glad to make her laugh for a moment with his remark, partly in jest, that she had the benefit of unwitting subjects to analyze around her at home, all the time.

Danielle ended up going to the student union party that weekend with Trevor, dancing with him to the rubato rhythms of hip-hop music and sipping gin with tonic in between. After a while, she switched to non-alcoholic beer, not wanting to become a cliché. Trevor's eyes narrowed for a moment when he observed her change of beverage, then he relaxed, reasoning that she was not trying to distance or disconcert him, and that she was a young woman he intended to take the time required to know better. Danielle's ponytail swirled as she moved to the music, smiling, and she seemed so attractive to him in her slightly décolleté violet silk blouse, top button undone, paired with an ultramarine pencil skirt that he felt glad to be her partner at the party. Trevor's memory turned to their high school senior class, when he first began to notice her, and to the look in her brown eyes after he had kissed her deeply in an empty classroom. When he learnt that she was an intending freshman at London Metropolitan, he decided shortly afterwards to apply there as well, instead of pursuing his original plan to study at South Bank University, near his family's home in London, where he was born.

Trevor's parents had migrated from the Caribbean island of Grenada, and for most of his life, had kept discussing the possibility of returning to the island to retire, with its bright sunshine, aquamarine seascapes, and lush green hillsides reaching down to the beaches upon which their eyes could linger most days.

However, as their only son grew up in London, vacationing in Scotland, then Wales, during successive summers with his family, and as he became a young man overnight, it seemed, the family's dinner table talk turned to Grenada less and less. When Trevor mentioned Danielle's Jamaican heritage to his parents one weekend, in response to an inquiry as to where his friends were going to study after high school graduation, their response had been somewhat critical, until he disclaimed any immediate thought of asking her to go out with him. Now, Trevor and Danielle felt the music vibrate in their bones and smiled at each other. When the band paused, they returned to one of the tables, all decorated with tablecloths patterned in alternate red and white squares and rested for a while.

Meanwhile, Melody was engaged in reading Daniel Defoe's *Robinson Crusoe* to a small group of nursing home residents, who were hanging on almost every word, making her feel so appreciated that she took extra pains with her enunciation and paused, from time to time, for dramatic effect. When the protagonist's ship was captured by pirates a collective gasp from the audience was audible, and having escaped, when he was shipwrecked again, years later, near the Isle of Despair, off the Venezuelan coast, Melody looked around gratified to see that all of her listeners were on the edge of their seats. That night, David and Alessia were in bed at home upstairs, taking advantage of the absence of other family members. He was stroking Alessia's brunette hair, as she lay across his chest, her bare legs intertangled with his, almost drowsing following their most intense engagement in lovemaking for several weeks. David drew her head closer and kissed her partly opened lips gently, again and again, remembering a comment she had once made about the too often under-appreciated concentration of nerve endings in that location. After a while, he reached down with his right arm to stroke, lightly at first, between her legs and was gratified to encounter pooling moisture, rather than the tension that still all too often attended their togetherness. As he caressed her mons and vulva rhythmically, his mind turned to the moment when he opened the door to the room where she lay trussed to the bed in the South Quay building owned by Acerra, then to her brother Giancarlo's newly found employment. David held Alessia's breast with his left hand, circling her nipple and the delicate pink whorls of her aureoles, marveling at her lovely golden honey color and soft texture, and found himself praying incoherently and silently that they would be able to fulfil their dreams of life together without any repetition of the desperate moments caused by the interaction of her brother Paolo with Benito and Tomassini. As he did so, Alessia attained her release, crying out and panting in a way that encouraged her husband, after an interval, to enter her delightedly again, resting above her on his arms to avoid crushing her slim body.

Later, as a light rain began outside, David and Alessia pulled the cover over themselves, and talked about matters such as pending projects for their university classes, a number of staff members at the bank as well as the store who sometimes seemed to misunderstand or even deliberately ignore the requests they made, and her reiterated question as to whether Melody really meant it when she declared that they could remain at her home for as long as they liked.

Danielle enjoyed her dancing with Trevor at the student union party and was glad that when the time came to leave, he simply kissed her lightly on her lips, while hugging her warmly, reasoning that they were both beginning to know each other better and that he was evidently willing to take the time to do so, rather than to make assumptions. As she was on her way home on the bus from the Turnpike Lane tube station, her phone rang with an unfamiliar number. Upon answering out of curiosity – an action her mother had repeatedly warned her against – Danielle heard Ahmet's baritone voice greeting her. During the conversation that followed, he told her that since graduating from their high school, he'd joined a drama group, would be participating in a play called "*After the Fall*" in Soho the following weekend, and wanted to invite her to see the play and to dine with him afterwards. To her question as to the meaning of the title, he laughed, saying "If you were a member of the cast, would you give the plot away just like that?" Ahmet reminded her of a school drama based on the Wizard of Oz in which they had both played roles, and told her that since that time, he had realized that if you do something with all your heart and soul, it could create an internal river of joy. Danielle could not always hear him well on the telephone, over the noise of the bus in which she was traveling and the conversation of other passengers around her but recalled some aspects of their school play, including his portrayal of the tin man, and her own role as Dorothy, and was intrigued by his invitation. When Ahmet asked her about her university studies, she tried to explain the pull on her imagination created by looking at a specific building and imagining how it could have been designed differently or the growing excitement of beginning with a blank sheet and sketching form and function into being, in a unique way that could fulfill the aspirations of potential residents for a sustainable home in a particular location – even before their own awareness dawned. Danielle suddenly realized that her stop was rapidly approaching and ended the conversation after agreeing to let him know within the next day or two whether she could come to his play. By the time she arrived at home, Melody was watching television alone in the living room, inquiring why she had remained at her party so late, and offering her a leftover dinner of rice and peas with roasted beef. Danielle had not expected to have much of an appetite after the party, with the snacks and drinks that Trevor and herself had consumed, but she did, so accepted her mother's offer gladly, especially when Melody joined her at the table, drinking a cup of hot green tea. She took the opportunity to ask her mother again about the way in which her parents had met, and how she had known that Joseph was the one for her. On this occasion, Danielle mentioned a recently encountered theory of assertive mating, where couples with similar underlying physical characteristics tend to agree to link their lives and commented with a smile that she could not recall any such strong similarities in the appearances of her parents.

Melody sighed, then smiled after a few moments. "You were so young when your father left. Why don't you ask David for his take on that theory?" Indulgently, she went on to tell the story again of how she met her husband at a public library, where they were both returning books, and how he'd noticed she had a swimsuit under her dress, and was holding a beach bag, then immediately invited her to the beach. Danielle laughed with delight. "So that was the time you said you didn't know him, and he introduced himself, then just looked at you until you told him your name – then invited you again!" she recalled. "You do remember the story," said Melody, "but my decision to go with, and eventually, to marry your father had much less to do with his appearance than with the look in his eyes, the way he carried himself, his smile, voice and especially, my sense of what his very soul was like. He was always reading a book or article that had captured his interest, then talking with me about his readings and thoughts from time to time. If not love at first sight, I certainly had a realization, within only a day or two, that he was the one with whom my life should be spent." Danielle listened to her mother with a new fascination, eyes shining with upwelling emotion.

The next day, Danielle set aside a few moments to call Ahmet, and to accept his invitation to the play in which he was acting. That weekend, he met her at the Tottenham Court Road tube station, then they walked into Soho to a restaurant with an upper floor that had been converted into a stage, almost surrounded by audience seating, as well as overflow standing. As the play was not scheduled to begin for another fifteen minutes, Ahmet introduced her to a bearded Indian who was wearing a white Sikh turban as Chirag Bassi, saying "You wanted to know the meaning of the play's title – the playwright is just the person to ask!" then excused himself to visit the dressing room. Danielle turned to the playwright, with her eyebrows raised in question. He smiled benevolently and explained that the play was inspired by his religious beliefs, that God was wondrous, shapeless, timeless, incomprehensible, and invisible. For Sikhs, the highest virtue was truthful living. Human pride and commitment to material possessions often led to a fall from grace, and when this occurred, it was critical to seek reconnection with God. Chirag concluded that the title of his play was very much influenced by the intractable struggles of friends who had long emigrated from the Punjab in India to new environments, and who had almost always found themselves falling away from virtue, unable to resolve the contradictions in their lives that resulted from efforts to become like their new neighbors and friends. Danielle looked at him and asked, "So have you been able to resolve the contradictions in your own life?" "No," he answered, "but for me, the creation of the characters and the plot, including each act, represented a means of beginning to work towards this end, for both the audience and myself, through the scenes and dialogue on the stage." As the lights in the playhouse began to dim, and the audience gathered, Chirag ushered her to a seat near the front row and took his leave. Danielle turned her attention to the stage, where drumming offstage was rising to a tremendous crescendo, with the spotlights on stage changing color and increasing in intensity. The background consisted of the cream-colored internal walls of a room, with light shining through an open window. She identified a Buddha-like, gold-colored statue on the right wing of the stage as a probable representative of Virtue. It was not long before she recognized Ahmet in a velvet cyan costume sitting silently at a table with a crystal goblet, glasses, and plates, along with two female actors.

Other *dramatis personae* eventually filed on stage, some chanting, some arguing. As it turned out, there were three Acts, but Danielle was sometimes unclear about the characters portrayed, the issues addressed in the rapid-fire dialogue, or the resolution. Afterwards, Ahmet invited her to a vegetarian dinner at the restaurant downstairs and once they were seated in a booth looking out on the street outside, posed the inevitable question as to what she thought of the play.

Danielle paused as a waiter arrived with the menu, and after they both ordered a lasagna with a meat substitute that turned out to be somewhat desiccated, along with chilled pomegranate juice, asked him, "Well, what did *you* think, having had the distinct advantage of reading the script, preparing for your role, and acting in the play?" Ahmet chuckled. "In the beginning, I thought the characters seemed credible, that the setting was clear, while the plot moved the dialogue and action forward towards audience understanding, if not necessarily applause - although appreciation is always welcome!" He stopped to sip his juice, and continued, while looking at her lips. "My character as an Islamic immigrant here in London was consistent with my experience but it was not evident to me that some of the other characters, such as the two Sikh immigrants and the human personifications of Pride and Greed, were comfortable with their lines. Perhaps some of the other actors did not take the opportunities to practice as seriously as they should have." Danielle heard his remarks but focused first upon his religion. "So do you pray five times a day, go to a mosque on Fridays, and fast during the month of Ramadan?" she inquired. "And have you been on pilgrimages to Mecca?" Ahmet sighed. "Not every believer has had the opportunity for a pilgrimage to Mecca, and it can be quite difficult to pray at work during weekdays here in London – but I certainly visit a mosque each holy day, fast during Ramadan, and find myself physically as well as spiritually healthier for it." For a few minutes, they enjoyed their meal in silence, and then Danielle answered his original question. "I did not always recognize the characters in the play, or the intended psychological conflicts, if any, but Chirag's prior comments made me understand that the plot was supposed to demonstrate how they could readily fall from grace, in his perspective, and what the actors would need to do to resolve their internal contradictions." A group of patrons at the next table began to argue vigorously about their favorite national politicians. When she fell silent again, Ahmet added, "So you were unable to follow the inner story to its conclusion, correct? Not to worry – you won't hurt my feelings – the cast certainly needs more practice, as I've just mentioned, and perhaps the plot needs more careful development. But I certainly will not stress Chirag by presenting him with such a blunt assessment!" Danielle listened to Ahmet, while thinking of Trevor, and comparing them. Each was such an interesting man, handsome and energetic in distinctive ways. She recalled news earlier in the year about riots in Jos, Nigeria, between Christians and Muslim groups, leading to some two hundred deaths, and also remembered the case of a Muslim gunman in Egypt, who fired into a crowd of Coptic Christians, then returned to Ahmet's comments about the challenges of practicing his religion as a migrant at work in a non-Muslim society. Was a sustained cross- cultural relationship between people from such different worlds really practicable? Consciously turning at least partly away from this line of thought, perhaps for a later discussion with Alessia, she asked Ahmet whether he had yet seen the reportedly spectacular movie "*Avatar*," which had recently generated a new world record in box office earnings. "Are you actually inviting me to see this science fiction movie with you?" he asked in turn, making her feel suddenly shy.

Danielle explained that she had simply been wondering what sorts of other artistic productions and genres appealed to him. She caught his questing eyes lingering on her lips, then traveling to her low-cut, cream blouse, and her nipples suddenly tightened. As the restaurant was becoming more crowded and they had completed their meal, after making payment, Ahmet walked with her to the Bond Street Station, while inquiring further as to her plans for a career in residential architecture, and about her relatives. The night was warm, and the traffic intense. They paused now and then to look into the brightly decorated store front windows. In passing news vendors, Danielle noted headlines about heavy rains in Madeira, Portugal, that had caused floods and mudslides, leading to many deaths – the worst such disaster in the archipelago's history. She remembered a conversation with her brother on the increasing impacts of climate change, when a violent earthquake in Chile recently killed over 500 people, injured thousands, and led to a tsunami that struck Hawaii soon afterwards. What did such natural disaster trends mean? At the station, amid the hurrying crowd, Ahmet lingered over their handshake, looking into her eyes, and telling a somewhat distracted Danielle that he hoped she would accept when he invited her out again soon.

Meanwhile, Melody was sitting in her living room with David and Alessia, over a supper of chilled white wine, wheat biscuits and cheddar cheese, discussing the assertive mating theory that Danielle had mentioned to her. She smiled while retailing her daughter's renewed interest in the way in which she had met her husband, and reiterated the comment then made that her decision to marry Joseph had much more to do with his bearing, attitude, values, and her sense of his soul than with his actual appearance. David remarked that he understood, and looking at Alessia, went on to say that the first day when he glanced along the gleaming black marble counter at the bank where they were working and saw her only in profile, he felt very impatient to see her face fully. The opportunity to do so only occurred when they happened to go separately to a nearby sandwich shop. "Yes," interrupted Alessia, "that was Pret-À-Porter, where we ended up ordering prawn sandwiches and sat together for the first time." David nodded, sipping his wine appreciatively, after enjoying a bite of biscuit and cheese, and reminisced that when he finally looked at her face fully, he had felt both suddenly drawn to her, and convinced that such an elegant lady with a lovely skin tone, beautiful brunette hair, and fascinating gestures could never be interested in him. Alessia commented that for her part, David's face, voice, and mannerisms were captivating, especially because she had never talked with a man alone before, all the more so one with his intensity, and delightful complexion, and because she found herself wanting to run her hand through his hair. David looked amazed. "Now that is something you have never told me before!" Melody broke in, smiling "But you were both meeting for the first time, and would naturally be nervous, in your own ways." She went on to tell them about her first day at the beach swimming with Joseph, and how uncomfortable it felt initially when he seemed to stare at her blue one-piece swimsuit. David nodded. "But going back to that assertive mating theory, Danielle was explaining what she read to me as well and went on to say that the longer-term health of a couple becomes similarly impacted by shared lifestyle factors, such as the daily routines and rhythms of a relationship. Did you find that with Dad?" Melody continued to reminisce. "I wish we had been able to spend more time together, but Joseph was always working, and when at home, apart from dinner time, he frequently took you out to the park - in your perambulator to begin with - where he would sit and read to you for hours." Alessia smiled at David. "So that was how you first developed a taste for reading in my case, it was my mother who used to read to me, beginning with bedtime stories, and continuing with local folk tales, sometimes in dialect."

Danielle arrived home while they were still in the living room, sat beside Melody and took the last biscuit with cheese left. As she munched, her mother got up and returned with a glass of wine for her, asking "How was your evening at the theatre with Trevor?" Danielle explained that she had not really been to the theatre but to a playhouse in Soho, and that her evening companion had been Ahmet rather than Trevor. "Interesting name," commented David. "Where is his family originally from?" His sister took off her beige high heeled shoes and relaxed on the sofa. "The entire evening was interesting. I will come back to Ahmet but let me first tell you a little about the play, which was called '*After The Fall*,' written by a Sikh playwright named Chirag Bassi. "Naturally, it had nothing to do with the Biblical Garden of Eden story, but rather, the ethical challenges and moral conundrums faced by fellow immigrants practicing his religion in locations such as London, where community lifestyle choices lead to a frequent fall from virtue, especially from what is called *truthful living*." David interjected "But many members of immigrant host communities will argue that someone who wants to practice his or her religion in its purest form should not consider migration." He turned to his mother, "When you arrived in London with Dad, didn't you both do your best to adapt to the customs, practices, and traditions here?" Melody responded that they had been glad to have an opportunity to earn more money and to improve their lifestyle while doing all they could to adapt to their new environment yet retain their identity. Alessia remarked that perhaps it came down to how identity was defined. Her siblings and herself expected to function in a very different environment to Reggio Calabria, upon arrival in London, and tried in their own individual ways to change their attitudes and actions to fit in, without abandoning the culture into which they had been born. David looked at Alessia and held her hand, adding that he entirely understood, but the results had been very unfortunate in Paolo's case. Danielle continued to recount her evening. "I promised to get back to Ahmet, who acted in Chirag's play, but evidently has his own issues, where work and the practice of his Islamic religion are concerned, such as his daily sequence of prayers, for instance." It was Melody who asked her daughter thoughtfully "But do you see Ahmet as a potentially close friend? How does he compare with Trevor?" Danielle looked somewhat uncomfortable. "I like them both, for entirely different reasons, but please be reassured that I'm not about to settle down with either or convert to a new religion of any kind!"

Later, David and Alessia lay in their queen-sized bed, luxuriating in the afterglow of joyous lovemaking, and smiling with exchanged memories of the day after returning from their honeymoon, when they found that Melody had moved Alessia's belongings into David's bedroom, citing its comparatively larger size and en suite bathroom. They were just beginning to become accustomed to being regarded as a married couple, so Alessia still tended to look towards Melody when they were all together and someone said "Mrs. Armstrong." Indeed, on several occasions when out on their own, and her new surname failed to attract her attention, both had found themselves laughing. This evening, Alessia snuggled up to David, burying her head in his neck and kissing him tenderly, as it began to rain outside. However, when his left hand wandered invitingly between her legs once again, she swatted it away, smilingly warning him not to bite off more than he could chew. "I've been wondering whether we can find a few days in the summer to visit my parents in Reggio Calabria," said Alessia. "They have been inviting us to visit for a while now, and it seems that my father is not very well." David responded that he was sure they could each manage a summer vacation week, while London Metropolitan University was not in session. He went on to ask, "Do you think they are now prepared to welcome me as your husband?" while holding their contrastingly toned hands up to the lamplight. Alessia held him more closely, commenting that her elder brother Paolo, in particular, had been praising him in conversations with their parents, telling them that he'd never seen their sister so happy, and that she was sure the projected visit would go well. David mused, "Well, we each have our twenty-three chromosomes, with genes from both parents, even if mitochondria are passed on only through our mothers – when you think of it, if an average lifespan is let's say seventy years, with a turnover in generations at that point, leaving aside a perhaps more realistic overlap after thirty years - in the course of going back just four centuries, a couple accumulates some 354 grandparents, or 177 each. We are not only a part of all that we have met, to quote Tennyson's "*Ulysses*," but also, of all that our collective grandparents met!" Alessia kissed him tenderly again and again. When she inquired whether he would really be glad to meet her parents he nodded, and hugged her more closely, while holding her buttocks tightly. "Mrs. Armstrong," he declared, "you possess the loveliest *derrière* in the world!" She sighed contentedly, stroking her husband's forehead, as they admired her wedding ring.

The following day, as David and Alessia returned from work, they paused to clear the mailbox near the road in what had become a daily ritual. A large manila envelope attracted Alessia's attention as she pulled out the contents and sorted through them, with her husband looking on over her shoulder. He frowned, noticing that the envelope was addressed to 'Ms. Alessia Amato.' She opened it as they stood just inside the gate, on the neatly bordered pathway through Melody's beautiful red, white, and yellow rose garden where bees buzzed lustily through the blossoms, leading to the front door. They both exclaimed in shock as a set of glossy black and white photographs of a nude Alessia spreadeagled on a bed, with the ropes that had bound her while she was abducted '*photoshopped*' out, to create the impression that she had posed for the camera willingly. David hastily bent to collect the photographs from the ground, and found a short, printed note as well, saying that the photos would be released to the media, unless the police were kept out of this matter, and Alessia agreed to visit a location to be advised separately, alone for a day, with the date to be also provided at that time. In shock, the couple went into the house, placed the other items of mail on the table, greeting Melody who called to them from the kitchen, as usual, then headed up to their room to sit on the bed. Alessia took the photographs and laid them out, shaking her head in amazement to see how erotic and revealing her posed figure appeared. David looked at the photos and clenched both his jaws and his fists. For a few moments they were silent. Alessia began to quiver and bent her head, as tears rolled down her cheeks. David hugged her shoulders, folded her into his arms and told her, "We are not going to submit to this attempted blackmail on the part of Benito Esposito or Tomassini Rossi, but will report this immediately to Detective Inspector Jeffries," he said grimly. "There is only one newspaper in London that would be likely to publish such photographs, and he will surely be able to head off any such action on their part. If not, we will take preemptive legal action." Alessia looked at him wide-eyed, her face still wet. "What if the police are too slow to act, or these evil men decide to publish these horrible photos elsewhere, for instance in Italy?" she asked. David paused and responded that there might also be a way to trap them, using the further information pending, if they were given the impression that they were going to have their way with her. She looked shocked for a moment, then asked "You mean, that we should contact the Detective Inspector but also appear to be too frightened to do otherwise than carry out their instructions, so the police will have an opportunity to discreetly plan a trap?" As David nodded, Melody called from downstairs that dinner was ready. They packed away the photographs and hastened to shower, toweled each other, dressed somberly, and went to dine.

The next morning, David called Detective Inspector Jeffries from work on several occasions, until he was finally connected with him. It took a few moments for the Detective Inspector to remember David and Alessia, but as soon as he was reminded of the kidnapping and the devastating fire at Melody's former home, his immediate question was "have there been any further issues?" When brought up to date, he followed up with a request to have the photographs and the accompanying note as soon as possible. David hesitated, then responded uncomfortably that the photos consisted of very graphic nude photos of his wife, and wondered whether sworn statements, together with the printed note could not suffice. The detective congratulated him on his marriage, then insisted that there was no substitute for the photos as evidence of intended blackmail, as well as the prior abduction, adding that they would be kept securely and used only for legal purposes. "However, in the circumstances, we should not meet at any police station." Pausing for a moment, he went on to say that they could meet that afternoon at a hotel in the vicinity of his office where meeting and conference rooms were available, and he would be accompanied by a colleague who could draw up and witness their sworn statements. David inquired whether it was absolutely necessary for his wife to be present and to sign a statement as well and sighed deeply in resignation to be advised affirmatively. The couple ended up taking two hours of urgent personal leave away from their workplaces to travel to Covent Gardens, where they found the agreed hotel without difficulty. Detective Inspector Jeffries had left the required meeting room location, and welcomed them there, then introduced his colleague. David handed over the manila envelope and the two officers reviewed the contents silently as Alessia looked down at her hands, folded in her lap. They were then requested to write their statements, which were then signed and witnessed as planned. To David's query as to what next, Detective Inspector Jeffries confirmed that Alessia should plan to keep the expected appointment when a location, date and time was indicated and shared with him by telephone. He declared that she would not be in any danger, as a carefully concealed team would move in upon her arrival, while taking the necessary measures to safeguard her. Looking at David directly, he added that he should plan to be engaged in his normal routine and should on no account attempt to intervene as he did when Alessia was held in South Quay.

Another manila envelope arrived for Alessia within two days, with a printed note indicating an address in St. John's Wood, providing a time of 9:00 am to 6:00 pm, and the date of the following Saturday. It was evidently intended to prepare her to spend nine hours at the site, and perhaps to also provide some assurance as to her eventual departure. When David contacted Detective Inspector Jeffries, the next morning, they agreed that the note should be faxed on this occasion, and that Alessia should make herself available at the entrance to the stated address and time, dressed attractively – but after ringing the bell or knocking at the door, should appear to hesitate to enter. "That will not be difficult," David commented grimly. "My wife is now experiencing regular nightmares in which she is once again abducted and assaulted." During the following days, Melody and Danielle wondered aloud on several occasions why the couple seemed to have such limited appetites, and always seemed so tense. Melody became worried that her son and his wife might be quarrelling, or otherwise at odds with each other. On the morning of Alessia's planned travel to St. John's Wood as a decoy or bait, she found it difficult to decide what clothing would be appropriate, and eventually settled on a silk cream blouse with a lime-green skirt, a crimson belt, a set of strappy brown shoes with four-inch heels, and a matching handbag. Alessia insisted that David should at least travel with her to the tube station, remaining seated on the arrival platform until she telephoned him, as a compromise with the instructions they had been given. When they arrived, she clung to David, kissed him passionately, and then reluctantly, climbed the stairs to the exit. He settled down to wait, a Metro newspaper in hand, reflecting that if matters went wrong, his wife could indeed be kidnapped again – or alternatively, the photographs at issue might be published, if not in London, then as Alessia had suggested, perhaps in Italy. In his mind's eye, he ran through the seemingly sultry pictures of her posed invitingly and felt pained to his core at their existence, as well as the need to have handed them over to the police for their viewing. As he watched the trains pull in and out of the tube station, brakes sometimes squealing, accompanied by an acrid smell, with a succession of passengers hurrying out of, then crowding into each one, David also considered the possibility with a sense of dread that Alessia could be caught in crossfire, should the police raid be inefficiently executed, and might end up injured or even dead.

Benito was jubilant. He slapped Tomassini heartily on the back and told him that it was always his plan to return to London quietly, once investigations into Acerra Import/Export PLC had become dormant, and to have an opportunity to enjoy Alessia properly, after all. Tomassini inquired "But why did she make such an impression upon you over six months ago? She married the man who rescued her at South Quay, returned to work, began her further university studies. It seemed probable that you would simply forget her, so I was surprised when you asked me to keep track of her." Benito looked thoughtful. "I agree that it would be simplest and perhaps safest to just move on and to focus my attention upon what is now an increasingly successful New York branch of our company. But one of the lessons I learnt from my early days in Campania was that your reputation builds your personal and business brand. A leader must be remembered with fear! Once we are done with this young lady, her family will never forget the name of Benito Esposito – or Tomassini Rossi. At the same time, a leader must always '*look around the corner,*' and plan for contingencies." Tomassini wondered "Did you ever think that she might just have followed instructions and planned to arrive without alerting the police?" Benito shook his head and inquired whether the Acerra security team had fully implemented the disinformation instructions given them, that they should use their networks to advance the date on the police case documents, after the directions given by Detective Inspector Jeffries. Upon Tomassini's affirmative answer, he reminded him that the company had always controlled their targets effectively by identifying and skillfully exploiting their greatest fears, while remaining several steps ahead. He added that in Alessia's case, her greatest fear was clearly public exposure and the loss of her reputation, so the photographs sent her catalyzed the entirely predictable actions of the couple. He chuckled, commenting that by the time they both finished enjoying her, and taking additional compromising photographs, she would become putty in their hands, and there would be no way in which her husband, however proactive and creative, would be able to help her, this time. While awaiting Alessia's arrival, Benito and Tomassini logged on to their laptop computers and confirmed their travel arrangements, then each concentrated on their corporate reports.

Tomassini shook his head, noting Benito's shaking hands on his computer keyboard. In answer to his unspoken question, Benito muttered that his doctor was now thinking that his TDK or tardive dyskinesia might be linked to either gastrointestinal issues or to bipolar disorder, whatever that might be. Meanwhile, Detective Inspector Jeffries was in office with two colleagues, reviewing the photos of Alessia spread on his desk. The three men were exchanging ribald comments on the erotic nature of her poses, when one idly inquired, "Isn't it tomorrow that she will be the bait for the raid in St. Johns Wood on the gang members who are planning to assault her again?" Detective Inspector Jeffries stopped short and commented that he was sure that Mrs. Armstrong was scheduled to visit the address indicated that very day, and about the time that they were all talking, then directed an immediate cross-check. Within the next five minutes, he was reviewing the fax received from David, and swearing a folder containing follow-up instructions for the same time on the coming day. He demanded that the intended team be deployed immediately, adding that the evident error in the case folder would need to be investigated subsequently.

Alessia arrived at the address she was searching for in St. John's Wood and looked nervously around for any signs of the expected police team, before climbing the steps to the green door with an antiquated brass knocker, accompanied by a doorbell under a spyglass. On the first step, she paused again, checked in by phone with David, who was briefly concerned that she had observed no indication whatever of a concealed police presence, and then ascribed this to trained skill in concealing their presence. When Alessia completed her climb up the six marble steps and rang the doorbell, the door opened promptly. Seeing no one at first, she hesitated in the doorway, attempting to focus her vision as she looked into a dimly lit entry hallway, pervaded by a musty smell, with two plush cream sofas and a red carpet. Suddenly, someone grabbed her Alessia's right arm, pulling her forward, closing the door behind her and turning on a light switch that enabled her to see the smiling, expectant face of Benito, then to realize that Tomassini was behind her. Alessia tried to control her fright and to reopen the door just behind him. However, Tomassini pushed her towards Benito, and the two lifted her by her arms and legs to a large oak desk in an adjoining room, where they expertly tied her down, using already prepared cords, so that each limb was absolutely immobilized, firmly flat against a sturdy desk leg. Alessia had been so shocked initially that she'd hardly struggled, but now she screamed loudly, again and again. Benito quickly placed a rubber gag on her mouth, blocking any further sound, leering at her, as he unbuttoned her silk cream blouse and thanked her for accepting his invitation, dressed so attractively and irresistibly. Meanwhile, Tomassini used his penknife to cut her bra straps deftly, leaving her delicate breasts exposed within a few seconds.

Benito smiled more widely, as Alessia's eyes darted around the room in terror, and she visibly fought to calm herself. He massaged her left breast and squeezed her pink nipple appreciatively. "If you're not used to us by now, you soon will be," her commented, then told Tomassini to take off her shoes and the rest of her clothing – an action undertaken with such alacrity, including the removal and replacement of each bond as necessary, that Alessia rapidly found herself nude and trembling, spreadeagled on the desk, both wondering why the expected police team had yet to arrive, and deeply embarrassed at the state in which they would find her if and when they did. She felt completely constrained and exposed. Her thoughts were interrupted when Benito took out a camera, reminding her of the one he'd used to take similar photos of her before that had led to this point. He snapped a few shots of her from a number of angles, including several close-ups, then put aside the device, and told Tomassini that he was free to enjoy Alessia above her waist, smiling even more broadly, while spraying her vulva with a liquid that smarted, then settling down to massage her intimately. "This time, you will climax, whether you wish to or not – and you will learn to enjoy anything we choose to do with you!" Benito declared. He penetrated her digitally, making slow and determined rhythmic efforts to stimulate her, while Tomassini alternately squeezed her breasts and circled her aureoles, bending to suck one of her now alert nipples from time to time, and to nip at her neck. As she found herself becoming increasingly excited despite her resolve, Alessia recalled reading about cantharidin lotions and wondered about the chemical content of Benito's application, given his determined remark. Glancing at him, she noticed his triumphant and somewhat amused expression. Alessia was closing her eyes and ardently thinking of David's loving face, increasing her efforts to regain calm, although moisture was steadily gathering inside her. She was breathing, and her heart was beating, more and more rapidly, while frustrated tears filled her eyes, when the hallway door suddenly opened, banging loudly against the wall. She opened her eyes to see what appeared to be several policemen, some plain-clothed and one uniformed, two with revolvers pressed against the slack-jawed heads of Benito and Tomassini, who had their hands up in shock, and another who was covering her considerately with a thick green drape just pulled from a nearby window that opened on the street below where oblivious drivers continued on their ways.

Alessia closed her eyes again, experiencing both relief and acute embarrassment, as her two assailants were handcuffed and led away. It appeared to be a hallucination, when she heard David's voice in the hallway, inquiring about the safety and location of his wife, and demanding to know why the police team had taken so long to arrive, given the plans made by Detective Inspector Jeffries. She wanted to call out to him, but the rubber gag was still in her mouth. David entered the room angrily, but his expression changed to deep dismay when his eyes met those of his wife. He realized that she had been tied down and her clothing removed, noting the remnants of her bra as well as her crumpled blouse and skirt on a nearby chair, along with her shoes. David felt a dizzying sensation of *déjà vu,* as he approached Alessia, lifted the gag off her mouth, and asked what exactly the two men who had lured her to this location had done to her. Alessia still could not speak, so he asked the remaining team, which included a policewoman to leave the room. The men complied, but Constable Sheila Thwaites introduced herself as a psychologist and indicated that her instructions were to help in relieving Alessia's trauma and to document the actions of her assailants in detail for the purposes of their prosecution. David nodded understanding, and they both turned to the task of untying Alessia – no easy task, as the knots had been expertly tied, so tightly as to affect her circulation.

Constable Thwaites ended up using her official issue Swiss army knife to cut each bond, and David hastened to help Alessia into the remains of her clothing and her shoes, then massaged her hands and feet. When she was somewhat composed, Constable Thwaites requested a recorded statement, to be transcribed and signed later. Alessia explained what had occurred step by step, beginning with her action in ringing the doorbell. When she completed her account, the psychologist asked a series of questions concerning her current state of mind, then turned to David.

Before she could continue with her questions, he once again demanded to know why the police team had been unable to deploy as planned, in time to foil the intended attack on his wife, noting her estimate that at least forty minutes had elapsed from the time of her entry to the arrival of the team. It was then that the horrified couple learned how close Benito and Tomassini had come to abducting and transporting her elsewhere again, after probably subjecting her to repeated rape for the remainder of the day in that St. Johns Wood apartment. It was Alessia who first surmised that at least one well-placed member of the force had been working for or taking instructions from Acerra Import/Export PLC. Constable Thwaites could neither confirm nor deny this surmise but commented that this issue was under urgent investigation. By then, Alessia was able to ask David what had led him to arrive when he did, allowing him an opportunity to explain that nagging doubts as to whether she would be safe, after her call, led him to leave the tube station eventually and to observe the address from a distance, perhaps five minutes before two marked police vehicles silently arrived at speed and the strike team entered the building, leading him to rush in immediately afterwards. Constable Thwaites recorded this explanation, and asked David how he felt about arriving to find his wife restrained as she was on the desk, where the green drape and the remains of the ropes that had bound Alessia had been left on the floor.

The Leica camera used by Benito had had already been removed as evidence. "I wanted to kill those men myself, in any way possible," he responded. "But I realize that they need to be prosecuted in court and hope that they will end up in prison for the rest of their miserable lives, so that we can at last get on with ours." Alessia added her concurrence, then Constable Thwaites asked them to take a swab of the liquid that had been sprayed on Alessia, storing the result in a provided container as further evidence, then waited in the hallway to provide privacy. Upon David's indication that the process had been completed, she returned, and nodded in answer to his wife's question as to whether the company led by Benito and Tomassini would be thoroughly investigated and probably deregistered as well. She closed her notebook, turned off her recorder, and invited the couple to ride home with her, an offer that was readily accepted.

Chapter Eight

Melody relaxed alone in her four-poster mahogany bed at home, looking through the window at a full '*hunter's*' moon that was low in the night sky, with most stars dimmed by the light pollution of the city. She mused about the close association between moon phases, the rise and fall of tides, and the changing stages of human life and love, reflecting that age brings wisdom only to the fortunate. Another night lit by such a magical moon after a cinnabar sunset came to mind, at Joseph's home in Montego Bay, Jamaica, seen from their shared bed perhaps two weeks after their marriage. The couple had continued their journey of discovering each other, as well as themselves. Melody lost herself for a while in a veritable river of lambent memories, where her husband lifted her from their bed to the bathroom, soaped, showered and then made love to her; where she first made herbal tea with cream, sugar and fresh buttered toast for her new husband, only to discover that his dietary preferences included neither sugar nor butter; and where he had purchased a fluffy pink cotton night gown as a surprise for her, and was so distressed to find that she would much have preferred a cream or turquoise night gown in silk. Cirrus clouds scudded across the glowing moon as she reflected upon the ways in which they had learnt to love each other more and more, by warmly appreciating their spouse's most enjoyable qualities, understanding each other's motivations and concerns as they came or were brought to attention, and accepting areas in which their approaches and tastes might differ – rather like a three-legged stool. During their early years in London, they had grown not only to love but to actively like each other, providing a sense of shared meaning and purpose in life, as first David and then Danielle were born. Melody had since been forced to live without

Joseph, while drawing a key reason for *being* from her children as they grew. Sometimes, she personified time as wicked – like a thief in the night, stealing the youth, beauty, and energies of its unwitting human targets. More often these days, however, she realized that her contentment was not so much determined by what her son and daughter were doing, and how they related to others, especially herself, but more by her inner reactions to her own life. For instance, Melody enjoyed the continuing process of decorating her home, tending the rose bushes in her garden, even when thorny, and gaining a new sense of purpose from her volunteer work and her reading. On occasion, she recalled Henry Thoreau's observation that progress occurs when we unlearn, and then learn anew, what we thought we knew before. When she read dramatic scenes from a book that captured the attention of her almost palpably fascinated audience, observing how caught up they were in the audibly imagined world that the sound of her voice allowed the author to project, afterwards, Melody often hummed a few bars from a childhood hymn such as "*Amazing Grace*" in her kitchen, as squirrels nickered while playing in a neighbor's leafy elm trees outside, and plashing waves of incipient contentment soothed her soul.

Meanwhile, Danielle was looking at the same moon from another angle of the house, while sitting up in her queen-sized bed with several fluffy mauve pillows, listening to a Sony Walkman recording of one of her favorite bands – *Abba* – a taste she hardly ever shared with friends, out of concern that such predilections made her seem out of step with their tastes. She moved her hands in the air, not to the music, but rather, as she silently depicted to the restless satisfaction of her mind's eye, an image of a mostly glass-walled two-storey home, built into the side of a grass-covered hill, with a roof containing both a red-tiled patio, and an array of south-facing solar panels, as well as a rainwater reservoir fitted with a filter.

She thought about the spate of news concerning natural disasters in a range of countries, such as the newspaper reports that had come to her attention near Bond Street Station during her recent evening with Ahmet and renewed her internal resolve to focus her work upon sustainable residential architecture. Danielle recalled Kahlil Gibran's verse…" *all our hours are wings that beat through space, from self to self.*" As she continued listening to music, her reflections turned to Trevor, and she languorously relived their slow kiss in that deserted classroom, stretching out her legs and curling her toes in the pleasure of retrospection and a measure of anticipation. Stimulated by both her ardent thoughts and her nimbly cunning hand, Danielle lost herself for a few minutes in a sensual haze and was settling down to sleep when rain began to beat more and more insistently against her windowpanes. She noticed that the full moon had been completely obscured in what seemed like an instant. Suddenly, a loud bang outside made her tense. Danielle got up and went to her window, recalling the night of the fire, heart instantly racing. Under the amber streetlight outside, she could see that their metal garbage bin had been overturned on the pavement near the gate, with some rubbish spilled, and then glimpsed at least one deer – perhaps also a stag - probably from Alexandria Park. Had the lid been left loose or off? Returning to bed, Danielle's memories strayed to various *National Geographic* articles about crows in Tokyo dropping nuts into the middle of the road before traffic lights, so they could retrieve the opened nuts when vehicles come to a stop; Parisian pigeons who picked up crumbs within a tube station, and having exhausted the available supply, jumped onto an incoming train, then emerged at another station, to resume crumb picking; and magpies that managed to collaborate with each other to remove tracker harnesses placed on them by investigative scientists. She also remembered a Canadian friend recounting that raccoons in Toronto were quite capable of learning how to open locked rubbish bins by turning and rolling them over. Danielle had mixed feelings about her few zoo and aquarium visits and mused that so much was yet to be learned about animal intelligence, especially in the cases of species such as dolphins, whales, and octopuses. Later that night, one of her restless dreams included a vignette of her father in a black leather jacket with a warm fur collar, pushing her in a green perambulator through a herd of attentive bucks and does, lined up in evident anticipation on either side of their unpaved walkway.

The next day, when Danielle met Trevor at the Campus Library as agreed, he invited her to ride with him on his new cobalt Harley motorbike that weekend to Hampstead Heath. She hesitated, then told him she had never been on a motorcycle before, while wondering whether it would not be an uncomfortable experience. "Wear shorts and short sleeves," he told her cheerfully. "I'll bring a picnic, and we can take a walk, then lunch on the Heath." Danielle looked up into his sparkling brown eyes and decided to accept his invitation. When she mentioned their plan to her mother on Saturday morning, Melody paused, then asked "Do you feel very comfortable with Trevor? If you brought him to dinner one evening, would our family find him agreeable?" Danielle smiled and nodded, then went upstairs to dress. Trevor arrived at the gate with a modulated roar of his engine, and Danielle went to meet him, dressed in one of her favorite cream shorts and a lavender blue blouse, with running shoes. She stood for a moment tentatively, after greeting Trevor, waving to Melody gaily, while looking dubiously at the relatively small seat upon which she was expected to sit. With Trevor's smiling encouragement, she sat, donned her aluminum helmet, placed her arms around his waist somewhat tentatively, and they were off. Streets and traffic became a blur, with interludes when they had to slow down, and Danielle soon found herself gripping Trevor's hips firmly, both riders vibrating to the roar of the engine. Trevor reduced speed when a light shower of rain sprinkled them near Kentish Town West. After a while, she relaxed enough to enjoy the ride, and remarked as they parked near Hampstead Heath that she had never previously covered such a distance in London so quickly. Trevor beamed, dismounted, and took her hand, helping her off the motorbike, while collecting his gray backpack, and they walked together into the sprawling park, where grassy slopes with occasional benches alternated with tangled bushes, stands of elm, poplar and oak trees, lakes, and meadows where boys were playing soccer, and families, as well as couples strolled by. Trevor found a cool location with a bench near a lake with blooming purple water lilies, and taking off his backpack, he invited Danielle to sit.

Once seated, helmets off, they relaxed for a few moments, listening to the thrushes and chaffinches tweeting in the nearby trees. To Danielle's comment about the cheerful songs of the birds, Trevor remarked that they were mostly males demarcating their territories with their syrinxes. "What exactly is a syrinx?" Danielle inquired. "This is your opportunity to expand my vocabulary!" "It's the avian equivalent of the human larynx in a way, but located lower, where the trachea forks into the lungs – birds have syrinx muscles that modulate vibrations independently, producing more than one sound at a time," he replied. "She looked at him appraisingly for the first time that day, noting his cyan shirt and cerulean shorts, commenting that he had evidently carefully color-coordinated his outfit that morning. Trevor laughed, moved closer and remarked "You are looking very pretty today – I can't claim to compete!" Danielle was quietly charmed but wary. After their motorbike ride together, was Trevor planning an effort to take advantage of their secluded location? She felt ready for an enjoyable snack and pleasant conversation but was concerned that their location appeared so isolated. He spread a small tablecloth from his backpack between them, taking out wheat biscuits, Gouda cheese, cashew nuts and salmon sandwiches, together with chardonnay wine and paper cups. As they sat, a pair of red admiral butterflies flew nearby and they were admiring their attractive red stripes when a single painted lady hovered over a honeysuckle flower, all dramatic orange with black tips. While eating sandwiches and sipping wine, they chatted about Trevor's management courses and his interest in building a sustainable seafood restaurant business of his own someday, as well as her latest architectural project, involving the reverse engineering of a major apartment building in Croydon, with a focus upon correcting any design issues identified after the fact. In answer to Danielle's question as to why he had decided to purchase a motorcycle, Trevor grinned. "How else could I have brought us here from Alexandria Park so quickly?" he asked. She countered "But we could have arrived feeling like wet rats if the rain had turned into really heavy weather and might even have been forced to turn back. Speaking of bad weather, do you remember the news last spring about that freak storm in the Afghan mountains that triggered a wild series of avalanches, trapping thousands of travelers and killing some two hundred people?" Trevor looked thoughtful. "I don't recall that report, but recently, a major mudslide in China killed well over a thousand people. Do you think there may be a global pattern in such events?" "Yes, I do," she earnestly responded, "there are far too many destructive windstorms, earthquakes, floods, mudslides, droughts, and natural catastrophes all over the world that continue to happen, for them to constitute simple coincidences. Human beings are actively destroying our wonderful planet home." When Trevor nodded in agreement, remarking that perhaps the well-known Simon and Garfunkel song with lines such as…" *a rock feels no pain and an island never cries…*" was making unfounded assumptions, and reached for her hand, she stiffened for a moment, then relaxed again. "If it is really true that one person with courage makes a majority," he averred, "perhaps we have a majority coalition for more sustainable practices in every economic sector around the world right here!" Danielle smiled, and they continued to sip wine, although it was now somewhat less chilled, munching the biscuits and cheese he had brought. They began to discuss their respective families, and their shared interest in traveling to the Caribbean one day, in a form of heritage tourism. Once the picnic was completed, Trevor repacked the remains in his backpack and edged closer to Danielle. When he leaned forward to kiss her, she turned her face away for a moment, then finally accepted his warm embrace.

They held each other closely, losing themselves in a sensuous kiss that began tentatively, settled into tongue caresses that exploded tendrils of warm sensations throughout their bodies, with both ending up panting and trembling. Danielle sat up, self-consciously wiped her mouth with a little embroidered linen handkerchief, then restored her lipstick. Looking closely at Trevor, she noticed a little smudge of red on the right corner of his lips, then giggling, used her handkerchief on him as well. When she told Trevor that it was time to return home, he nodded, almost absently, and getting up, they walked back, hand in hand, to his motorcycle. It began to rain again, this time more heavily, so they paused at a covered bus stop in Highgate for shelter where there was sufficient space for riders and the Harley and sat looking out at the street in silence for a while, until Trevor asked whether Danielle would be willing to go out with him again soon. When she nodded, his eyes lit up, and he hugged her for a few moments, until a pedestrian in a bright yellow raincoat joined them. When the rain petered out, they replaced their helmets, remounted and Trevor gunned his engine exuberantly, increasing speed rapidly after a right turn – then suddenly lost control in an unexpected oil slick on the road, skidding on to the left sidewalk into a brick garden fence. As the motor bike hit the fence and recoiled, both riders flew off into the road, and Danielle shrieked as the vehicle's rear fell on her left leg. Trevor lay stunned for a few seconds, then got up and lifted his now battered Harley off Danielle, who was moaning almost continuously. He took her up out of the road as a lorry approached, noticing that her leg was bleeding severely from a deep laceration, and removed her helmet. Trevor was frightened and very worried about her status. "I'm so very sorry," he said. "Are you hurting anywhere else apart from your leg?" She grimaced and shook her head but winced upon trying to stand. Pulling the Harley out of the road, he saw that the front fender was twisted, and the handlebar scratched. "If this is still working, let me take you directly to the nearest hospital for treatment," Trevor told her. Danielle shook her head, saying in a shaken voice that she would prefer an ambulance or at least a taxi. He found his phone undamaged in his backpack, called for urgent assistance, tied the blue-checkered picnic tablecloth as a substitute torniquet around her bleeding leg as she gasped, and had her lean on his shoulder until an ambulance arrived. Danielle's cream shorts were now blood-stained, and she was quivering. When she was placed on a stretcher, and secured inside, he followed the ambulance to its home hospital on the Harley, finding that it could still be driven.

Once at the hospital, Danielle was placed on a mobile bed and admitted to the emergency ward where a physician cleaned her wound and applied a tight bandage to stem her bleeding, then checked her vital signs. As she eventually informed Trevor, Danielle needed a type O+ blood transfusion, had suffered a number of bruises on her torso, and was in a state of shock – but had no broken bones or sprains. Trevor's offer to donate blood for her, which turned out to be AB- in his case, was instead accepted for the hospital's supply, as there was no match. He called an immediately alarmed Melody. She arrived shortly after Danielle's initial examination had been completed, when she was scheduled to be given six stitches on her upper left leg, along with an intravenous line in her left arm for blood transfusion, to counter the blood loss arising from her injury - already in process. Melody found her hospital room and rushed in, hugging her daughter. When her mother exclaimed at the sight of her bandaged leg and her attached intravenous drip feed, Danielle said tearfully that she deeply regretted distressing her mother so much. While Trevor waited with Melody down the hall for the stitches to be inserted, he tried to explain how the accident had occurred. She listened patiently then asked, with a measure of exasperation - "So you were speeding with my daughter when the accident occurred?" In response, he showed her the oil residue that had remained on his backpack, and attempted to defend his actions, saying that he was riding within the speed limits when an unexpected oil slick on the road caused his motorcycle to skid. "Trevor, you both could have been killed!" Melody remonstrated. She took a deep breath, reflected upon the saying that that age brings wisdom only to the fortunate, then continued.

"However, we are all blessed in that nothing worse occurred, and I thank you for getting Danielle medical assistance as soon as possible. Did you sustain any injuries?" Trevor explained that he had a number of bruises on his arms and legs, but their helmets appeared to have protected them from any concussion, as intended. Ambulance sirens kept wailing outside and the hospital intercom echoed with messages to doctors, interns, and nurses. Noticing a drink dispensing machine in a corner of the waiting room, Trevor offered to get them both a cup of coffee. In the event, they had to pool resources to locate the required coins, under the flickering fluorescent lights, and eventually succeeded in returning to their metal seats with lukewarm coffee. Melody took the opportunity to ask Trevor about his family and his university studies, and engaged him in an extended conversation, until a nurse finally arrived to invite them back to Danielle's room. Trevor wondered aloud whether he should wait while Mrs. Armstrong went to see her daughter, but she patted him on the shoulder, telling him to join her. Danielle's bed was raised, allowing her to sit up in her pink-striped hospital gown. Her attending physician explained that the properly bandaged stitches were now in place and the blood transfusion completed, so she could be discharged into her mother's care, with pain relieving tablets for use as necessary during her recovery. She was advised to rest completely for at least two days as an initial step, by way of recovery from her blood transfusion, and then to allow time for her wound to heal, before engaging in any running or rapid walking. After her physician's departure, Danielle smiled at them both, saying that she was glad to have completed the emergency room outpatient treatment, and to be going home. To Trevor's stammered apology for the accident, she said somewhat impishly "Perhaps I've already had too much pain sedation, but I still want to thank you for a very pleasant picnic at Hampstead Heath, and I'm so glad that nothing worse happened to either of us when your motorbike went off the road."

David and Alessia were each attending classes when Melody called with the news concerning Danielle. They agreed to return home early as soon as they were free. On the bus from the Turnpike Lane tube station, Alessia looked out the window while passing the park where they had been assaulted, for a moment, seeing the very bench where they had been sitting at the time. David's eyes followed her gaze, and he asked whether the news received during the prior week that Benito and Tomassini had been arraigned for trial, had been helpful in beginning to put her experiences with them behind her. Alessia smiled a little sadly and held his hand tightly. "My first abduction was an absolute nightmare," she commented. "But at least I was able to call upon my inner defenses until you arrived to rescue me. With the second assault, I felt absolutely helpless and numb. It was as if an evil spirit had taken over my life and it seemed that I was completely at the mercy of those men." David held her close and remarked that when they finally had the opportunity to testify at the trial, and to see them sentenced to many years of prison, at least, it would help to exorcise the nightmare. Alessia responded that in order to testify, she would have to revisit the tormenting torrent of accumulated memories. David kissed her lips reassuringly, observing that as the writer Paolo Coelho accurately advised, we must make peace with our past, so it cannot destroy our present. He pressed the stop button so they could disembark almost opposite their home. Upon entering the house, they heard voices coming from Danielle's room upstairs, and ran up the sixteen-step wooden staircase to join Melody in tending to their newly invalided sister. Soon after they greeted her, Danielle found herself retelling the story of her accident, displaying her bandages and some of her bruises. "But you both could have died in that crash," declared David. "How could Trevor have allowed that accident to happen? You should never ride a motorbike again." Melody commented calmly that she had initially said the same thing to Trevor, who had explained that an oil slick on the road caused a skid, although he was riding within the speed limits. Danielle chimed in that it would be quite unfair to blame Trevor, adding that with all of the medication taken since her return home, she hoped to be forgiven if she were to snooze for a while. Alessia hugged her, telling Danielle that they all wanted her to rest and to get better as soon as possible, and were ever so grateful that she was able to do so.

Melody warmed up a dinner that was mostly composed of savory leftovers while David and Alessia showered and dressed for the evening. During dinner, they spoke in hushed tones about Danielle's accident and injury, not wishing to awaken her, and then Melody moved on to ask about the arraignment of Benito and Tomassini, to Alessia's quiet discomfort. "I suppose that you will both have to testify. Will your brothers be invited to do so as well?" When David responded on her behalf that summons had evidently been sent to Paolo and Giancarlo, Melody realized that Alessia was visibly tense. Changing the subject, she talked about her experience with her class during the previous evening, when she read extracts from Jonathan Swift's "Gulliver's Travels," and found her audience hanging on every enunciated word evoking the contrasting countries and cultures of Lilliput and Brobdingnag, with their eyes often dilated. She had David and Alessia smiling with her, as she recounted several of the questions asked – for instance, '*just how small were the Lilliputians really?*' - and the wide-eyed wonder displayed by some of the senior citizens in her group. Melody mentioned her efforts to underscore the importance of hope in unpredictable circumstances, and her conversations with listeners about the ways in which individual thoughts and responses to events echoed across time, whether intended or not. David remarked that he remembered his father talking about the ways in which thoughts led to actions, generating habits that created the character and destiny of individuals. It was drizzling again outside, and a light breeze from the west was rattling some of the windows.

They were all silent, enjoying the residual odors of Melody's cooking and watching the news of the day on television in the living room, when a sudden scream from upstairs echoed through the house. Melody led the way in running up the stairs to Danielle's room, where she found her daughter in what appeared to be a waking dream, breathing rapidly and trembling. Melody hugged Danielle gently, while Alessia stroked her forehead repeatedly, until the recently injured young lady relaxed again. Later, once they had retired, it was David's turn to soothe Alessia, whose emotions had been triggered by their conversation about the impending trial, when returning home on the bus, and then again by Melody's question during dinner. He regarded the etiolated shadows on the floor from the streetlight outside and realized that he was himself profoundly disturbed by his now overlapping memories of finding Alessia bound on the single bed in the room at South Quay where he found her, and subsequently, trussed to the oak desk in the house at St. Johns Wood, after entering behind the police team. How best could they each deal with the accumulated trauma created by these experiences, from their divergent yet convergent perspectives? He hugged Alessia more tightly, after feeling a tear drip onto his forearm, as she lay across his chest.

In an eventually successful effort to distract her, at least in part, David recounted some of his recent challenges with the staff as well as the customers at the store where he worked. There was the lady in a mauve dress with a pearl necklace that accentuated her plunging neckline, who methodically tried a spray or two of every perfume and cologne sample in that department – then cursed crudely, demanding to be left alone, when politely asked by a staff member whether she could help find a particular brand for her. That staff member fled in tears to the restroom and refused to emerge for nearly an hour - then gave her immediate supervisor her notice of resignation. Alessia answered thoughtfully that she recalled from her cognitive psychology readings that effective managers consistently projected a sense of confidence, competence, and compassion to their customers and well as their staff, and that they continually set out to learn from prior management experiences, together with those of other managers.

David assented, commenting that regular, in-depth self-assessment, with the goal of learning from experience, was both uncomfortable and potentially counterproductive, because so many managers tended to learn too much from their own, perhaps imperfectly analyzed experiences, and too little from those of counterparts. He then told her he thought he'd defused the situation recounted by offering the customer, who had continued to linger in that department, a complimentary bottle of perfume, on condition that she apologize to the offended and stressed staff member who had tried to intervene. However, despite promising to apologize, the customer took the offered gift and walked swiftly out of the store; and the affected staff member did not return to work.

Alessia stroked his head and commented that he might have had better results if the two ladies had been first brought together, so the staff member could have heard the intended resolution, and the perfume had been provided only after the apology was offered and accepted. When David nodded, then added that in any case, the perfume had been an inexpensive "*knockoff*" brand, they both chuckled. Alessia remarked meditatively that his story reminded her of the day she accompanied her mother to a perfume store near their home in Reggio, in either the Via del Salvatore or the Via Trieste, and ended up purchasing an attractively shaped violet bottle of perfume, with a sweet fragrance that was quite noticeable in the store – but the scent had entirely dissipated within a few days. Alessia mused, while accentuating her thoughts with her hands in a way that David continued to enjoy so much, that sometimes, life seemed so circular, in multiple ways, whether from the perspective of her current anxiety about her unwell father, who used to take care of her on family excursions, as a little girl, or from the point of view that she now had a loving life partner who was always taking care of her, in place of her aging and ailing father. David hugged and kissed her deeply, touched by her comment, and when Alessia stroked his thighs, he returned the gesture, until they were eventually lost in the throes of rapidly increasing passion, followed by drowsy caresses, and refreshing sleep.

It was a fortnight before Danielle was able to return to her classes, wearing jeans and a beige blouse instead of her typical dress or skirt as a result of her bruises, when she saw Trevor briefly on campus, near the Library, in between her morning classes, for the first time since their motorcycle accident. She had missed several lectures and assignments, and so spent some time catching up, with the aid of her classmates. David and Alessia met her at the cafeteria, to share the prior day's experience in court with her, over a lunch of sauteed prawns and noodles with chilled pineapple juice. Alessia was subdued as they collected their lunch trays. When Danielle shook David's shoulder, impatient for an update, amid the buzz of conversation in the cafeteria, he began by describing the sight of Mr. Benito Esposito and Mr. Tomassini Rossi in handcuffs, looking defiant while seated beside their barrister. He continued on to the bizarre statements they initially made under oath, that they knew nothing about Alessia's kidnapping at the park, and had been busy dealing with difficulties in sourcing sufficient supplies of cold pressed, extra virgin olive oil for their business when police officers arrived with questions, at Lancaster Gate in the case of Mr. Esposito, and later, at South Quay in Mr. Rossi's case. It was only under cross-examination, when Mr. Esposito's camera and the photos that they had taken of Alessia were introduced as evidence that their testimony began to fall apart.

Even then, the defendants tried to contend that as Mr. Esposito and Ms. Amato had been engaged, and their marriage was imminent, her bondage and the photographs taken had really been the result of consensual erotic encounters between them. It was at this point that Paolo and Giancarlo were ushered into court and sworn in to testify.

David told Danielle that only while Paolo Amato was providing clearly articulated details of their meetings and conversations with the defendants that he noticed both Benito Esposito and Tomassini Rossi perspiring somewhat, despite the relatively cool temperature in the courtroom, and that Mr. Esposito's hands were shaking. When the witnesses from the police team that had forced their way into the building at St. Johns Wood and discovered Alessia trussed to a desk made their statements, the barrister for the prosecution appeared to be quietly triumphant. The final witness was Detective Inspector Jeffries, who provided testimony concerning the investigation conducted into Acerra Import-Export PLC and reported that given the evidence indicating the company's involvement in human trafficking, it had been deregistered, and several other senior staff members had been held in custody.

By prior agreement, neither Alessia nor David were called to the witness stand. Instead, their signed and witnessed statements were admitted as evidence. Alessia held her hands tightly in her lap, with her head bowed, and her face pale, while David was speaking. She felt more and more nauseous. Noticing her demeanor, Danielle inquired whether she wasn't relieved that the outcome of the jury's deliberations was already clear. In answer, Alessia looked at her plate, which was still almost full, then at Danielle. "I felt as if my abductions and assaults were occurring over and over, during the testimony – all the more so when the prosecuting barrister handed the folder with those horrible photographs to the foreman of the jury." Both Danielle and David put their arms around her, as she began to cry, and accompanied her out of the cafeteria to the nearest female restroom, allowing her an opportunity to compose herself. Danielle hastened to her next class, limping a little, while David waited for his wife just outside the bathroom.

When Alessia returned to David, she was smiling ruefully, and still downcast. "I'm sorry to have become so emotional and distressed while you were sharing yesterday's courtroom testimony with Danielle," she told him. David pulled her close, telling her that he fully understood her reactions, and that he still had nightmares, now and then, about the attack upon them in the park in Hornsey, her abduction, and the aftermath. "So, is that the reason why you sometimes shout inarticulately, while sleeping, shaking your arms and legs so wildly that I often have to move to the edge of the bed?" Alessia inquired with a broader smile. David grinned, encouraged that she appeared to be recovering. "What time do your classes end today? I know we have to be at work tomorrow, but if we can go home a little early, perhaps you can give me the back stories to more of your paintings – in return, I would be glad to give you a massage," Alessia pretended to pout, saying that his hands were all too gifted, as he always relaxed her in one way with such massages, while managing to get her all hot and bothered in another way. David enjoyed the way in which their conversation was developing. When it was established that her classes would be finished by mid- afternoon, he took Alessia back into the cafeteria, and encouraged her to order a replacement lunch of hot onion soup with toast. Later, while traveling on the bus from Turnpike Lane to Alexandria Park, Alessia commented that not only did they both have to be back at work the next day, but neither would have any time off – unpaid in her case – for their university commitments for a week. On this occasion, they deliberately avoided looking at the park bench where they had been assaulted and were careful to exit the bus on time. As Danielle was still at London Metropolitan University and Melody was shopping, they first settled downstairs with Alessia's folder of oil paintings. David wanted to know the backgrounds to several other small canvases, beyond those already discussed, and Alessia's mood brightened further as she responded, eloquently gesturing with her hands, as usual. "This is the only one portrait I ever attempted – my parents dressed and preparing to go to Mass with the three of us, one Sunday morning, when I would have been about fourteen years old," she explained.

David remarked upon the clarity of its composition, as well as the two burgundy armchairs seats and sofa with cushions depicted in the living room, with the sun shining brightly on them through a bay window, casting shadows elsewhere. He noted that both her parents seemed very healthy and youthful, and then asked why her mother appeared rather wistful. Alessia smiled. "Mama always had so much housework to complete, although I was always trying to help, and she was probably thinking about matters such as the dinner menu, and grocery purchases that she may have forgotten to make." Looking at the painting again, David asked whose black and white dog was sitting expectantly near the entrance door, commenting that he could see the muscles very clearly delineated in its forelegs. Alessia responded that Rico followed Giancarlo everywhere, and her brother was always glad to play with the dog - but never gave any attention to feeding or otherwise caring for his pet. When he asked whether she had encountered any foreigners, while growing up in Reggio di Calabria, she first complimented him on learning to pronounce the name of her hometown properly, then commented that she'd actually never spoken to anyone who did not look like the members of her family, before meeting her husband-to-be. Looking at David, she asked teasingly, "So am I ever going to get that massage you promised me? We will always have opportunities to look at these paintings together again!" Arising immediately, David lifted Alessia up, as she quickly clutched the folder, and took her upstairs, where he delightedly removed her clothing and settled down to massage her back, legs and arms with lavender and jasmine oil on their bed.

When he turned her over to continue, she looked up at him sensually and remarked that he'd got her where he always wanted her. David smiled. He still had difficulties in believing that Alessia truly belonged to him, and began massaging her beautiful breasts tentatively at first, circling her pink aureoles, and squeezing her nipples lovingly, then settled down to his task with growing gusto, lovingly spreading oil evenly on her torso, enjoying her contented sighs as he warmed up to his task – sighs that soon turned to panting as she squirmed and moaned under his ministrations. It was only later they realized the need to change their bed sheets, now soiled and fragrant with his applications.

Danielle arrived late for dinner that evening, explaining that she had been catching up with her class projects, including a team presentation that required library research after class. Everyone at table was in a genial mood, enjoying a pasta primavera with spicy sauteed shrimps that Melody had prepared, together with chardonnay wine, after her grocery shopping that day. In response to David's question about her team presentation, Danielle explained that they had to prepare an architectural design for an imagined new town in the Scottish highlands, to be constructed on sustainable principles, while explaining their assumptions explicitly – and that they might even have to travel by train to view possible sites soon. When Alessia asked how her left leg was feeling, Danielle stood in the white shorts donned after arrival at home and demonstrated that the stitches and the bruises she'd sustained were fading satisfactorily. After an apple crumble dessert, she asked her brother whether he would be willing to play some music on his guitar, having not heard him play for quite a long time. Alessia enthusiastically seconded this request. When David asked what type of music would be most enjoyable for the family, Melody suggested with a smile that he choose whatever his fingers felt ready to play. He returned, sat in a crimson armchair in a corner of the living room, begun to strum idly for a few minutes, then launched into a rendition of "*Red Sails in the Sunset.*" As the last bars faded away, and Danielle asked for an encore, David tried his hand at Saint-Saen's "*Carnival of the Animals.*" His listeners clapped as David beamed with pleasure. To Melody's comment that she'd always thought the volume and bass of his guitar to be remarkable, David answered that it was called the "dreadnought" because of those features, compared to "grand concert" or "auditorium" acoustic guitars, for example. He was about to replace his guitar in its leather case upstairs when Alessia asked him to explain the difference between an acoustic and other types of guitars. "The main difference to keep in mind is between acoustic and electric guitars," David responded. "Where electric guitars use electronic pickups and a speaker to amplify sound, when I pluck one of the six strings on this acoustic guitar, its vibration is transmitted through the top of the instrument, as well as the sides and the back. Sound resonates through the air in its body. A fine metallic thread is wrapped around four of the metal strings, enhancing its bright, driving sound." To her further expressed hope that someday he would teach her to play, David smiled, arose to hug his wife closely, feeling himself to be the most blessed man in the world, and proceeded upstairs as previously planned. Both Alessia and Danielle offered to take charge of cleaning up after dinner, enjoining Melody to relax and to watch a movie. In the kitchen, while washing up, when Danielle apologized for encouraging her brother to report on the prior day's courtroom proceedings while they were in the cafeteria, Alessia told her that she knew it was time to begin turning away from the searing memories of her abductions, and that she was attempting to do so, with David's loving assistance.

The next day, Danielle was hurrying to her first class at London Metropolitan University when she received a call from Ahmet, who wanted to invite her out to dinner that weekend. She hesitated, mentioning her recent accumulation of class projects, without recounting the motorcycle accident that had occurred while riding with Trevor, then suddenly decided to accept, telling Ahmet to text her the details. A few nights later, she was in a short turquoise dress with a broad white belt, seated in a Turkish Kebab restaurant with her former classmate, dining on roasted garlic lamb with rosemary, and sipping lemonade. Ahmet politely asked about her family, as well as her studies, remarked that she looked beautiful that evening, and inquired whether she had seen any plays since "*After the Fall*" in Soho. At first, Danielle felt mildly uncomfortable, then after reminding herself that she had made no commitment to Trevor, consciously settled down to enjoy the evening, asking about Ahmet's family and his work, in turn.

He was the oldest of two brothers and two sisters and had secured part-time work as a traditional London taxi driver, after passing an intensive examination about the city's streets known as "*The Knowledge*." Ahmet also worked in the family bakery near their home in Willesden Green, with his father and younger brother, while his sisters were still completing high school. "How do you ever manage to pray at all, during the days while driving your taxi?" inquired Danielle, with genuine curiosity. "You will remember that I described the fulfilment of this duty as difficult in London, "he answered. "However, a true believer will always find ways to meet his obligations to follow the five pillars of Islam – the confession of faith, prayer, *zakat* or charity, fasting during Ramadan, and the *Hajj* or pilgrimage to Mecca."

Ahmet went on to explain that he sometimes used his prayer rug in the back seat of the taxicab, while parked and waiting for passengers, or more frequently, under a grove of trees in a park, when there was a measure of seclusion, after meditation. As Danielle completed her entrée, he added that such prayer was essential to the maintenance of a connection between the soul of a believer and Allah. "But how exactly do you define a human soul?" she followed up. "Common definitions have variously included consciousness, sense of identity, character, sentience, perception and memory." Ahmet told her that she'd asked a very good question. Jutting out his bearded chin in sequential emphases, he asserted that Islam viewed the soul as an immortal, incorporeal essence, that would leave its human body after death, to be rewarded or punished by Allah, depending upon the merit or the censure accumulated during life. He added that *Islam* itself meant the soul's surrender to the will of Allah, and that the common greeting, "*Salaam,*" denoted believers' submission and peace. Danielle was intrigued at the parallels between major world religions, remarking that his approach appeared similar to that of Hinduism, where the soul is treated as an incorporeal essence, undergoing cycles of birth, life, death, and rebirth – *samsara*. Souls generate energy, whether good or bad, that pervade their next cycle of existence. When eventually purified, a soul will be reunited with Brahman or God, in the state of *nirvana*. Ahmet looked at her animated face, and her eyes, with deep interest.

Danielle continued, musing that in the case of Buddhism, where human suffering results from attachments and desires, the soul is either rejected as a concept, or sometimes seen as "*life energy*," and that suffering can be overcome when individuals reject attachments. The Buddhist injunction is to follow the path to enlightenment, including understanding, wise thought and action, mindfulness, and concentration. When Danielle paused, she looked around the busy restaurant, with waiters bustling to take and deliver orders, thinking it very unlikely that any other diners were engaged in a similar conversation. It felt somewhat warm, and she wondered whether her dinner companion was paying more than desultory attention to her thoughts. Upon completing his entrée, Ahmet remarked that believers in Islam had a clear, distinctive understanding of the soul, and that she would be most welcome, whenever ready, to listen to his Imam's regular discussions of this topic at the mosque. When she asked whether he would expect his wife to wear a burka, niqab or the hijab, he shifted uncomfortably in his seat, then answered that he would need to reflect prayerfully upon this topic. Danielle turned to the dessert menu, selected a pomegranate sorbet, and inquired as to his choice. Ahmet reached across the table to hold and stroke her hand, jesting that she would be his preferred selection, but if truly unavailable, he would assuredly have her recommendation instead. They both smiled, self-consciously in her case, and Danielle suggested that they each should enjoy a sorbet, in that case, then gently pulled her hand away, noting a flicker of disappointment in his eyes, when doing so. As their meal came to an end and they left the restaurant, she thanked Ahmet for his invitation to dinner, and left, reflecting upon their interesting discussion.

The following weekend, David and Alessia were on the tube from Camden Town, where they had been visiting with Paolo and Giancarlo, *en route* to Turnpike Lane, and the bus to Alexandra Park. The visit had been very interesting for Alessia, who had been recalling the six months when she lived there with less and less clarity.

Some of her old clothing and shoes were still in the room from which she'd escaped, running at full speed from Paolo, heart pounding. Now, they all sat together drinking limoncello while enjoying Giancarlo's *pasta arrabbiata* and talking about Reggio di Calabria. Paolo told them that his father's physician thought that he might be experiencing the early onset of Alzheimer's disease. From their mother's reports, he sometimes had difficulty recalling the names of his children, the location of his vineyard, or some of the streets in the vicinity of their home, and she regularly had to remind him to tie his shoelaces. In intermittent moments of clarity, he kept asking for Alessia in particular, and whether it was true that she was married. At the same time, other family members reported that their mother seemed increasingly frail and required help to manage her housework. During the visit, Paolo apologized again for having made his sister such a tempting target for Benito and Tomassini, while reiterating his delight to have learned, after their trial, that the cumulative testimony provided had led to a guilty verdict, and a sentence of at least twenty years each, as well as the dissolution of their company. The visit had also been fascinating for David, who had the opportunity to observe the Amato family in a relatively relaxed manner for the first time, and to note resemblances as well as decided differences between them, in appearance as well as personality. Giancarlo talked about his new job at an accounting company, where he had learned to avoid conversation unrelated to work, causing Alessia to ask, "So you haven't told a single joke in the office yet?" Her youngest brother somberly shook his head – then suddenly brightened. "Why is the time of day with the slowest traffic called rush hour?" he inquired. Everyone smiled, and Paolo patted his brother on the shoulder, then becoming more serious, asked David when he intended to go with Alessia to meet their parents, to be given the reply that they would work on practicable dates. It was eventually agreed that, if possible, they would all plan to travel to Reggio di Calabria together. During their tube journey from Camden Town, the couple was still discussing their visit animatedly. Alessia had such bittersweet memories of the life she had lived with her brothers, as well as eidetic images of her abductions, sometimes surfacing when least expected, and the conversation made her anxious to go with her husband to meet her parents, if fearful as to their reactions to David – but also ashamed to be experiencing such anxieties. As it was indeed rush hour, they found themselves standing and talking or embracing – occasionally both - all the way, while trying to secure some tunnel ventilation from the window at the end of their carriage, given the oppressive heat generated by the crowded passengers, with only partial success.

To the couple's shock, a man in a corduroy jacket with a visibly missing canine tooth and breath redolent of beer suddenly shouted at David, "Hey you spade! Why don't you leave our women alone?" A nearby, bearded companion with a menacing scorpion tattoo on his neck added, "Yes – you should look for your own kind. Aren't black women good enough for you?" Taking David by the hand, Alessia rapidly tugged him away from the spot, and they made their way to the center of the carriage, then alighted at Kings Cross St. Pancras. "I'm so very sorry you were subjected to that situation," Alessia said shakily. David hugged her on the busy platform, consolingly, replying that he deeply regretted having placed her in that situation. "What do you mean?" she asked immediately. "Are you saying that you regret our marriage?" He hastened to clarify that his regret was at having located her at that end of the carriage, near the abusive men – then inquired whether she thought they should take the next train six stops north or take a bus or a taxi home from Kings Cross St. Pancras. It was Alessia's turn to be very practical about their finances. "David, you are always saying that we are saving for a home of our own. Why would be take a taxi unless it's essential? Let's just take the next tube from here." Within five minutes, they were on their way again. However, on this occasion, they remained tense, neither touching nor talking with each other. It was only when they were seated in the upper deck front of the bus home that they looked at each other. David clasped her right hand and told her that they could not allow bigoted blowhards to dictate how they should relate to each other. Alessia nodded her complete agreement, and kissed her husband, twice quickly, tentatively – and then led the way into a long, increasingly languid kiss. David was only briefly surprised, upon raising his head to look around, to see that they had passed their intended stop once again. Upon leaving the bus at the next stop, they began walking downhill, and soon realized that the remaining distance home represented more than ten minutes' walk.

At dinner that evening, they told Melody and Danielle about their visit with Paolo and Giancarlo, without getting into their subsequent tube ride. When the conversation turned to Melody's most recent reading to her class from Dicken's Oliver Twist, they were all interested in the engaging reactions of her 'students' to memorable characters such as the manipulative and conniving Fagin, the coarse Bill Sykes with his dog, Bulls Eye, Nancy, his lover and victim, and the unforgettable Artful Dodger; then Danielle, who was no longer limping, shared her visit that day to the local fitness center, where she spent thirty minutes on a treadmill and a further fifteen minutes using 15-pound free weights, before swimming a dozen laps in the pool, then going to the library to work on two class project team assignments. After dinner, it was the couple's turn to wash up in the dual white enamel sinks of the kitchen, which looked out upon a darkened neighboring house behind, and only then did they continue their conversation, speaking quietly about the leave from university classes as well as work that would be required for them to travel to Reggio di Calabria. They settled on a week in the following month of August when this visit might be practicable for them both. Alessia undertook to convey this timing to her brothers as soon as possible. Upstairs in their bedroom, talking even more softly, they turned to the burning question of what to expect from her parents, once introduced to David as their new son-in-law. Alessia tried to reassure David as to the expectations and behavior of her parents; but found it difficult to comfort herself, especially in the light of that day's experience. She vaguely remembered two or three young men from families in the region to whom her mother had tried to introduce her, after her studies at the Università Cattolica del Sacro Cuore – one, in particular, talked mostly to her parents, having assumed that her father would make the choice.

Another appeared to focus upon her bust, to the exclusion of her eyes, even in the presence of her father, and tended to stammer. The third had brusquely announced his desire to father a large family like the one in which he'd grown up and inquired whether she'd had any recent medical examinations that confirmed her ability to give birth, to the consternation of even her mother. If one had been Greek, they were all clearly Caucasian natives of Reggio di Calabria, and Alessia remained concerned that however she might have attempted to prepare her parents, there might be no means of avoiding a deeply distressing meeting with her husband, for all concerned. Turning to David, she kissed him, picking up from where they left off in the bus, and found her somber mood changing almost instantly, as they caressed each other, and rapidly removed their clothing.

David was taken aback when Alessia, after gently stroking between his thighs, inquired whether he had any twine or even rope available. In response to his immediate query, she hesitantly explained her interest in exploring how she would feel if he tied her up to the bed, constraining her completely. At first, David was put off by the idea, recalling the soul-searing scenes that greeted him after her assaults by Benito and Tomassini. However, after she explained further that if they could jointly create a sensual new memory, this might be a catalyst to drive out her existing recollections, he became more willing to experiment, and indicated that he had a few old ties in his wardrobe that should work. Linking the thought to the deed, he tied her hands tightly to the top legs of their bed, then at her instruction, her feet to the other two legs, in such a way as to stretch her out fully, then enquired whether she could move. Alessia shook her head, then asked whether he had another old tie that could serve as a blindfold. By now, David was falling fully into the spirit of their experiment, and quickly complied. There was no need for her to provide further instructions. Locating his lavender and jasmine massage oil, he settled down to work, beginning with her breasts and working down to her bound feet, then up again to her shoulders and hands. Alessia first trembled and squirmed, then began to pant. As she cried out her initial release, she asked David to remove her blindfold so she could see him, and he readily complied, then continued to play with every available square inch of his increasingly excited and delighted wife's body, mounting her several times in between. After untying Alessia, he held her close and asked whether the experiment had met her expectations. She was silent for a few minutes, then kissed his face repeatedly, telling David how much she loved him. As they lay in a close embrace later, she whispered "you really trussed me up so tightly that it was completely impossible to move - and you took charge of me so fully that I'm sure to begin discarding the terrible memories that were created by those awful men, and to stop worrying so much about how my parents will react to us." David was elated at her comments, stroked her wrists and calves gently, where his bonds had left visible marks, and then settled down with her into a sound sleep.

That very night, Benito and Tomassini found themselves out at the same time, in the congested exercise quadrangle of the prison where there were located. Each concluded that they would probably be able to converse discreetly for the first occasion since their entirely unexpected arrest and subsequent trial. Incandescent lights were trained from above on all corners of the field. The evening was warm and oppressive, with darkening cumulus clouds in the sky as the pink and purple glow of sunset faded. Benito looked around at the men in numbered orange coveralls, some walking repeatedly around the perimeter, others playing an impromptu game of soccer, some staring at their surroundings blindly, yet others smoking in small groups, and a few, including both the former Acerra Import/Export PLC executives, taking the measure of the enclosing walls and guard posts, and the ubiquitous CCTV cameras, as they considered their chances of escape -more as a reaffirmation of individual identity, hoping against hope, than as a practical proposition. He reflected bitterly upon his decision to return for a short visit from New York to London, partly as a result of his obsession with Alessia, and his burning desire for revenge against her immediate family. Benito found an alcove near a group of men who were arguing loudly about a proposed passage of legislation allowing same-sex marriage in Britain that had been mooted during the television news that day, and once there, nodded at Tomassini, inviting his visit, if only for a few moments. Once they were within earshot, despite the continuing dispute in the vicinity, he inquired, with studied casualness, "Is your attorney still in touch with any of our team?" When Tomassini nodded, he continued, "tell him that the evening breezes on Sicilian beaches are still the most refreshing in the world. He will know what to do." The two men promptly separated, and paced on different sides of the quadrangle, mingling with other prisoners who were similarly occupied. Benito reflected that although his own attorney had returned to Campania, there was at least a line of communication that Tomassini's attorney could activate, without suspicion, in such a way as to set in motion the contingency plans that he had made for his searing revenge upon David and Alessia Armstrong when they least expected it.

Chapter Nine

A week later, during another leisurely dinner conversation, when David mentioned that he was planning to travel with Alessia and her brothers to visit their parents in Reggio di Calabria during the coming August, Melody commented that Danielle and herself had yet to meet Alessia's brothers. This discussion led to Alessia's promptly provided and accepted invitation to Paolo and Giancarlo to visit her home for lunch with David and his family, on the following Saturday. The two brothers arrived dressed formally in charcoal grey suits, white shirts, and ties – a teal tie in the case of Paolo, who brought a bottle of tart limoncello, while Giancarlo's was red with a sunburst icon. Melody welcomed them at the door, and immediately sought to put them at ease, inviting the brothers to remove their jackets, even before they hugged their sister warmly, then exchanged handshakes with David and Danielle. Paolo and Giancarlo were immediately seated at the table, as Melody had been timing their arrival, and a lunch of shrimp cocktail followed by spaghetti bolognaise and rhubarb tarts was ready in her kitchen. The sun was shining brightly, and a light breeze coming in through the partially opened entrance door wafted in the scents of Melody's lovely rose garden. When Paolo remarked that he could not believe Alessia and David had been married for almost a year now, the conversation took a turn down memory lane, to their wedding, the honeymoon that followed, as well as their respective university studies and their work. Everyone carefully avoided any mention of Benito and Tomassini or their recent trial, having been made keenly aware of Alessia's continuing efforts to put the dark clouds of all related memories behind her.

When they turned to the projected visit to Reggio di Calabria, and Danielle inquired about the construction of homes there, Giancarlo smiled and brought out several charcoal drawings, in which he'd captured distinctive views of his parents' home and the surrounding neighborhood with such artistic flair and zest that warm commendations accompanied them around the table. "*Madre mia*," said Alessia, using her now favorite form of address for Melody, "this brother of mine has always liked drawing, but I've never seen such accomplished work!" Melody smiled in agreement. When the circulated drawings came to Danielle, she spent some time examining them, and scrutinized Giancarlo with interest. "These homes all seem open to the south - the wooden window lattices probably invite cooling breezes indoors during the summer, although the terracotta roof tiles detract from this effect, unlike white tiles" she commented. Giancarlo responded that in Reggio, older residences all had built-in natural cooling and heating construction arrangements, whereas newer homes depended upon air-conditioning and heating. "I've never before met an accountant with such a gift for drawing," remarked Danielle. David followed up by commenting that artistic ability seemed to run in Alessia's family, and mentioned as examples her oil paintings, which his mother and sister had now enjoyed reviewing on more than one occasion. After lunch, Danielle and Giancarlo ended up on Melody's orange sofa, discussing the relative cost savings to be derived from sustainable architecture, and some of her university class projects, as well as Giancarlo's impressions of London, and his daily accounting challenges at work, while David talked with Paolo on the patio overlooking the garden, and Alessia helped Melody to clear up in the kitchen.

During this first conversation by themselves, Paolo wanted to know whether it would likely be much longer for Alessia to recover from her appalling assaults by Benito and Tomassini, apologizing sincerely, once again, for his role in creating the interactions leading to these terrible experiences. David smiled warmly, saying that he fully realized that these involvements had begun with good intentions, and that Paolo had made up for introducing these warped men to his family, by actions that included standing in so willingly for their father at the wedding, and his forceful testimony at the trial. A shadow crossed David's face, when answering his brother-in-law's query about Alessia's recovery, as he explained that she was still trying her best to *'turn the corner'* on those episodes, and that her healing process might take a while yet. They both gazed at the gorgeous red, white, and yellow roses in Melody's garden for a while, in companionable silence, sipping the remains of Paolo's limoncello, and enjoying an afternoon zephyr that made several cream cirrus clouds scud across the pale blue sky. David took the opportunity to ask Paolo, in turn, how his parents had received the news that she was married to a *mente nero*, having learnt the term from his wife. Paolo was embarrassed. "You must have heard that upon seeing you for the first time in Hyde Park with Alessia, I used that unfortunate term," he said wryly. "At the time, it would never have occurred to me in my wildest dreams, as it is often said, that my little sister would end up marrying anyone other than an Italian from our region." Paolo went on to explain that while there was a community of people of African heritage in Sicily, often involved in trade with North Africa, hardly any such persons had been seen in Reggio di Calabria while they were growing up. He hastened to add that having met people from many nationalities and ethnic backgrounds since their arrival in London – and especially, having recognized that Alessia and David were deeply committed to each other, his previously ingrained attitudes had fundamentally changed. David recalled several related conversations as a young boy with his own father, including a reiterated laconic remark that *'we believe what we see, and see what we believe.'* After sharing this memory with Paolo, he asked, "So do you think that your father and mother, as well as your other relatives in Reggio di Calabria, will accept our marriage?" Paolo responded directly "At first, not at all. The celebration of mixed-race marriages is simply alien to their culture. This is probably why Alessia has yet to send the wedding photographs that our mother, in particular, but also our aunts, have been begging for. However, Giancarlo and I will continue explaining the circumstances before we travel and set the stage for your visit. The atmosphere might be a little tense, at first, but I'm absolutely sure that once our parents actually meet you, and realize how happy you both are, all will be well." David responded quietly and hopefully, "From your lips to God's ears."

Meanwhile, indoors, Giancarlo asked Danielle "So what exactly is sustainable architecture?" In a moment, she was off and running. "Any approach to architecture that most efficiently and effectively uses development space, local as well as recycled or recyclable building materials, and energy, can be sustainable," Danielle began. She continued by explaining the importance of taking sun location and wind direction into account in designing homes or other buildings, mentioned that an air gap between internal residential structures and the exterior shell reduced heating and cooling expenses, and highlighted the importance of rainwater management. "Take the term *biomimicry*," she added. "In sustainable architecture, this means using structure to change functions, and focusing upon passive energy use, in a way that emulates nature, for instance, using planted trees and shrubbery to reduce summer temperatures and to provide shade, while enhancing air quality." As Danielle spoke, her brown eyes dilated, and her voice became more alto rather than contralto. She also gestured with her hands, perhaps unconsciously emulating Alessia.

Giancarlo was fascinated, as he listened to her, while paying increasing attention to details of her appearance, such as the mauve silk blouse and the short crimson skirt that she was wearing, showing off her now bruise-free, tanned legs, the copper highlights in her hair, and the way in which she smiled from time to time, while speaking. Suddenly, Danielle stopped in mid-flow, feeling self-conscious. "You probably realize that sustainable architecture is one of my passions, but I must be boring you with all of these technical details," she commented, then squared her shoulders and suddenly sat up, "Did you actually work for that human trafficking company run by those awful men who abducted and assaulted your sister?" Giancarlo stammered his response, "It was only for a few weeks, when Paolo was insisting that I should begin working in London. I was an olive oil sales manager and had nothing to do with any such executives." Danielle did not seem entirely placated by his answer. "So please tell me what drew you to accounting," she inquired. Giancarlo hesitated for a few moments. "My father produced large quantities of excellent, very succulent black grapes in his vineyard," he finally explained, "but as I grew older, and helped him in dealing with purchasers, it increasingly seemed that the prices they offered him were very unfair, taking no account of production costs." As Giancarlo told her, upon realizing in his senior high school year that accounting was the key means of systematically measuring business results and making this information available to users, including purchasers, investors, and creditors, he decided to study accounting - the language of business - when accepted into a university. During his freshman year at the University of Palermo, he encountered management, government, financial, tax, and forensic or internal audit accounting, and ended up specializing in internal audit accounting by his final year.

"So, were you able to help your father with the accounts for his vineyard eventually?" Danielle asked. "Not really," Giancarlo replied. "During my vacations from university, I was always trying to catch up on my class projects, readings and required exercises. For a while after graduation, I was actually fed up with accounting. Then, a few months ago, after coming across a recruitment advertisement for a forensic accountant – a staff member who could help companies manage risks by systematically evaluating their operational processes and recommending improvements, I applied, was accepted, and am actually enjoying my work – so my studies are being put to good use here in London, after all!" Danielle noticed how animated he became while answering her question, enjoyed the scent of his cologne, redolent of aquatic and citrus notes, as he moved almost imperceptibly closer to her while talking, and noticed the light brown stubble on his chin, as well as his increasingly defined moustache.

Changing the subject, Giancarlo asked Danielle whether she had any interest in soccer and was intrigued when she mentioned following the fortunes of Arsenal, using their nickname of '*The Gunners*.' However, when he launched into a detailed discussion as to the achievements of strikers and goal keepers in Italian teams such as Juventus and AC Milan, Giancarlo realized that Danielle was becoming less attentive, and instead asked her "If vegetarians eat vegetables, what do humanitarians eat?" When Danielle chuckled, then laughed outright, he joined her, and Melody called from the kitchen, "Do you want to share what is amusing you both so much?" Neither answered, as they were still beaming at each other. Danielle looked at him and asked, "What does Giancarlo mean anyway?" When he responded that it was an abbreviation for the name 'John Charles,' she commented that the double-barreled *'John Charles'* sounded like a serious and perhaps staid professional whereas *'Giancarlo'* sounded like a warm, fun-loving person. He paused for a moment, inquired whether she thought that two such persons might perhaps enjoy a dinner together soon, and was elated when Danielle nodded, smilingly. Giancarlo could not resist an effort to make her laugh, by telling her about recently read news that a man had been jailed for assaulting a fortune-teller who'd predicted that he would go to jail. When Danielle politely nodded, he added a vignette about a young lady who said to a recently re-encountered young man, "I've decided I would like to know you better. Let's start with your bank details." As she laughed, he felt vindicated.

In the kitchen, Melody and Alessia had finished washing up after lunch, and were sitting at a kitchen table, next to a bay window, each sipping a cup of coffee and enjoying the resplendent white narcissus and the pale violet hydrangea flowers just outside. When Melody asked Alessia whether she felt that her mixed ethnicity marriage had been fully accepted by her brothers, and received a smiling affirmative in response, she went on the inquire about other people encountered at the university or at work. "We've had no cause for concern really," Alessia told her mother-in-law, "except for the way some people look at us when we're traveling together." She went on to recount the occasion when they were returning from visiting her brothers and were verbally abused by two men on the tube. Melody was horrified. "David did not share this distressing incident with me," she said. "One or both of them could have pulled out knives or some other dangerous weapon." Alessia reached out to hold Melody's hand, asking her not to let David know about their discussion. "He is trying so hard to ignore such people and to establish the foundations for a happy future together, including our own home someday," she explained. When Melody followed up this exchange by inquiring whether she could expect a grandson or granddaughter anytime soon, Alessia blushed and responded it was much too soon for them to have children.

Melody smiled, telling her that she had given birth to David within about a year of her marriage to Joseph. "You must miss him so very much, *madre mia,"* said Alessia, squeezing the hand she was still holding across the table. "What was he like? Does David remind you very much of him?" Melody sighed, then rose to get them more hot coffee. "Yes, on both counts," she answered, sitting in pensive silence for a while. "How did you meet him?" asked Alessia. So, Melody took a deep breath, and told her the story of their meeting in a public library in Montego Bay, Jamaica, where they were both returning books. She had planned to go swimming and was wearing a blue swimsuit and holding a cream cotton beach bag with a purple hummingbird design. "He was so tall and handsome, so self- assured, and introduced himself so smoothly that I could no object when Joseph invited himself along for a swim," she explained. "We identified so many interests in common, beginning with swimming and reading, and ended up exchanging ambitious dreams about the future soon after meeting," Melody said, as salt tears sprung to her eyes. Alessia pulled her chair closer and hugged her warmly. "You brought up two absolutely wonderful children after he *left*," she said, consciously using the word that David had taught her, "and you've accomplished so many other things since then, such as the purchase of this comfortable home in which we all live," Alessia went on. "You've been so strong. If something were to happen to David now, I simply would not want to go on living," she declared. Melody told her quietly that she had felt exactly the same way when told of Joseph's terrible accident at work.

Two very busy weeks ensued, before Danielle was able to accept Giancarlo's invitation to dinner. They ended up at a steakhouse in the vicinity of Oxford Street. Both had given careful thought as to how best to present themselves for the occasion. Giancarlo met her in a new light blue sports jacket and a recently purchased bright yellow long-sleeved shirt, with a white bow tie – but not before enduring a barrage of witticisms from Paolo about the young lady whom he evidently was hoping to impress, and repeated queries about her identity. Danielle met him in pearl earrings, a modishly low cut, frilly cream blouse, a green mini skirt, with a light brown Prada handbag. She had also not confided Giancarlo's identity to any of her family members, despite the temptation to discuss him with Alessia. Now, they looked at each other in a booth, across a gleaming black marble table with a lit candle and a red rose in a white crystal vase, hesitating after exchanging greetings and placing their orders from the menu. Danielle was the first to break the silence. "What made you decide to invite me to dinner?" she asked. "I remember that we were joking about warm, fun-loving people after you came to lunch with Paolo, but here we are – Alessia's sister-in-law and David's brother-in-law, settling down to a dinner date." Giancarlo responded, "I invited you to dinner simply because you are the most attractive young lady I've ever met." Danielle responded that his declaration seemed to be one that he habitually made to each female that he encountered.

Giancarlo had to speak up to be heard across the table, and above the noisy conversation in the restaurant. "Would you be comfortable if I sat on your side of the booth so we can speak without shouting?" he asked. When Danielle nodded, he lost no time in relocating himself, then told her that he had never in his life met anyone so lovely, vivacious, and pleasant, so focused upon her planned profession in sustainable architecture, yet such a joy to converse with, even about soccer and his own rather dry field of forensic accounting - so complimentary about his simple charcoal drawings, and able to laugh so readily at his jokes.

Danielle saw that he was speaking sincerely and enjoyed the sparkle in his brown eyes as he looked at her with full attention. She asked, "Does Paolo know that we are having dinner tonight?" Giancarlo shook his head and asked in turn whether she had shared this information with David or anyone in her family. Danielle smiled. "I am still learning about you, so it is much too soon to talk with anyone in my family about spending time with you." Giancarlo found her direct approach truly enchanting. He sat up straight, hoping that she was pleased with his posture and choice of attire. In turn, Danielle looked at him appraisingly, and realized that she was enjoying their time together much more than she had expected. At that moment their entrée arrived, accompanied by cabernet sauvignon wine. The aroma of their hot food invited them to eat.

Danielle was thinking about her first impressions about Giancarlo, which had been initially conditioned by varied comments made in passing by David and Alessia, during conversation. She realized that she'd taken special care with her appearance this evening because by the time that they last took leave of each other, she had been in a daze. Almost unconsciously, she leaned forward as she ate, affording Giancarlo a better view of her cleavage. After raising their wine glasses in a toast to their evening together, and agreeing that the entrée was quite tasty, they enjoyed their meal in silence for a while. Giancarlo looked at Danielle, and asked, "If you will allow me to take a leaf out of your own book, do you have any boyfriends?" She smiled, nodded her head in assent, then added impulsively, "But perhaps I've recently met a new one!" Giancarlo was encouraged. "I would like to be your only boyfriend," he responded, somewhat impetuously. "But how do you define the role of any kind of friend?" Danielle asked. He paused to think. "I once read that a friend is someone who will recall the words and tune to your favorite song, and should you ever forget, can sing it back to you." "Very poetically put," she riposted, "but I think of a friend as someone who is present throughout my joys and sorrows, able to share fully in my pleasures, and patient and compassionate when I'm dealing with troubles or torments." Giancarlo felt a new respect for her ability to articulate her thoughts so astutely. "If that is the kind of boyfriend that you wish, you have found him, and will require no others." Danielle parried again, "You must be aware that nothing is often considered most certain as that which is least known. Don't you think that we should become more acquainted with each other before you make such statements?" Giancarlo flushed with some embarrassment, finished eating his last piece of steak and vegetables, put down his utensils, and reached for her hand. "You are right," he said. "We have a lot of catching up to do. Why don't you tell me all about yourself, beginning with your childhood and teenage years, and then, allow me to do the same?" Danielle slipped her hand from his, telling him that she needed to finish her meal as well, and that friendship could not be hurried, only encouraged to grow over time. He watched her ending her meal and wine with evident gusto.

When she had finished, Giancarlo looked at his watch, then turned to her and said "It's still early. How would you enjoy a walk by the Thames?" Danielle told him that she really ought to be returning home, to rest before presenting a major class project on the following day – then relented, and agreed that given the balmy weather, and the meal just completed, it might be pleasant to take a walk. So it was that they ended up on the South Bank, ambling along the Thames from London Bridge. As they walked, Giancarlo said that he would be glad to tell her all about himself, and when she nodded her agreement, which he was barely able to perceive in the shadows between restaurants, other businesses, and exhibits, he began to speak of his years growing up in Reggio di Calabria, a story that included Paolo, Alessia, their parents, other family members and friends. Danielle listened in increasing fascination as he described locations such as the Castle of Caccuri, where he once was lost for over an hour, and told her stories about the town of Sano and Precacore, the thick woods of Sila Greca, which she'd encountered in Alessia's paintings, and searching for porcini mushrooms, or "Calabrian Gold," in the Serra mountains. He regaled her with tales about exhilarating family outings to the bonfires on the beach during the nights of San Lorenzo, where he sometimes sprinted excitedly between them, and traditional Tarantella music festivals with dancers in colorful costumes, playing the mandolin, tambourine or the accordion. Giancarlo also shared memories of getting up very early on Sundays for the family to go to Mass, and their parents' concerns about the occasionally reported financial extortion activities of the *'Ndrangheta* or Mafia, close to the neighborhood where they were living. When Danielle shivered slightly at this reference, Giancarlo hastened to say that no one in his family had ever encountered such gang members themselves, and taking off his sports jacket, he placed the garment around Danielle's shoulders. She did not object, and they continued walking. Eventually he paused, just short of the National Theatre, and they stopped to look over the Thames. "Don't you agree that it's your turn now?" Giancarlo asked. "OK," said Danielle, "where do you want me to start?" "What were you like as a little girl growing up?" he asked. "Where did you live and go to school, and did you enjoy it?" So she began telling him about her abbreviated memories of her father, who used to lift her from her perambulator to hug her regularly, the bedtime tales he often read to her – recalling how stories such as "The Three Little Pigs" and "Little Red Riding Hood" had her running from wolves in nightmares for weeks afterwards – and how she cried bitterly when told that he had *left*. Danielle talked about days in school when classmates teased her as a *'tomboy'* because of her preference for playing soccer, table tennis or netball with the boys, rather than showing off prized dolls with the girls in her class during their lunchtimes, and how David regularly protected her when a classmate would pull her plaited hair, pinch her surreptitiously, or hide her lunchbox.

Danielle began to enjoy her story telling, as she went on to her teen years, and regaled Giancarlo with incidents such as the time when she first learnt how babies were conceived, recoiling in disgust, and her increasing absorption with architectural solutions that could contribute to reducing the dangers posed by climatological changes occurring around the world. Giancarlo was mesmerized, in turn, sometimes smiling and at other times frowning, as Danielle continued, talking now about more recent events, such as the day that her mother and herself met David in a nearby park, with his head bruised and bloody, after the assault on Alessia and himself, and the night of the fire at home that caused them to flee to a hotel in the middle of the night. As she spoke, they both looked out at the lights dancing on the river, while smelling hamburgers, hot dogs, popcorn, and pizza cooking in the vicinity, as vendors attempted to attract customers.

When Danielle paused and commented that it was good that they'd already had such an enjoyable dinner, Giancarlo put his left arm around her, drawing her close. Tentatively, he turned her to face him and leaning down towards her, kissed her lips lightly. Almost automatically, Danielle kissed him back in the same manner and ended up opening her lips to his increasingly urgent kisses, as the crowds passed behind them. Their lissom tongues tantalized and excited each other. She finally pulled back, coming up for air, and they looked into each other's eyes, recognizing that they had already become much more acquainted with each other that evening, than either previously expected, and that the night was growing quite late.

As Giancarlo and Paolo were completing a lunch of pasta primavera at home together on the following Sunday, after returning from Mass, the two brothers moved on from a discussion of required grocery shopping to Giancarlo's '*mystery date*,' as his elder brother phrased it. When Giancarlo eventually relented, after parrying the question expertly several times, and told his sibling that he had actually dined with Danielle, Paolo was stunned. "Didn't you say that you ended up taking a long walk on the Thames afterwards?" he inquired. "You came home looking so pleased with yourself. Are you going to tell me that you are actually developing a relationship with a *donna nera* who is your sister-in-law?" Giancarlo gave a mischievous smile. "Why should Alessia be the only family member to enjoy the company of someone who looks different from us, and who is not from Reggio?" Paolo explained his concern that their parents and other family members would already be asked to adjust to Alessia's marriage, and that now, assuming that Giancarlo was uncharacteristically serious, and he ended up introducing them to Danielle – perhaps as his future fiancée - also, they might well find themselves coping with an extended period of stress for all concerned. Giancarlo tried to make light of the situation. "We have only had a single dinner, followed by a walk together. Why are you jumping to conclusions?" They both flinched for a second when the engine of what was evidently a sports car misfired in the road outside. "Let's clear the table and continue talking in the kitchen while washing up the dishes," Paolo suggested. As they cleared up after lunch, when his elder brother tried to probe further, Giancarlo asked him whether he really had yet to meet an attractive young woman, perhaps even an Italian, in the course of his work at the Tottenham Court Road bookseller, if not before or after mass at St. Peter's Italian Catholic Church - and chided him for engaging in recreation only in various pubs, from time to time, placing Paolo, at least temporarily, on the defensive. "Your younger sister has been married for more than a year now," Giancarlo remarked, "Why don't you have a fiancée at least, of any kind you wish?"

At almost the same time, Danielle was fielding questions from Melody after lunch. "You took such unusual care with your appearance when you went out last night, and when you returned, looked happier than ever before. If your dinner companion was neither Trevor nor Ahmet, who was it?" Danielle smiled and looked shy, but her eyes sparkled. David pulled up an armchair close to his sister and jocularly joined in the questioning. "So, my adventurous sibling is '*playing the field*' these days? Be careful to avoid dangerous men who give you the impression that '*butter would not melt in their mouths*'," he warned. Danielle laughed heartily. "Honestly, you all are getting so wound up about nothing!" she remonstrated. Nevertheless, a little smile curved her lips as she got up, saying that it was time to put some clothing in the washer, and to clean up her room, in preparation for the week ahead. While Danielle was busying herself in her bedroom upstairs, Alessia knocked on the door and entered. Taking Danielle's hand, she hugged her lightly for a moment, then asked directly "Are you in love?" Danielle paused, looked out through her window where puffy cirrus clouds were sailing lazily through a clear blue sky, and told Alessia that she had been thinking about the time when they had discussed the nature of love in Alexandra Park. Alessia looked into her eyes, and declared, with sudden intuitive insight, "I was just remembering how animated you were in talking with Giancarlo on the living room sofa, that day when my brothers came to lunch. Could you possibly be dreaming about him right now?" When Danielle nodded, breathing deeply, Alessia hugged her more closely. "Have you two actually made love together?" she asked. Danielle shook her head, then added softly, "We've only kissed so far." The two young women sat silently for a while, with the bedroom in disarray around them. Then Alessia sighed and told her sister-in-law that she would join her in completing the chores at hand in return for a detailed account of her evening with Giancarlo. In the course of telling that evening's story to Alessia, who was listening attentively and sympathetically, Danielle found herself reliving the occasion, especially their extended walk along the South Bank, and the mounting excitement she had felt during Giancarlo's increasingly passionate and confident kisses. When this recollection actually brought tears to her eyes, Alessia hugged her again, murmuring "Don't worry.... I'm sure that my little brother feels exactly the same way about you, although you both should take the time to get much better acquainted with each other. He will probably invite you out again soon." When David called from downstairs to remind Alessia that they had agreed to go to a movie adaptation of Shakespeare's "*Coriolanus,*" starring actors who included Ralph Fiennes and Vanessa Redgrave, she kissed Danielle on each cheek and hurried out to meet her husband, who was already dressed and awaiting her.

David and Alessia were just in time for their movie. They settled down together to watch, holding hands as usual, During the intermission, Alessia told David about her conversation with Danielle. "And there I was half joking about her apparently adventurous spirit and cautioning her about safety!" he commented. "If my sister develops a relationship with your younger brother, what would your family think of such a situation?" Alessia placed her head on his left shoulder and sighed. "My mother has a romantic streak and might come to find such a set of relationships appealing – but my father, and most of my other family members might not adopt any such positive perspective." David kissed her lips and stroked her cheeks. "The feelings of family members who know and care about you are always very important," he commented. "Such relationships help to give us all a sense of meaning and purpose in life. Let's do all we can, when visiting, to help your family in Reggio di Calabria see that we're truly happy together. If that comes to apply to Danielle and Giancarlo as well, perhaps we can join in demonstrating how critical such circles of love and deep contentment are. When I spoke with Paolo about the reactions of your parents to our marriage, he was sure that, given a little time, we would be fully accepted," he assured Alessia, lifting her right hand to his lips and kissing it. They watched the tragedy of Coriolanus unfold, for a while, with both wishing they'd had an opportunity to also see Ralph Fiennes in his seminal role as Heathcliff in Emily Bronte's "*Wuthering Heights.*" As the movie ended with the death of Coriolanus, after his mother, together with his wife and son dissuaded him from destroying Rome, they were exchanging thoughts about the philology of the characters' speech and the layers of cultural history upon which the plot was based. When Alessia remarked upon the changing connotations and denotations of concepts such as courage, morality, duty, patriotism, fidelity, and revenge, over time, and the ways in which these concepts had influenced recorded or imagined historical events, as well as related literature, David agreed, commenting upon the saying that people often '*become what they see of themselves in the eyes of others.'* At the same time, tendrils of memory sprouted.

He dimly recalled, with chagrin, racing away from a supermarket with stolen groceries, as a young boy, and regretted not having then had the courage to reject either his own thoughts, or the suggestions of his friends that led to that action. While awaiting the train on the platform, Alessia asked David whether he planned to travel with his electric guitar to Reggio di Calabria, as he usually kept his musical instrument at hand. While he thought about it, she followed up with the comment that if an opportunity presented itself, perhaps he could play some music for her family. He smiled and nodded. David and Alessia took the tube home from Regents Street and found themselves on the alert for any recurrence of the hostility encountered after their visit to Paolo and Giancarlo. Relaxing somewhat as they exited at Turnpike Lane, David asked Alessia whether she really thought that Giancarlo and Danielle could be happy together. "Well, notwithstanding his jokes and enjoyment of soccer, and despite his profession of forensic accounting, Giancarlo has a sensitive, thoughtful and artistic soul. You have known Danielle all of her life, but I've observed her to be very much an idealistic and sensitive person at heart, wanting so much to make a difference to the world, using sustainable architecture as her means, and most of all, dreaming of loving and being loved." David responded that in such a case, they would seem to fit each other well, but would need to decide for themselves, and to have the time to do so. Alessia softly inquired, "Do you still think that we fit each other well?" In response, David lifted her up into his arms, surprising other passengers waiting at the bus stop, and covered her face with kisses as she laughed in pleasure. When the bus arrived, it almost left them standing there, still focused upon each other.

Either before or after her volunteer activities at the local nursing home, Melody often spent time in her garden pruning her rosebushes, luxuriating in the smells and the colors of the pink, white, yellow, crimson, and scarlet blossoms now surrounding her. She regularly thought of her children, occasionally worried about them, and reflected upon how much she yearned for Joseph. At first, she had thought that his passing would leave a scar on her heart and soul that would become somewhat less pronounced with time, the healer of wounds. However, she still often woke up at night, longing for the warmth of his loving hands on her body, feeling very much as if they had only recently been married. She reminded herself of a passage from a writer whose name remained tantalizingly on the tip of her tongue…." *Make peace with your past, so it cannot destroy your present,*" and reflected, not for the first time, that age brings wisdom only to the fortunate. Then again, apart from the times that Melody studied her face and figure in the bathroom mirror, noting that despite her prematurely graying hair and the extra weight gained since the birth of her children, at age forty-five, she still frequently felt vital and youthful. Even so, she could not imagine remarriage to anyone she had met. As she chided herself for holding so fast to the memories of her years with Joseph, instead of living in the present, a thorn pricked her right thumb, and another saying came to mind…" *we may be sad that roses have thorns, or glad that thorns have roses…"* She was happy that David and Alessia seemed to have settled down together well, and it warmed her heart, when her slim and pretty grey-eyed daughter in law called her "*madre mia*," so much so that she had asked Alessia to teach her a little Italian, beginning with "*mia figlia*," or "my daughter."

The news Melody had received about the sentencing of Benito and Tomassini to twenty years of imprisonment for their abhorrent assaults upon Alessia, as well as the human trafficking in which their now deregistered company had engaged, had been very welcome, although the thought occurred to her, now and then, that perhaps when these men were eventually released from prison, the accumulation of simmering resentment over the years might lead to renewed attacks upon her family. Meanwhile, Melody worried about whether the attitudes of some of the racially prejudiced people who traveled by tube or bus with her son and his wife might explode in perhaps deadly attacks, when least expected.

Recently, most of all, she worried about Danielle – her little baby girl, whom she had fed and burped and bathed and changed so tenderly, who had grown up overnight, to the point where she was well on the way to her baccalaureate degree in architecture, with dreams of helping to change the world, but also, a young woman who was seeking a life-partner, the way she had unconsciously sought for Joseph years ago, not knowing that her search was about to end at that small lending library with the fans whirring in Montego Bay, the day that she entered on a routine visit. A part of her mother's heart insisted that Danielle was still far too young to be entrusting her future happiness to any man, especially her Italian brother-in-law, when David and Alessia had yet to be accepted by the latter's family in Reggio di Calabria. However, her questing mind, recalling a recent encounter with the writings of Henry David Thoreau, told her that she had to unlearn and then learn anew what she thought she knew before, in order to make progress in life. As Melody expertly snipped a set of crimson roses for the vase on her dining table, deciding that it was time to begin preparing dinner for her family, she squared her shoulders, breathed deeply, and set out to release her accumulated anxieties.

Several weeks later, soon after flying to Tito Menniti Airport in Reggio di Calabria, close to the city center, and checking into the Mediterraneo Guest House, David and Alessia, accompanied by Melody and Danielle, as well as Paolo and Giancarlo, were seated in the Amato family's living room. Dazzlingly bright sunlight fingered across the polished wooden floor, and an occasional breeze whispered through the blinds. Sparrow hawks cawed in the Neapolitan alders outside. Mr. and Mrs. Amato were flanked by her equally aged sister and brother. Upon their arrival, Mrs. Amato had hugged her children warmly, and both parents shook hands with their visitors, as did the uncle and aunt in attendance. Once the guests had accepted limoncello, wine or tea, and answered polite questions about their journey, Paolo attempted to "break the ice" by commenting that he'd never seen Alessia so happy and glowing as she had since her marriage to David over a year ago. "More than a year ago?" responded Mr. Amato, with trembling indignation. "But why were we not asked for our prior permission, and at least invited to the wedding of our only daughter?" When Giancarlo tried to support Paolo by explaining that they had proposed a visit to Reggio rather than having them try to undertake such a long journey, given the state of their health, especially that of his mother, Mrs. Amato declared that she would have wanted to be there to participate in her daughter's wedding, even had it been necessary for her to be taken in a wheelchair or stretcher. Alessia's Uncle Luigi attempted to pour oil on troubled waters by saying, "Now, now, Lucia, you know that your physician has been reminding you not to exert yourself – the same applies to Matteo – neither of you could have traveled to London." Mrs. Amato persisted, "Very well, but Alessia, you could at least have considered making your wedding arrangements here, so that your family and friends could participate." Melody felt that it was her turn to intervene. "Mrs. Amato, we have all come a long way from London to meet your family and are sure that you join everyone in celebrating the happiness of my son and your daughter – we also know how glad you are to see Paolo and Giancarlo, as well as Alessia again," she said soothingly, looking directly at her host and hostess.

Danielle wondered for a moment when she would be introduced, or at least mentioned, while commending patience to herself, glancing at Giancarlo, who appeared uncomfortable. Meanwhile, Paolo supported Melody's initiative by embracing his mother again, and telling her how glad everyone present was to see her in an alert and vibrant frame of mind. Lucia Amato smiled, in spite of herself, given her 'soft spot' for her eldest son, and transitioning to a more welcoming tone, invited the visitors from London to come to dinner the following day, then turned to her daughter, saying "Come and give your old mother a chance to look at you, and another hug as well." After exchanging kisses on both cheeks, Alessia and her mother sat in quiet conversation for a few minutes, then calling David and Danielle over, she introduced them with a measure of formality to both her parents. Lucia Amato asked her daughter, "Are you really happy, child?" Alessia nodded in response, eyes shining, pretending not to hear her father grumbling in his rocking chair about all the eligible young men in the region that she could have considered as a husband. When Alessia introduced Danielle to her parents as well, they each greeted her politely. Mr. Amato gazed at her for a minute, and mumbled, "*Che bella signora nera*!" - "what a lovely black lady!" Giancarlo sighed as he overheard and glanced at Danielle, who was listening closely to his tone.

Later, at the Mediterraneo Guest House, Melody, David, Alessia and Danielle dined on *Pasta e Patate Ara Tijeddra* (Baked Pasta and Potato), at Alessia's recommendation from the menu, wearied by their journey, and assessed their first meeting with her family. Danielle was somewhat disconsolate that Giancarlo had not only been notably uncomfortable during the visit, but was unable to be with her now, having remained with Paolo at their parent's home. After asking his reluctant wife to translate her father's *sotto voce* comments, David was reflecting that it really was important to be careful what one asked for and would almost have preferred not to realize that his father-in-law was still at least as reserved about his ethnicity as previously expected. However, the meal itself, with its spicy sauce, cheese, and breadcrumbs, all baked to a crunchy surface texture, and the Chianti wine that accompanied it, improved the mood of the diners. They retired to their rooms – the couple in one bedroom with Melody and Danielle sharing the other, ready to rest, if not yet to sleep. David looked out through the window at the still busy traffic on the street below and tried to assimilate the fact that he'd really arrived in Reggio di Calabria with Alessia. For her part, she sat on their double bed, combing out her long, brunette hair, attempting to sort out her feelings about their visit with her family. David turned to her and asked, "Do you think your mother believed you when you told her that we were truly happy together? If she did, is it possible that she will convince your father to accept us?" Alessia smiled fondly, telling him that he usually asked one question at a time, allowing for responses in between. "Yes, I believe that she accepted my response to her request to know my feelings about our marriage. We will have an opportunity to evaluate my father's attitude further tomorrow evening – but he has been rather set in his ways for at least the past decade." David was both pleased at her answer where her mother was concerned and apprehensive about her father's perspective. Sitting beside her, he gave her a long, warm hug and taking her favorite tortoise shell comb from her, settled down to complete her evening hair treatment, before massaging her shoulders with jasmine and lavender oil, kissing her ears, as she leaned back against him and relaxed. David untied her mauve silk dressing gown, stroking her aureoles lovingly, then just grazed her taut cherry nipples lightly, with hands, then lips, before they retired.

Danielle sat in a carved wooden armchair in her hotel room, while Melody took a warm shower, remembering the days and nights after the fire at their prior home in London, when David and Alessia shared a room with them. They seemed to have settled down, not into domesticity, but into routines demonstrating loving support – and clearly continued to share extremely ecstatic passion, judging from the moaning, excited cries and panting regularly heard, when she listened at their closed bedroom door these days. Danielle wondered whether it would affect their marriage, should most of Alessia's family indicate lack of support, and if so, in what ways. Her thoughts turned to Giancarlo. It was amazing how quickly he had replaced Trevor and Ahmet in her thoughts and feelings. Those two young men had each occupied special places in her life for quite different reasons, and now she found herself repeating uncomfortable excuses as to why further dinners, lunches or other engagements together did not fit her schedule. Meanwhile, she had met with Giancarlo for three meals, followed, respectively, by a movie, a play, and even a soccer match, and allowed herself to feel actually jealous of her brother and his wife for a few moments, missing Giancarlo acutely, here in his home country, where the sights and sounds of the streets appeared so exotic.

As Danielle continued her reflections, Melody came out of the shower, preparing to go to bed – then stopped, looking at her pensive daughter. Pulling up a chair from an escritoire in the room, Melody sat beside her and inquired as to why Danielle appeared to be so thoughtful. When her daughter hesitated as to her answer, Melody added, "I've seen the way that you looked at Giancarlo during today's travels, and our visit with his family. Have you two become physically close?" Danielle nodded her head. But it was only after she showered, in turn, and joined her mother in one of their rather lumpy twin beds, that she was able to talk about her relationship with Giancarlo. After telling the story of their memorable Southbank walk, following dinner, and the way in which they ended up unexpectedly sharing so many details about their lives for hours, followed by deep, lingering kisses, Danielle went on to tell her about the intensive petting and cuddling in which they'd engaged, during their visits to a cinema complex and a theater that had followed. "Do you love each other?" asked Melody gently. "I think so," replied Danielle, "He wanted to be here with me tonight and only reluctantly accepted my assertions that neither you nor his parents would be happy about such a scenario." The night felt uncomfortably warm, despite the hum of the room air-conditioner. In the relative silence that followed, she tossed and turned languorously on her bed for a while, then got up to make some herbal tea, sipping it slowly until she began to feel drowsy. Meanwhile, Melody took a walk down memory lane, thinking of Danielle's birth, Joseph's late arrival at the hospital, the times that they took turns rocking their daughter in her green perambulator – and going further back, her own earliest weeks with Joseph, before and during their marriage. She recalled a fragment of the lyrics and tune to a song that had been popular in London during her early years, that resonated in her when heard on a Jamaican radio station: *'All of life's a circle, Sunrise and sundown, The moon rose through the darkness. While the day is coming round...'* Melody found herself praying inarticulately for the contentment of her son and daughter, who represented all that physically remained of the truly incandescent love that Joseph and herself had shared. Why do we so often realize too late how important special people are in our lives? It was a long time before she fell asleep.

Giancarlo lay on the bed in his boyhood room, thinking of Danielle. In his mind's eye, he walked with her again by the Thames that amazing evening and stood looking out at the flowing, light-speckled river while they shared stories that echoed with past resonances. As a light wind stirred the blue linen curtains over his partly opened window, and the waning moon stretched lambent, etiolated fingers of soft light across his bedsheets, Giancarlo recalled their visit to the cinema, when he guided Danielle to a seat at the back, where only a few patrons sat, and they watched a re-run of a movie called "The Seduction of Inga" that included music from the famous Swedish band, Abba. He'd thought she might hesitate at his suggested selection, but Danielle, who was once again dressed very appealingly, this time in an ultramarine dress with straps ending in a bow behind her neck, and a cerulean belt, appeared comfortable with his choice. As the movie unfolded, they found themselves kissing again, with increasing intensity, after lifting the seat arm in between. Giancarlo remembered stroking Danielle's upper torso through her dress, then realizing to his delight that when the bow-tied strap at her neck was pulled, her full, bare breasts became available for him to caress and to suckle her responsive nipples. They heard rather than saw snatches of the movie after that point, and following an impatiently received intermission, recognized just in time, resumed their hugging and nuzzling as soon as possible. When someone arose to visit a nearby bathroom, Giancarlo turned, and found himself envying Alessia for having managed to settle down with David, with the apparent acceptance of their mother. Thinking of his father, he whispered to himself indignantly that Danielle was not a "*signora nera*," but rather a "*signora marrone miele*," a truly lovely lady with sensitive, honey brown skin, together with a fascinating mind and soul. Returning to memories of their times together, he marveled at the perspicacity with which she'd told him one evening that happiness was usually much less determined by what is happening in one's environment, and much more by what is occurring within an individual. Danielle had continued to laugh at his occasionally contrived jokes, even those that after the fact, seemed inadequately articulated to him. She really admired his pastime of freehand drawings, accompanied him to a Tottenham Hotspurs soccer game, despite her limited interest in the event, and most important of all, he regularly saw warm appreciation, whenever she looked at him. Another resonant remark of Danielle's came to his mind..." *We become what we see of ourselves in the eyes of others,*" and Giancarlo reflected that perhaps he was actually becoming more like the person he really wanted to be, changing as a result of her companionship. By the time that dawn broke, after a quite fitful sleep, Giancarlo had decided that he would ask Danielle to marry him soon, regardless of his family's potential reactions.

The next evening, Melody, David, Alessia and Danielle arrived at the home of the Amato family shortly before the appointed time of seven p.m., when the old high- beamed wooden kitchen with its traditional stone oven was still buzzing with activity. Alessia immediately went to join her mother in the kitchen, where she found her directing a local maid in the final stages of preparing swordfish, or *pesce spada*, seasoned and roasted with olive oil, garlic, parsley, oregano, and water, chili pepper and onions, as well as tomatoes, capers, and olives. Mrs. Amato was also preparing *lagane pasta*, cooked with salt water and flour, without eggs, seasoned with sauteed olive oil, red pepper, garlic, and chickpeas; to be followed by *caciocavallo cheese* and *crema reggina*, a creamy, rum-based pastry. Alessia soon found herself put to work, after pulling on an apron last used when she lived with her parents. Meanwhile, Mr. Amato, Paolo and Giancarlo sat in the living room's sofa and arm chairs with Mrs. Armstrong, David, and Danielle, sipping limoncello, listening to their host's old Calabrian folk tales about matters such as *malocchio* who tried to cast an evil eye on his vineyard on more than one occasion, years ago; the legend of the lost treasure of Alaric, King of the Visigoths, who was reportedly buried in Cosenza, Calabria; another legend of *Madonna Della Corona*, where nearby villagers lowered themselves into a dangerously deep grotto near Monte Baldo, following a dazzling light, to find a statue of Mary holding the lifeless body of Jesus; and stories about *Tarantasio* or dragons with a taste for devouring children, who roamed the Po Valley centuries ago. Paolo and Giancarlo had heard some of these stories from their father before but could not recall seeing him as animated as he appeared to be with his current guests, although they also noticed how his voice trembled and rasped from time to time.

When dinner was served, his sons helped him to the table, and Mr. Amato offered a prayer of gratitude for the meal before everyone else sat and began to eat, with Alessia and her mother serving hearty portions. The weather was still quite warm, made more so by the heat rising from the oven, so Paolo turned on two living room fans. Mrs. Amato fed her husband solicitously, as his hand shook with palsy. She shared recollections about the day of their marriage some sixty years ago, when he fed her with a traditional cake, then asked David about his work. After explaining that he helped to manage a large department store in the center of London, David mentioned his master's program in international business studies, and expressed pride in his wife's master's studies in cognitive behavioral therapy at the same university, as well as their plans to purchase a home of their own soon – inadvertently opening up a round of rather pointed questions from Mrs. Amato regarding his mother's residence and the remaining time before he could make '*proper provision for Alessia*.' She hastened to explain that they had planned all aspects of their lives together, and to express her appreciation to a quietly smiling Melody for her warm hospitality. In turn, Melody Armstrong asked Lucia Amato about the recipes for the meal that they had enjoyed, leading to a new conversation topic. Alessia took the opportunity to look from David to his guitar case standing in a corner of the living room, and arched her eyebrows, questioningly. David stood and asked Mrs. Amato whether he could play any music of her choice, as a way of expressing appreciation for the dinner provided. She looked up at him appraisingly, inquired whether he could play "*Santa Lucia*," and shortly afterwards, was regaled with the plangent notes of a melody she'd enjoyed since her own girlhood. Everyone smiled and clapped as David concluded. Meanwhile, Giancarlo and Danielle were looking – surreptitiously, they thought – at each other, and Paolo watched them both, with a measure of anticipation and concern. Later, David and Alessia shared with her parents an album of photographs memorializing their wedding ceremony at St. Peter's Italian Catholic Church, as well as a few views of beautiful scenery from their honeymoon location in the Isle of Wight. When the evening came to a close, the Armstrong and Amato families exchanged embraces and the travelers made arrangements to meet at the airport early the following morning, for their return to London.

Once back in London, it was not long before Giancarlo and Danielle made arrangements to meet again, this time, for a sunny weekend picnic lunch in Richmond Park. Giancarlo had recently purchased a bright yellow Ford automobile with brown side stripes and was happy to take Danielle for an extended drive, during which they discussed their recent two-day visit with his family in Reggio di Calabria. She was convinced that his parents would not welcome a relationship between them. As the warm summer breeze streamed in through the Ford's half-opened windows on the drive south from Charing Cross, Giancarlo tried to project optimism. "Didn't you notice how my mother smiled when David was playing his guitar, and how my father felt glad to tell his stories?" Danielle riposted, "But what about the way in which your father muttered and looked somewhat sour when Alessia introduced me?" Giancarlo's explanation that he was actually describing her as a 'lovely black lady' made matters worse, as Danielle grimaced. "He may be willing to follow your mother's lead where my brother and your sister are concerned – but simply sees me as an exotic black woman – and might even have a stroke, if he knew that we're going out together!" They traveled in silence for a while, before Giancarlo remarked that Danielle was not at all black, but an absolutely irresistible golden brown in color, and that he was not about to let his parents dictate whom he should be with. She focused almost exclusively on his adjective '*irresistible*' and smiled, first inwardly, as her mood lightened. Danielle had found herself dressing with extra care whenever meeting

Giancarlo, and today was no exception, as she was wearing a new silver halter top leaving her midriff uncovered, and white shorts that showed off her long legs to advantage. As they entered the town of Richmond upon Thames, she was once again reflecting upon just what drew her to Giancarlo, more than to Ahmet, for instance - a vibrant, intense, and very handsome young man, but one so wedded to an Islamic interpretation of life and so dogmatic about the superiority of his faith to all others that he made her distinctly uncomfortable. By contrast, Giancarlo had clearly been brought up as a Catholic, but like his sister Alessia and indeed herself, he was evidently willing to adopt an ecumenical approach to religious beliefs. Danielle's thoughts turned to her Hampstead Heath picnic with Trevor, and she remembered the longing with which he always looked at her, their Caribbean heritage discussions, his interest in planning to open a sustainable restaurant, and especially, his searing kisses that afternoon, followed by their motorbike accident. She glanced at Giancarlo, who was concentrating on traffic near the entrance to the park and felt a pang of regret to be next to such a charming, warm, and excitingly sensual young man – one with whom she'd exchanged so many stories about their younger days – and to be thinking about other men. The term 'soulmate' came to mind, and Danielle wondered whether she had actually found such a person in her brother-in-law as he parked, and they entered the park on foot.

After strolling through the Isabella Plantation Woodland Gardens, visiting King Henry's Mound, then horse riding along a trail with carefully selected mares – she pretended to have ridden before, and paid particularly close attention to the reminders provided, such as the side from which to mount - Giancarlo and Danielle found a quiet location for their picnic, with red deer roaming nearby. Giancarlo spread a red and white checkered tablecloth brought from home on the grass and took out the French baguettes with gouda cheese and smoked salmon, along with custard pies, and cabernet sauvignon wine that he had purchased for the occasion. They sat and munched for a while, watching the stags and does grazing a little distance away, enjoying the provisions at hand with gusto.

Afterwards, Giancarlo brought out his sketch pad and pencils, then set out to draw two of the deer. Danielle was impressed with the speed and dexterity with which he completed his first drawing. After admiring it, she asked, "Could you draw me equally well? Giancarlo smiled, and to his response that such a drawing would require the right pose, Danette invited him to suggest one. They spent some time in experimentation, accompanied by recurrent laughs, and she ended up lying on the verdant grass, supported by her right elbow, legs and bare feet extended towards him, chin supported by her hand. Giancarlo was in his element, as he rapidly sketched her, capturing both Danette's relaxed posture and her meditative gaze. Upon review of the drawing, she was pleased with the result and warmly praised his skill, once again. Giancarlo smiled broadly, elated, and moved closer to her. "Would you share some of those thoughts with me in return?" he asked. Danielle was unprepared for this query and hesitated for a moment, then answered directly "I was thinking about us." Giancarlo lifted her hand to his lips, kissed it, and commented that she had a very promising subject. They were both momentarily startled when a buck ran by, following a doe, then laughed heartily – suddenly stopping to look into each other's eyes. "I was wondering whether we really have a future together, and just what you see in me," Danielle elaborated.

Giancarlo turned to look at a stand of maple and oak trees in the vicinity, then returned his gaze to her. "I see before me the most charming and desirable woman ever met in my life, one with strong and informed opinions on a variety of issues, including what can be done to improve the future trajectory of human life on Earth – someone who lost her beloved father at an early age, and has nevertheless managed never to lose sight of her dreams." Danielle was deeply touched by Giancarlo's remarks, recognizing his sincerity, and lifted her face up to kiss him gently. He pulled her closer still, and for a while, they simply held each other. As the sky suddenly darkened and a few raindrops fell they hastened to pack away the remnants of their picnic, discarding rubbish, and ran just in time to the shelter of a cafeteria on the other side of the road, arriving thoroughly sprinkled but not soaked, then took advantage of the adjacent restrooms to dry themselves.

A few weeks after David and Alessia returned from Reggio di Calabria, she awoke one morning, and rushed to the bathroom, feeling extremely nauseated. They were shocked, as she had been taking medication to prevent conception, given their repeated agreements that they should complete their master's degree programs and move into their own home, before having any children. Thinking about her physiological symptoms, she realized that it had been over eight weeks since her last period, and that her slightly tender breasts felt larger than usual.

Alessia suggested that David should take her to a gynecologist before talking to anyone else about the possibility that she might be pregnant. David hugged her comfortingly, lifting her blouse to caress the soft cream skin of her abdomen, and reassured her that if she were indeed expecting, they would find a way to implement their plans, while welcoming a baby into the family. She held him close in return, saying teasingly, "You have been exercising me so much, almost every night and every morning, until I'm orgasmically exhausted – we really shouldn't be surprised if our preventative measures might not have been up to the task!" David answered affectionately "I can't help wanting to enjoy my delectable wife, who represents my needed and preferred sustenance every day!" As an initial step, she suggested a home pregnancy test kit, which David purchased from a pharmacy later that day. When this test appeared to confirm her condition, they made an appointment to seek a medical assessment of her condition the following afternoon. Alessia was quite nervous to have her first full-fledged gynecological examination, feet in stirrups, and she held David's hand tightly. Afterwards, her specialist invited them to her office and confirmed that her fetus was healthy and approximately ten weeks old. That evening at dinner, when they shared the news with Melody and Danielle, both were delighted, especially Melody, who began to suggest names for her grandson or granddaughter almost immediately, gravitating towards options such as Grace and Joy for a girl and Paul or Joe for a boy, before they all agreed that there would be a lot of time in which the couple could decide. It was Danielle who inquired first about the way in which they would manage work and their studies with a new arrival in the family.

Lightheartedly, David told her, "That's exactly what aunts and grandmothers are for – did you never encounter the saying that '*I'm going to have children while my mother is young enough to care for them*?'" They all laughed uproariously, and he added, more seriously, that Alessia would explore her bank's maternity leave arrangements with the human resources manager within the next few days. They ceased conversation for a while, listening to a television evening news broadcast about the completion of a sustainable, 43-storey skyscraper in Southwark that incorporated wind turbines into its structure, and the shocking shooting of twelve people in Cumbria. Once upstairs and in bed, to David's surprise, it was Alessia who took the initiative in kissing his face, stroking his manhood, and stimulating him, delighted that she was going to be a mother, who would no longer have to remember her contraceptive medication, and evidently, more readily aroused than ever before, as she urged him to mount and enter her as soon as possible.

Melody sat in the living room for a portrait at Alessia's request. Since the announcement that she would soon become a grandmother, she had been alternately elated and depressed – glad that her son and his wife were expecting a son, now that their gynecologist had revealed the gender, and sorrowful that Joseph was unavailable to share this milestone with her. Looking closely at Alessia, who was concentrating upon the canvas on her easel, paintbrush poised over an array of oil paints, Melody saw a beautiful, fair-skinned, usually smiling young woman, despite her current frown of concentration, wearing a light blue polyester dress that hugged her curves, including a now perceptibly distended abdomen and enlarged breasts, brunette hair cascading over her shoulders in waves. She considered it a decided blessing that her son and his wife appeared to have settled down into a contented domestic routine, with David working and studying all week, while Alessia was on three months of maternity leave from her bank, mostly studying from home, and still insisting on helping her protesting mother-in-law with meal preparation as much as possible. As they had few occasions to be out together on public transport these days, Melody was less worried about the possibility of invectives or attacks directed at them by other passengers. She was, however, quite concerned about Danielle, who was going out with Giancarlo every weekend, and sometimes coming home late, looking both happy and somewhat stressed. Melody sighed and turned in her armchair, earning a pained reproof from her artist-in-residence – who then excused herself to visit the bathroom. Looking out through the open front door to the patio and to her cherished rose garden beyond, she reflected that these days, Danielle would not say much about her relationship with Giancarlo but was evidently seeing no one else. Her thoughts turned to the prior day, when she read the final chapters of Gustave Flaubert's Madame Bovary to her class, and the multiple questions that had eventuated. "If he really loved her, why didn't Emma try harder to convince her husband, Charles Bovary, that she needed more attention? How could he possibly have been so unaware of her increasingly deep unhappiness, the substantial debts that she was accumulating, her affair with the Marquis d'Andervilliers, and afterwards, with his successor, the law clerk Leon Dupuis? Who was most to blame for her eventual suicide?" Melody had been very pleased with her students' intense engagement with Flaubert's work, but also concerned that they appeared to have rejected most of her attempted explanations as inadequate. She ended up asking herself, who was to blame for Joseph's departure from her life? Returning to her seat, Alessia observed the tears rolling down her cheeks, put aside her paint brush, and came to hug her, sitting on her lap. "*Madre mia,* are you missing your husband again?" she asked. She embraced and soothed her mother-in-law until Melody began to smile wryly, and then got up to bring her easel over. "I wouldn't normally show you a painting until it is completely finished – but thought it might be good for you to take a look now," she said. Melody was stunned. Alessia had not only captured her physical likeness, including her green floral cotton dress and the crimson armchair with cream armrests upon which she sat, but most of all, her wistful, deeply brooding, and lonely spirit, mirrored in her eyes and mien, not quite checked by a conscious determination to emphasize the blessings remaining in her life. "You really are quite an artist," she commented. "Did you say that you never took any lessons?" Alessia answered, "David and you have always been so kind about my hobby.

When I was a young girl at home, I spent many hours in my room, absorbed in experimenting and practicing. However, my parents always thought I was wasting time, instead of studying or helping my mother in the kitchen. When we saw her in Reggio di Calabria, she asked me whether I was still painting, instead of attending to my work, my studies and taking care of my foreign husband."

Giancarlo and Paolo were sitting at home in their living room, after dinner, and found themselves once again in a discussion about Danielle. Paolo was somewhat frustrated, because his younger brother wouldn't or perhaps couldn't explain clearly whether - if so, why, and when, he was actually planning to marry his sister-in-law, an action that seemed vaguely incestuous to his elder brother, although he'd not been able to identify any Church doctrine that prohibited such a marriage. Now that both their parents had grudgingly accepted Alessia's marriage to David and were aware that the couple would soon make them grandparents, Paolo thought it unfortunate to complicate matters by requesting further significant attitude adjustment within their family. Giancarlo, who had lost some weight and acquired a more sober attitude since their arrival in London, maintained that his relationship with Danielle was an issue neither for the Church nor their parents, but rather, for them to work out themselves. Paolo placed a hand around Giancarlo's shoulder. "I hope you understand that in raising this matter, you are my most important concern. Even the phrase that you just used, 'an issue to be worked out,' suggests that in spite of yourself, you need your elder brother's council." Giancarlo lightly clapped Paolo on his back and rose, telling him that he worried far too much, and that he would be sure to ask for any advice that might ever be required, while clearing the dining plates from the table. Just then, the doorbell rang.

Giancarlo hastened to respond, welcoming Danielle inside. They all sat for a while in the living room, while Paolo made herb tea for everyone, talking about the progress of Alessia's pregnancy and the health of their parents in Calabria, the most popular works of fiction sold at the bookstore where Paolo worked, and the forensic audit difficulties sometimes encountered by Giancarlo, arising from the temperaments of some of his colleagues, who wanted to query even the smallest transactions, regardless of whether or not they were material. Soon after Paolo tried to hide a yawn and indicated that he needed to go to bed so as to be prepared for the next day's work, Giancarlo invited Danielle up to his room. She demurred, asking whether there was any reason not to talk to each other in the living room, adding that she'd come to see him, but not to sleep with him. Giancarlo hastened to answer that he was mainly seeking to ensure that their conversation was private. Danielle smiled. "Every time there is an opportunity, those hands of yours find themselves all over me, and you're so good at kissing me that if I weren't a practical person, you would end up doing whatever you wish with me!" Giancarlo protested that she was so attractive, in body, mind and spirit, that she made his head spin, and that they now knew each other well enough, and that his income was sufficient, for them to agree upon making their lives together. "Is that a forensic accountant's proposal, Giancarlo?" she asked, "You know that we've repeatedly talked about the need for me to finish my degree, and to find work in a sustainable architecture, rather than to become a kept housewife. Besides, your parents seem unlikely to support any such plans. After all, they have just barely managed to accept David and Alessia's marriage." Giancarlo held both her hands and asked "How much longer do you have before graduation? Isn't it at least another year?" When Danielle nodded, he continued, "Alessia is still studying for her degree, even late in her expectancy. Couldn't you do so also?" She leaned back in her chair, retrieving her hands, and looked at him. "What you really want is a wife like your mother – someone who will concentrate only upon taking care of your home and raising your children," Danielle challenged him. It was Giancarlo's turn to smile. "Your remark reminds me of an old joke about an elderly teacher telling her students the story of Adam and Eve. One student keeps falling asleep, and the mischievous boy behind keeps touching her bare shoulder with a pin to awaken her. The teacher asks the class what Eve said to Adam after she had given birth to Cain and Abel. The sleeping student is awakened suddenly once more, and shouts, '*if you stick that thing in me one more time, I'll break it in half!*' - then the absolutely shocked teacher fainted." They both laughed, then Danielle recovered her sense of decorum and told him that she hadn't realized that his repertoire included such ribald jokes. Giancarlo protested that he simply wanted them to be more relaxed about their future together.

By the time that he walked her to the Camden Town tube station, after a series of kisses and affectionate cuddles, they were both simultaneously smiling, hand in hand, and saddened to be parting.

Alessia's water broke without any warning, while she was preparing a tomato and cheese omelette with French toast for David in the kitchen. Melody was still asleep, and Danielle had already left for London Metropolitan University. For a moment, she wasn't sure what was happening, then screamed for David, who came running, while still dressing for the day. He hastened to collect her already packed little brown suitcase with clothing and toiletries, called a taxi and still incompletely dressed, left with her for the maternity ward of the local hospital where her obstetrician was registered, urging the driver to increase speed. Alessia was promptly admitted. David sat with her and attempted to reassure his wife, when her first examination indicated insufficient dilation. It was later that day that she experienced her first truly painful contractions, without the ability to complete the process, and began to moan loudly, then scream intermittently, made more frustrated by the repeated injunctions of her obstetrician and her husband to push. David felt increasingly stressed and helpless as she suffered. By the second afternoon, Alessia was almost too exhausted to scream any longer and David was dizzy with fatigue and fear. Her obstetrician had begun to arrange for a caesarian section, when she suddenly cried out, and the crown of their son's head unexpectedly emerged, lightly tufted with brunette hair. When her afterbirth had been addressed, the baby was washed and given to an extremely weary but relieved Alessia, who was aided in sitting up. David was seated in a metal armchair, partly resting on her bed, in in a disoriented nap, when he heard her say huskily, "*È proprio come suo padre!*" (He looks so much like his father!) as their copper-toned son latched on to her distended right nipple and looked up to see him properly for the first time. David smiled wanly and held Alessia's hand. As she fed her baby, she felt incredulous that her ordeal was actually over, memories of the severe pangs suffered already beginning to be somewhat attenuated by the pleasure of nursing. It was David who continued to feel absolutely shattered for a few more hours, until a nurse brought lasagna for them both, and gave him an opportunity to hold his son. When he remarked upon the goosebumps on Alessia's areola, she took pleasure in teaching him what she'd learned from Melody – that he was actually observing Montgomery's glands, which exude lubricating moisture to facilitate their son's feeding. Smiling wanly, he commented that he would clearly have to allow the newly born infant priority access to her nipples for now. The quiet of completion spread across the room like a blanket, as mother and child dozed, and David watched them in wonder. He mulled over name options, and found himself gravitating towards Oliver, thinking of his mother's recent related comment, and his father's middle name.

A few days later, Melody sat in a new bright orange, wooden rocking chair in her living room, her grandson tucked safely in her grateful arms, while Alessia rested upstairs, David was at work, and Danielle in a university class. She beamed at Oliver, thinking about his departed namesake in a less stressed manner than she had for a long time. Melody counted her blessings, which almost seemed borne by the light breeze now wafting the subtle fragrances from her rose garden. David was enjoying his job as a store manager while making progress with his graduate studies, and had fathered a healthy, evidently currently dreaming baby boy, with five perfectly formed fingers on each hand, and a set of five little toes on each foot. As she rocked contemplatively, Melody heard Alessia call her softly, and hastened up the staircase, to find her sitting up, more than ready to nurse her son, spurts of milk overflowing. As she sat on the king-sized bed watching Alessia feed her son, Melody's thoughts drifted through the mists of the years since her own son's birth, remembering the lusty determination with which David had fed at her breast, leaving her feeling both perennially sore and recurrently fulfilled. She went to the kitchen and returned with a cup of cocoa, honey, and milk, as Oliver finally finished his meal, and cooed with satisfaction. Melody placed Alessia's cocoa on a bedside table, next to the lamp that she'd purchased early in pregnancy, its silver stand depicting an angel with outstretched wings, and taking her gurgling grandson once again, asked her daughter in law, "How are you feeling today?" In the pause that followed, as Alessia sipped her hot cocoa gratefully, she noticed a new relaxed maternal glow pervading her, full breasts incompletely covered, green nightgown damp with milk, brunette hair in disarray, eyes still drowsy with sleep, but cheeks ruddy with health. "It feels so strange to be suddenly empty here," patting her abdomen, "and to be so full of milk that it is painful, when accumulated," Alessia answered, adding that David sometimes seemed afraid that his son would be hurt if he did not hold him correctly – and that he also treated with her very delicately, as if she were an easily broken ceramic decoration.

Both women smiled, as the cream silk curtains lifted in an incoming gust. "Danielle is still learning how to hold her nephew as well," Melody told her, as she deftly corrected the sticky pads on the baby's nappy. Later that day, when David returned from work, greeting his family ebulliently, immediately after showering, he took a dinner tray with rice risotto, broccoli, and stewed beef, accompanied by warm milk, up to Alessia, feeding her tenderly, while she nursed his son. Only after Oliver was sleeping soundly on his stomach in the newly installed baby crib with a line of colorful little toys strung across it, near their bed, and after he'd helped Alessia to shower, then settled her back in bed to watch a television musical, did he join Melody and Danielle at dinner downstairs. Their conversation revolved around the sleeping baby upstairs for a while, then at Melody's request, her children shared with her some of the contours of their day.

A few days later, Giancarlo arrived at London Metropolitan University and made his way to a lecture theatre where he had understood that Danielle and her classmates should be listening to a midterm assessment of architectural styles. He paused in the entrance for a few moments, located her in the front row, then went to sit in the back. Giancarlo carefully read notes on the chalk board concerning aspects of classical, neoclassical, Greek revival architecture, and nineteenth century Italianate architecture, then listened attentively to the lecturer as she discussed Bauhaus architecture, among other styles, with its emphasis upon simple, rational, functional design, contrasting this with buildings constructed under the influence of the Art Deco movement of the 1920s and 1930s, as well as the Modernist focus upon designs where form followed function, using materials such as steel, concrete, iron, and glass. Giancarlo noticed that when the lecturer turned to sustainable architecture, using 3-D printing and laser cutting technology, Danielle appeared to become even more animated, taking notes at a rapid pace.

After the lecture, he waited for her while she talked with the professor and enjoyed her clearly pleased surprise as she came up to the door of the lecture hall. "I didn't think that you were serious when you said you would like to come to one of my review lectures," she remarked. Taking her hand, Giancarlo walked with Danielle to the cafeteria. "I was glad to have the opportunity to understand a little more about your professional passion, when my office closed for an urgent renovation project today," he responded, as they weaved through groups of students and passed through successive halls. She nodded, when he added his assumption that the Barbican, where they had gone to a musical performance a few weeks before, represented an example of Brutalist architecture. Danielle noticed Trevor sitting with a lively young lady of Chinese origin, upon entering the cafeteria, and experienced a twinge of searing regret that she'd never been able to satisfactorily explain her reason for refusing multiple invitations from him, after their accident – so he'd evidently ended up thinking she blamed him for her injuries so much, upon reflection, that she wished to have nothing further to do with him. Giancarlo did not notice the direction of her gaze, but sensing her sudden discomfort, offered to take her to lunch elsewhere. They ended up eating a spicy curried prawn meal with sauteed vegetables at an Indian restaurant on Queensway, adding a glass of Chianti at his urging. Danielle noted approvingly that Giancarlo appeared to be a good listener, as she described her baby nephew Oliver, whom neither uncle had yet seen, and discussed her most recent class projects, together with the recent opening of the Thanet Wind Farm, while he eventually added a comment concerning Brazil's victory over Spain in the World Blind Football Championship. Towards the end of the meal, he surprised her by seizing her right hand, kissing her open palm repeatedly, and asking her whether she would become his fiancée.

If David and Alessia were besotted with Oliver practically from the moment of his birth, Melody was the epitome of the adoring grandmother. His crib next to his parents' bed was fitted with an audio alarm, with mini speakers allowing everyone to hear downstairs, should he cry loudly for long. Melody kept going upstairs to lift her grandson up, cradling him lovingly in her arms, while admiring his soft, tan skin, wispy brunette hair, and grey eyes like his mother's, despite Alessia's regular remonstrances that he needed to settle down to sleep. At the same time, David watched Alessia nurse Oliver as often as he could, and frequently took him to rub his back gently with the goal of getting his son to burp, while marveling at the almost translucent milk that sometimes continued to spurt from her visibly sore nipples. When he teased her about their damp sheets and pillows once too often, Alessia reminded David that he needed to equip himself with a pump and feeding bottles in which to store sustenance for their son, as her maternity leave from work would expire within another fortnight. Danielle was also fascinated by her nephew, pronouncing upon the several ways in which he resembled his parents, yet feeling quite timid when anyone suggested that she hold him for a while, demurring that she would do so in good time.

David was distressed when his inquiry about the possibility of paternity leave from his store yielded the response that no such policy existed, and he hurried home from work as rapidly as possible each weekday, after catching up with his lectures, while sharing the collection of lecture notes for Alessia with his sister. The weeks following Oliver's birth seemed to fly in a medley of meals interrupted by baby care routines, incipient arguments as to who would change his diapers or bathe him, check-up visits with the pediatrician, and the general enjoyment of his first clearly evident smiles and happy gurgles. David asked Melody more than once when he himself had begun using his first words, and she smiled indulgently, telling him once again the story of how Joseph had come home after work and was stroking David's head in his bedroom crib, and suddenly called her from the kitchen, saying excitedly that their son had vocalized "*Da-da*" as his first word.

Giancarlo was both pleased and disappointed, when Danielle accepted his sudden invitation to become his fiancée, but only informally, until she completed her degree program at London Metropolitan University. As he sat in his corporate office, attempting to focus upon a forensic accounting challenge involving a set of British and French hotel management partner companies headquartered in Jersey, one of the Channel islands, Giancarlo stretched his right leg, then his left, his mind wandering to his conversation with his brother Paolo that morning, over a rather English breakfast of ham, baked beans, grilled tomato, and toast with tea. Paolo had been pleased that Giancarlo had neither the immediate intention nor the need to communicate with their family in Reggio di Calabria about his intense involvement with Danielle. From Paolo's perspective, another year at least would allow time for his younger brother to reflect upon this relationship, and to meet other eligible and attractive young women - perhaps even a Catholic born in southern Italy - and if they both still wanted to become formally engaged afterwards, he would be willing to provide his support. During this conversation, Giancarlo once again inquired whether Paolo was destined to be a confirmed bachelor for the remainder of his life – and even teased his brother, to the latter's chagrin and articulated annoyance, that perhaps his interests ran to other men, in which case, their entire family would be devastated. Paolo ridiculed this supposition concerning his preferences, stated once again that although he was not easily pleased, he would eventually encounter the person that he wanted to marry – then changed the topic of conversation to Oliver, whom they had both met for the first time a few weeks before, when David and Alessia had visited them with their son. "A handsome young fellow to be sure," Paolo had commented, and then asked whether Oliver should not be saying at least a few words, a year after his birth. Giancarlo had responded thoughtfully that their mother had remarked on several occasions that her children did not begin speaking until after almost two years of age, making her concerned at the delay in vocalization each time this occurred. By the end of their breakfast, when the brothers were each hastening to take the Camden Town tube to work in different directions, they had agreed upon the importance of patience, especially given their nephew's evident vitality and almost non-stop activity when awake.

Several months later, David and Alessia were visiting the office of Oliver's pediatrician, Dr. Norma Foster, in Wood Green for a regular checkup. They told her of their concern that he slept most nights and did not cry much, even when he ought to be hungry, or was wet. Although their son seemed to smile regularly, at sixteen months of age, he still was not articulating the simplest words – David could not wait for him to say "*da-da*" or "*ma-ma*" - or pointing at items that ought to be interesting, such as the colorful wooden toys hung over his crib. Dr. Foster completed an initial physical examination, pronounced Oliver to be evidently normal in size, physique, and autonomic responses, then tried to stimulate his verbal or non-verbal reactions to a succession of colored patterns and objects.

Alessia was visibly stressed as her little baby appeared to ignore his pediatrician, and to rock gently in place, but to be startled and disconcerted by her clapping, and the light she shone into his eyes to check pupil response. At the end of the visit, Dr. Foster reassured his parents that babies developed at varying speeds, that it was still too early for a diagnosis of classic autism or autistoid behavior and suggested a follow-up appointment in six months' time. Afterwards, David and Alessia took Oliver in his blue pram to Alexandria Park and shared the spicy baked salmon and Stilton cheese sandwiches Melody had made for them that morning, accompanied by apples and cider.

It was a warm and quiet afternoon, with few other people in the park, and a bevy of green-hued mallard ducks swimming in the nearby lake. They regarded Oliver thoughtfully, as he sat quietly for a while, then once again began to rock repetitively. David tried to comfort Alessia, who was crying softly, even while trying to munch a brown wheat sandwich. He hugged her and counseled patience, telling her that perhaps another few months would make all the difference to their son's development. She wiped her eyes with David's offered handkerchief, his initials in blue on one corner, sighed, and said, "My parents, perhaps even my brothers, and some of my other relatives, are certain to say that our baby's behavior is the result of mixing our genetic heritages – we have never had any such developmental disabilities in the extended Amato family." David held her close stroked her hair and kissed her lips. "Well, what do you think? You know, we've never had any such cases in the Armstrong family either." Alessia looked at him tenderly and apologized for her comment. David offered her a paper cup with Somerset cider, telling her that it was a good idea for them to be prepared for hurtful if uninformed criticism, in a worst-case scenario – the best defense would be to hold fast to each other and to plan for an entire family of happy, laughing children running around their own home by the seaside, in the near future. Alessia smiled wanly, then giggled as David tickled her expertly. "Stop, stop," she cried as his mischievous hands roamed all over her body. "So, you really want to have me always ready for you in bed, bearing baby after baby, cooking barefoot in the kitchen, and concentrating upon taking care of our family, rather than completing my graduate degree in forensic psychology and setting up a successful consultancy!" David chuckled, his left hand now stroking her leg, under her pleated cream silk skirt – "I don't mind the part about enjoying each other in bed, but whatever happened to our plans for work-life balance?" he asked. "We can have successful consultancies and a rich family life if we organize our days and nights properly." The ducks quacked in a chorus on the lake, and blue jays darted rapidly from tree to tree. A passionflower vine curling securely around the trunk of a nearby elm tree caught their eyes. Alessia finished her warm cider, kissed him again, and while bottle- feeding, then burping Oliver, reminded David that they each had mid-term examinations in a week at London Metropolitan University for which she, at least, had yet to prepare. When David added that he also had to lead a management meeting at his department store the next morning, they made their way home.

Melody felt more distressed than even her grandson's parents that Oliver sustained his inability to articulate even the simplest words and continued to enjoy being left alone to rock in place, at almost two years old. After months of regularly reading stories such as Dr. Seuss's "I love green eggs and ham," or "The Three Little Pigs," or "Little Red Riding Hood" to him as her special mission, without any evident response, she could no longer reassure David or Alessia by quoting Dr. Foster's prior remarks that delayed development sometimes occurred, and that there was no need to worry – they were now mulling over readings that identified gene mutations that affected cell development in Broca's region of the brain, an area associated with speech, and environmental factors such as air pollution that might have caused Oliver's condition. Accordingly, Melody now counseled her son to model acceptance and appreciation of Oliver's physical health otherwise, his cherubic disposition, and beautiful eyes, which mirrored those of his mother. During one such conversation, David explained that now that Alessia and himself had managed to complete their Master's degrees, they had been contemplating a mortgage down-payment on a property in Hastings, which was conditional upon whether they could both find work there, or at least in the vicinity. When Melody inquired whether they planned to have any more children, he laughed, somewhat more exuberantly than necessary, told her that she would be the first to know when their son's brother or sister was '*in the works*,' and invited her to visit the property in Hastings on the following weekend, to help them decide whether to proceed. When told about the impending trip, Danielle enthusiastically added herself to the group, asking her brother how he could even imagine a visit to East Sussex for this purpose without including her. Melody reflected, disconsolately, but did not share the thought, that when David and Alessia were living in their own home elsewhere, and busy working, and when Danielle eventually got married and settled down also, she would find herself quite alone, in the three bedroom home in which they had all enjoyed building their lives together since that awful night of the fire in Hornsey from which they had barely escaped in time, with the aid of the police security team then assigned to them.

The next Saturday morning dawned bright and clear, with the first hints of autumn in the air, as Melody, David, Alessia and Danielle found themselves around a four-seater table in a first-class train compartment, with Oliver quietly seated in his pram, traveling from London Bridge to Hastings. Melody had packed breakfast as usual, and once they had left West Dulwich behind, took out a thermos with coffee and paper cups, accompanied by ample helpings of warm fish and chips with her special garlic sauce. David, echoed by Alessia, remarked appreciatively on the appearance, and enticing aroma of the food she had provided, while Danielle simply began to eat her share with an evident appetite. The rolling green meadows and woods of the countryside sped by the train compartment windows, interpolated with towns such as Sevenoaks, Tonbridge, and Tunbridge Wells. By the time that Hildenborough was passing by, they were replete, and the trip had taken on some of the feeling of a vacation, except perhaps for Melody, who was still reflecting upon the expected effleurage of silence throughout her home when all her family members had eventually spread their wings. Alessia fed her son his milk and expertly burped, then changed him. Several arriving or departing passengers looked at the group with special interest but made none of the offensive remarks they were semi-consciously braced to hear – except for Danielle, who simply could not accept that anyone had any right to make negative observations about people they did not know at all. Alessia had read every journal article and book that was available to her about autism, together with David, and they had counted their blessings, on more than one occasion, that Oliver had not evidenced any extreme behaviors, such as epileptic seizures – at least not so far – and that he was such a pleasant and quiet baby.

Now, as the train approached Battle, near Hastings, Alessia felt a mixture of resignation and anticipation, that once in their own home, with consultancies or other jobs that were professionally satisfying, David and herself could plan for a brother or a sister to Oliver, who could, in due course, help to take care of him. Upon arrival in Hastings – the first visit for any of the family - they looked around with curiosity after exiting the station, then finding a taxi rank, took a taxicab to the address that David had been researching with an estate agent.

He gave the address on Robertson Terrace to the cab driver, and they all settled down for the drive, which took them past the Priory Meadow Shopping Centre and the Town Hall, towards the Grand Parade area near the beach. When they arrived, both Melody and Alessia exclaimed with pleasure at the lush little garden that met their gaze, filled with pink and white peonies, purple asters, and red carnations. However, a note on the door from the estate agent presented apologies for her delay, with a promise to be available an hour later, so at David's suggestion, they ended up walking to the beach, Once they had crossed Grand Parade, they took off their shoes and enjoyed strolling on the sand. Danielle went up almost to her knees in the somewhat chilly sea, lifting her green skirt slightly and smiling broadly, while David and Alessia sat nearby, enjoying the tangy sea breeze and each other, with Oliver's pram at hand. In earlier days, they used to rock him regularly, with the goal of lulling him to sleep; these days, he either rocked himself or sat quietly inside the pram. Melody ended up rambling down the beach by herself, reminiscing about the days when she swam with Joseph at several beaches near Montego Bay in Jamaica, and realizing that she had not been near the sea since that time – and also, how distinctive these roaring, choppy cobalt waves were, coming in from the north Atlantic Ocean, compared with the aquamarine, ultramarine and cerulean blues of the tropical sea in which they'd swam, often in the resplendent light of lambent, cinnabar sunsets. Her thoughts turned to Oliver, with his unexpected developmental disability in the form of autism and merged into an inchoate prayer that his parents would have the wisdom and fortitude to enjoy him, rather than be stressed by his condition. She noticed that David and Alessia were talking quietly with each other and felt a renewed gladness that her son had found a wife, however different in appearance, ethnicity, and origin, who evidently joined him in mutual acceptance, understanding and appreciation. Melody also looked thoughtfully at Danielle, recalling their conversations about Giancarlo, whom she'd not mentioned for a while, and regarded her daughter as she now walked on the beach just above high tide line, collecting carefully selected seashells. She turned to look back at David and Alessia, hearing a peal of laughter from her daughter in law, and smiled to see how they were now playing a modified game of foot fighting, lying back on the sand with shapely white and larger tanned feet flat against each other, as her son pretended to struggle against Alessia's firm pushes. Looking at her watch, she noticed that over an hour had passed and hastened to alert her family that it was time to walk back to Robertson Terrace.

When they finally met the estate agent, she turned out to be a cheerful and sprightly elderly lady, who shook everyone's hands, and announced herself as Irene Donovan – "*please call me Irene*" - before taking them on an initial rapid tour of the cozy, three-bedroom house, with bay windows in front. Irene explained that the property was available for sale - furnished, partly furnished, or unfurnished. A well-organized little vegetable garden in the rear of the house, featuring lettuce and tomatoes in serried rows, caught Melody's attention.

Danielle was intrigued by the master bathroom, which included a local water heater, a bidet, and a large, chestnut-framed mirror, in which she thoughtfully contemplated her reflection for some time. She gazed at the young woman there, against a reflected background of marbled cream and pink wallpaper, with well- defined eyebrows, long lashes, sparkling black eyes, recently shampooed waves of black hair, and usually sensuous lips, currently set in a quizzical line. Danielle recalled some of the highlights of the sermons delivered by the pastor at the church to which Melody had taken her children on Sundays for years after the passing of their father, such as "*God is Love*," and "*We are all made in the image of God*." She remembered her father's habitual remark that even if we cannot change the world by our actions alone, we can adjust our own attitudes, creating the potential for transformation in people around us. Her mind then wandered from such thoughts about frequent inhumanity between humans, and the increasing environmental devastation of the Earth, to imagining God as the Soul of the Universe, creator of multiple types of intelligent and sentient beings with various forms of existence across a myriad of worlds, circling distant stars.

David and Alessia spent a good deal of time examining the master bedroom, featuring a double, four-poster mahogany bed, with an intricate carving at the top of each post that neither could quite make out, accompanied by an ornate Chesterfield dressing table with a matching red velvet chair, an antique chest, and two wooden rocking chairs. After reviewing the other bedrooms, with Oliver's pram in hand, they asked Irene about the schedule of purchase option costs, local banks that might consider a first mortgage, the normal expected down payment, and the date that the property would be available. This led to an extended discussion about their employment or business development plans. Irene alerted Alessia to a possible work opportunity at an organizational development consultancy company in St Leonard's-on-Sea, a nearby town, and mentioned a commercial bank in the Priory Meadows Shopping Centre that had recently advertised for a new manager to David. He indicated interest in purchasing the property, subject to the availability of employment for each, and a mortgage, and that the existing furnishings were fine as part of the purchase package – except for the dilapidated carpeting, which needed to be replaced. While he was speaking, Alessia took up Oliver, who had been rocking sideways serenely, and bottle-fed him. Irene looked keenly at him, and when told, in response to her inquiry, that he had yet to say any words, exclaimed, "I knew that your baby reminded me of one of my nephews, who is now a teenager of fourteen, and lives in his own little world, without ever speaking! Her parents worried about him so much when he only rocked and sat by himself, making no real eye contact with anyone. Why, Andrew didn't even want to be hugged!" David inquired with some anxiety, "Did he ever display any symptoms of epilepsy?" Irene immediately remarked that he clearly had been engaged in a good deal of ASD research, and that indeed, her nephew had to be given medication for epileptic seizures from time to time, after about age twelve. She added her understanding that up to 70% of people with autism spectrum disorder were never impacted by seizures, to his relief. During the ninety-minute train journey back to London Bridge, which actually appeared shorter than their outbound travel to Hastings, Melody and Danielle agreed with the couple that Robertson Terrace might well be made into a comfortable home for David and Alessia, should their employment and mortgage requirements fall into place.

Danielle was once again looking into a bathroom mirror, a small circular one at home on this occasion, as she prepared for an interview at an architectural consultancy company where the Managing Director had indicated an interest in her sustainable architecture background. When she had completed her baccalaureate degree program at London Metropolitan University, several of her classmates had announced an intention to continue on to a master's degree, citing the challenge of securing well-compensated and interesting work in the field without advanced qualifications. However, Danielle was impatient to put what she had been learning to work and had neither a scholarship nor wished to ask her mother to meet further tuition costs. In addition, Giancarlo had become impatient, inquiring how much longer it would now be before they could announce their engagement. As she put the finishing touches on her lip gloss, Danielle reflected that if David and Alessia had been able to settle down happily together, despite their obvious differences in ethnicity, color, and heritage, and all of the various extreme stresses encountered – most recently, including Oliver's diagnosed autism spectrum disorder – Giancarlo and herself should be able to build a life together as well. She felt confident in their mutually declared love, but uneasy about his evident preference for a wife who would remain at home, taking care of a family that he regularly assured her would eventually include many happy and healthy children. Danielle once discussed Giancarlo's preference that his wife focus her energies upon home rather than work with Alessia, who smiled and reminded her that throughout his adolescence in Reggio di Calabria, he had encountered almost no female professionals, and that all the married women in the family had modeled the lifestyle that he now projected. However, Alessia also attempted to reassure her, with mixed tenderness and amusement, that Giancarlo had encountered many professional women since arrival in London, including a few colleagues within his forensic accounting firm, and that given his reiterated remarks to his siblings about his feelings for her, he would be sure to adjust his attitude. Danielle snapped out of her reverie, completed her gray pants suit with a gold belt, and hastened to leave for the Turnpike Lane tube station, exchanging a hasty goodbye with a somewhat startled Melody on the way out the door. She ended up waiting for almost an hour at her interview location in Holborn, where she initially spent the time reviewing an array of abstract paintings on the walls of the office, by artists she couldn't recognize, and then found herself thinking about her mother, who seemed slightly frail these days, despite Melody's regular remark that she had been blessed throughout her life. Danielle reflected upon the implications of a recently read comment by Simone de Beauvoir, that one's life had value as long as one attributes value to the lives of others. Her mother had spent her life in caring for her family, raising her children, first with their father, and then by herself after his departure from this life, and continued to care for David, Alessia and herself at home, as well as in her work with her nursing home reading group. She was still lost in introspection when the receptionist called her name, and ushered her into a large, mahogany-paneled office for her interview.

Danielle encountered a panel of three elderly men seated around a conference table and was invited to sit on one side. She recognized Sir Henry Stanfield, who had once visited her university class to provide a guest lecture on the evolution of sustainable architecture, and immediately felt intimidated. Perhaps responding to her body language, the interviewer who was evidently chairing the panel smiled, and tried to put her at ease. "Good morning, Ms. Armstrong. Your application was very articulate and demonstrated a great deal of enthusiasm for the type of architecture that this company wishes to treat as its hallmark. Why don't you begin by explaining how your background, education, values, and attitude would enable you to make an excellent contribution, if recruited?" However, Danielle explicitly inverted her response, by first arguing that urban built environments inevitably tended to generate negative environmental impacts when extensive use of concrete, steel and glass was accompanied by paved areas for parking or access roads, and increased resort to private transport. She provided vivid examples of sustainable architecture in various regions of the world, such as open rainscreens in Japan, allowing air to vent through sidings; the use of natural or recycled materials such as wood in Scandinavia, where high rises were no longer necessarily constructed of concrete and steel, and the merits of small-scale, hexagon-shaped residential units, with abundant application of natural, or at least LED lighting; the importance of developing community outdoor spaces in locations that encourage appreciation of nature, as in some Swiss towns; the use of solar or wind, or thermal, or renewable hydraulic energy power, in a number of Caribbean or Pacific islands, when practicable; an emphasis upon passive heating as well as cooling; and the benefits of creating rooftop terraces with attractive plants and flowers along defined walkways or vertical fern or purple and white clematis gardens, within major urban areas, such as in London and New York. As Danielle spoke, she became visibly more relaxed and animated. By the time that she began to discuss the fit between the role at hand and her own background, each member of the interview team was nodding in appreciation of her remarks. When the interview ended with a review of the company's history and culture, and Danielle left the office with the sense that she might well end up working with the team, she called Giancarlo at work, to provide an update, as previously promised, speaking loudly against the traffic passing on the street, and they agreed to meet for a seafood pasta lunch in Knightsbridge.

David and Alessia were taking time off from work in his London department store and her bank respectively, for a day visit to Hastings, both to participate in invited interviews and to meet with a local mortgage banker. Meanwhile, Melody was taking care of Oliver, who was rocking gently in his highchair in the kitchen, where she was slow cooking roast beef, to be accompanied by vegetables and risotto for dinner that evening. On the radio, news had been succeeded by a music show featuring the 1960s, and she found herself humming to the tune of "*The Restless Wind*," almost unconsciously, as she prepared her vegetables for steaming and stirred her rice with milk, while checking on the progress of her roast in the electric grill. Melody abruptly stopped humming and picked up her ringing phone, to encounter Alessia calling from Hastings to inquire about Oliver, and reassured his anxious mother that he'd been fed, burped, bathed, and was giving his grandmother absolutely no trouble. To Alessia's further query as to whether he was making any sounds, or any type of eye contact, Melody sighed inaudibly and told her that she had a gentle, beautiful son, who greatly enjoyed hugs even if he had to communicate without words, and that he continued to be a blessing to his family. As the conversation continued, Alessia explained that her organizational development consultancy interview had finished, she hoped successfully.

However, David was still engaged in his bank interview, and they expected to have a meeting with a mortgage bank manager afterwards, to discuss possible financing options – knowing that any commitment was unlikely until either or both had received, and accepted employment offers. After ending the call, Melody reflected that Alessia's original Italian-accented English was changing, as she responded to her environment in London, including life with David. She imagined that her own accent had altered significantly since her days in Montego Bay, Jamaica and daydreamed again for a while about her first day on the beach with Joseph, to whom she had been drawn, initially without any conscious realization, from the first moments of their meeting in that little library.

Now the radio was playing another old lyric, "*Under the Boardwalk*" by a group of performers called "The Drifters," and she would have continued her daydream, had not Oliver gurgled and rocked more vigorously than usual, so that his chair was in danger of toppling over for a moment. She looked fondly into his charming grey eyes, mirroring those of Alessia, and tousled his unruly dark hair, which reminded her so much of David. After transferring her grandson to the safety of a playpen, Melody returned her attention to her cooking, encouraged by the rich odor arising from her almost completed roast, and remembered reading, in something of a reverie, that the taste of any meal was largely related to its smell and warmth. It also came to mind that smell constituted the only one of the five basic senses that was not mediated by a small, almond-sized gland in the brain called the hypothalamus. Since aromas were processed directly by the olfactory cortex in the front of the brain, odors had a unique power to bind and to communicate unconscious memories in a stunningly direct manner, within all human beings, across time and space. She gazed out of the kitchen window.

Now the rising aroma of the roast beef took her back to her wedding reception at the home of her parents in Montego Bay, where relatives and friends milled about in the living and dining rooms, as well as the verandah and garden, some eating and drinking with the new couple at the dining table, others using paper plates and plastic utensils – all exchanging jokes, their memories of past family weddings, and teasing or toasting Melody and Joseph. For what seemed a few moments, the present blended into the past, and the years in between vanished – then the insistent ringing of her living room phone ended her reverie and she found Danielle on the line, telling her that she had just agreed with Giancarlo that as soon as she had a confirmed job, they should proceed to provide twenty-eight days of notice to the local Registry Office and get married, in a civil rather than a religious ceremony. She held the blue landline phone away from her right ear, feeling disoriented for a few moments, looked at it, then caught her breath.

When Melody recovered herself sufficiently to congratulate Danielle on her plans, she asked whether Giancarlo would not prefer a religious ceremony, perhaps at the same church where David and Alessia had been married. Danielle readily responded that Giancarlo wanted them to settle down to a contented life together as soon as possible and accepted her as she was – an agnostic non- Catholic, who much preferred a wedding at an approved venue such as a hotel where the Registrar could be booked at the same time to perform the ceremony. Danielle told her mother, in a clearly excited tone, that she would like her suggestions as to appropriate readings and music to help make the ceremony memorable, and that she would also need assistance in planning a reception, she hoped, in the same location. Melody was touched, and promptly promised all her support, then inquired what documentation they would need. "Oh, just our birth certificates, proof of address, such as a bank statement, and perhaps photographic ID," Danielle told her. She added that they might consider a Catholic convalidation ceremony afterwards, for the benefit of Giancarlo's birth family.

Melody moved into planning mode. "For music, what about "*Claire de Lune*" by Claude Debussy, and Frank Sinatra's "*Moon River?*' she asked. I am just now remembering now how much, early in your teenage years, you used to enjoy "*Endless Love*" by Diana Ross and Lionel Ritchie, and Otis Redding's "*My Lover's Prayer.*" "Those should be absolutely wonderful, "answered Danielle, "but we may need a few more, for specific aspects of the ceremony such as the Processional, the Registry Signing, the Recessional, and perhaps, for transitional music before the reception." Melody smiled tenderly, "You really have been thinking a lot about this event, haven't you love? Before we get further into music, have you both thought about your rings, witnesses, guests to be invited, your wedding gown, the reception menu, a good photographer attuned to the memories you wish to create, and your honeymoon location?" Danielle sighed. "I'm just beginning to realize what a major project this matter of marriage is, well before the stage of actually settling down with someone for the rest of your life and navigating the kind of hate speech issues that David and Alessia have had to face." Melody listened keenly to the quaver in her daughter's voice and asked her whether she was absolutely sure that Giancarlo was the man with whom she wanted to spend the rest of her life, to be met with Danielle's cheerful, positive response "Yes, mother, he's the one, and we had better be sure of each other, because you'll become a grandmother again before the year comes to an end!"

Several weeks earlier, Giancarlo and Danielle were completing a lunch of spicy lentil soup and *pasta arrabbiata* just outside a small Italian restaurant in Camden Town. Giancarlo was away from office on a project that was scheduled at a nearby client's office, and Danielle had just received word concerning the positive results of her recent interview, so they were celebrating with a bottle of Chianti. Smiling over the vase of violet hydrangeas on the table, Giancarlo proposed a toast to his still secret fiancée – "May today's success become one of many stepping stones that you take in your professional life." In response she blew him a kiss, then asked, "If the only difference between stepping stones and stumbling blocks is the way we use them, which best describes your forensic accounting at this stage?" Giancarlo tried to avoid a direct response while introducing a note of levity, by commenting that one of his colleagues seemed to be always sleeping at his desk, and when awakened, repeatedly explained that he regularly worked on his case files after dinner. However, a tabloid photo of the same gentleman cavorting in a well-known Piccadilly nightclub, during the early morning hours, which had made its way to the office last week, did not support his explanation. Nor did his regularly totally relaxed demeanor, while asleep at work, mouth open. Danielle persisted. "But are you doing your own work with all your heart and soul, so that you can feel a river of joy flowing within you?" Giancarlo looked at her more seriously. "My river of joy flows most fully when we are together." After enjoying a fork full of *pasta al dente* followed by wine, he added "When are we going to get married?" Danielle asked him, with a mix of anxiety and sensuality in her glance, "Is that a proposal?"

Giancarlo stood up somewhat theatrically, went over to her side of the table and kneeling down, held her left hand and asked her to marry him. When she hesitated for a few moments, he kissed her hand, then she stroked his wavy black hair, looked into his eyes, and nodded. Giancarlo clasped both her hands, lifted her up from her seat and enfolded Danielle in a passionate kiss, as many of the other restaurant patrons on the sidewalk cheered. Giancarlo ended up inviting her to visit his nearby home, noting that Paolo was at work, called his client to reschedule the previously arranged meeting, and the couple soon found themselves seated on his living room sofa, drinking limoncello and munching walnuts, as they began to discuss the implications of their decision. "How do your parents feel about David and Alessia's marriage now?" asked Danielle. "Do they know much about Oliver's disability?" Giancarlo was uncharacteristically serious, as he looked up at the staircase that had featured in Alessia's imprisonment in her old room, and her subsequent escape, already more than three years ago. "I was waiting in the library of a client's office in Belgravia last week, came across a book dealing with quantum mechanics, put it aside, then eventually opened it to encounter an interesting comment on change." Danielle looked at him in surprise. "It would never have occurred to me that you would have reopened and read any book on a topic so far removed from accounting!" Giancarlo smiled somewhat sheepishly and continued. "I forget the name of the author, but he wrote that *change is more often a rapid transition between stable states than a continuous transformation, at slow and steady states*." He went on to explain that this thought had remained in mind, because people either generate or are subjects of change, whether continuous or rapid. Just as it had been time for David and Alessia to build their lives together, and for his parents to accept this choice, it was now their turn to promptly create a new 'steady state' of mutual love, support, and joy in the marriage they'd just agreed upon.

Giancarlo hastened to add that he realized she would probably prefer a civil ceremony rather than marriage in a Catholic church. In the silence that followed for a moment, Danielle told him that this was correct, but if it would help his family to adjust, she could live with a subsequent religious ceremony, in due course. She looked outside at the cerulean blue sky with stratus clouds scudding by, finished her limoncello, sat up decisively, moved closer to him, then began to remove his bright yellow tie and unbutton his crisp white polyester shirt. "What are you doing?" he asked, somewhat taken aback. "I'm removing your clothes to examine my husband-to-be properly," Danielle said pertly, as she inverted Giancarlo's prior erotic reveries, and he sat passively in pent-up tension, unsure how to respond. In another few minutes, she had briskly removed his outer clothing, black wing-tipped shoes, and socks, and turned her attention, moving more slowly and attentively now, to his white cotton underwear. Lifting Giancarlo's turgid manhood out, she stroked and eyed him appreciatively, for the first time, in the bright daylight coming through the bay windows, saying under her breath...."*so big and so beautiful*!" As Danielle examined him, after removing his underwear, Giancarlo became intensely excited – suddenly springing up, lifting her in his arms and carrying her up the staircase to his bedroom, where he lost no time in removing her dress and shoes, then placing her on his partly made-up, single bed. Making short work of her lacy underwear, he knelt between Danielle's outstretched legs, examined her admiringly in turn, and began to kiss her swollen vulva while reaching up to stroke her sensitive breasts. Even in her increasingly intense erotic haze, Danielle had the presence of mind to inquire whether he had a protective condom available, while repressing the questions that came to mind when Giancarlo nodded. He entered her with adoration, thinking of the life that they now intended to spend together – while taking a moment to look around his room critically, and to wish that he had made it tidier that morning. Danielle was increasingly lost in the sensation of his hard fullness rocking inside her, as he suckled her nipples and kissed her with abandon, ardor and passion rising to a series of ultimately shared orgiastic explosions that left them both drained. They relaxed in bed afterwards, sated, holding each other close and dozing. Only when the front door was opened, and Paolo called out "Are you here Giancarlo? Why is your clothing on the ground?" did they spring up. Giancarlo first helped Danielle to dress quickly then headed to the bathroom to remove his condom – only to return a minute later to say crestfallenly, to her puzzlement, "Somehow it broke."

David and Alessia returned from Hastings in good spirits, anxious to share their news about successful interviews and a home mortgage that had enabled them to make an accepted offer on their new Robertson Terrace home. However, they found Melody and Danielle engaged in excitedly planning a previously unexpected wedding that had already been scheduled with a Registrar in twenty-eight days.

After sharing their news in rapid fire fashion, the family settled down to a daily whirlwind of work, while arranging wedding gown fittings, guest lists and invitations, selecting a photographer, planning the reception menu and related music, and making hotel and honeymoon location choices – while teaming together to soothe the uncharacteristically recurrent anxieties and almost manic- depressive moods of the bride to be. It was only approximately a week before her wedding that Danielle realized with mixed feelings that she definitely was not an expectant mother, after all, and could settle down to focus upon her forthcoming marriage with Giancarlo, and her new job in the field of sustainable architecture, representing a passion pursued throughout her university studies. Meanwhile, David provided notice of his departure to the department store where he had been working and prepared to move to Hastings with Alessia and Oliver after Danielle's wedding. It was a time of high excitement and anticipation for the family, with the partial exception of Melody, who realized anew that in celebrating the expected joys of her children, she was also transitioning into a period when she would be living alone in the home that they were leaving. However, she buried such thoughts, at least for the time being, and concentrated upon helping Danielle with her wedding preparations, while continuing to encourage her son and his wife to enjoy Oliver as he was, and to count the blessings represented by the fruition of their plans for life in Hastings, several hours away by train.

On the day of the wedding, which was celebrated at a fashionable hotel in Kensington, a veiled Danielle was resplendent in her white wedding gown and Giancarlo positively glowed with anticipation in his best suit. This time, Paolo was his brother's best man and Melody, suppressing incipient tears, represented Joseph as well as herself in '*giving the bride away.*' She could not believe that both of the children created by Joseph and herself were now married adults, with spouses from the same Calabrian family, preparing to live their own lives, in their own homes. The Registrar reminded the couple that they were vowing to remain together, but not necessarily to remain the same persons, and that it was therefore important for marriage to bring together best friends. With gravity and efficiency, he then completed the civil ceremony within ten minutes and departed, leaving the reception to follow, heralded by artfully selected mood music, including the lambently soothing *Claire de Lune* and the lyrically stirring *Endless Love.* One of Giancarlo's younger aunts from Reggio di Calabria, a pleasant and quiet lady in fashionable Michael Kors glasses, with limited English, represented their parents and made a few comments intended to bless his union with Danielle. The bride was radiant, reflecting that she now had a husband who had also proven himself to be her best friend – someone who was present, patient, and compassionate. Giancarlo himself was remembering a quotation from Leo Tolstoy that his new wife had once shared with him – '*when you love someone truly, it is for the person they are, and not the person you would like them to be,*' thinking how very fortunate they were to have found each other. David and Alessia joined in congratulating the newly married couple warmly, with Oliver rocking in his stroller nearby, and most guests paused to tousle their baby's hair, commenting upon how well-behaved and good natured he was. Alessia's attention was attracted, for a while, by her son's serenity, as he took such affectionate gestures in stride. For a few moments, she reflected upon on her journey with him, from birth, to the eventual discovery of his disability, to acceptance, to deep, abiding love. However, the guests included an unassuming, now bespectacled Arkady, who had been tasked in detail through several loyal contacts by the still-imprisoned Benito with the pursuit of his yet remembered vendetta against Alessia and David. He remained nearby in the background, and as soon as Melody and Oliver's parents were distracted by an animated conversation, deftly and gently lifted the baby from his stroller, placed a sealed envelope there instead, and slipped away to his yellow Volkswagen automobile parked almost immediately outside, with temporarily altered licence plates.

Oliver quietly rocked in the front passenger baby seat, while Arkady made his way to the M-5 motorway, heading west to Cardiff. Arkady was prepared with milk formula in a thermos, as well as a nursing bottle, and diapers. He pulled off the motorway to add petrol to his vehicle and to feed Oliver after approximately two hours, while noticing with surprise that the baby neither cried nor spoke. However, he was pleased that he drank the offered milk without protest and relieved that there was evidently no need to change his diapers yet. Arkady took a moment to send Benito an indirect signal in the form of two mobile phone rings at a predetermined time, from a one-time use device specifically procured for the purpose, then discarded it carefully in a petrol station rubbish bin. Meanwhile, neither David nor Alessia registered the disappearance of Oliver for perhaps fifteen minutes. It was Melody who first noticed that his light blue blanket with a white fitted sheet were bundled up in the otherwise empty perambulator and called their attention to Oliver's absence. Both his parents immediately became absolutely frantic with anxiety and searched the hotel area allocated to the reception while attempting to avoid alarming the guests, or spoiling the occasion for Danielle and Giancarlo, who were dancing with abandon to the lyrics of *Moon River* and beaming.

It was David who looked more closely inside the perambulator, and found the envelope left by Arkady. He opened it with trembling fingers and read a message typed in capitals: *"We will know the instant that you bring your son's disappearance to the attention of the police, and that will be his last moment alive. On the other hand, if you wire £20,000 to the following bank account within five working days, he will turn up safe and sound at your mother's home shortly afterwards."* A series of SWIFT and account numerals completed the message.

Once it was evident that Oliver was really nowhere to be found, David located the telephone number of Detective Inspector Jeffries and connected to him quickly – but then had to identify himself more than once, before it became clear to the policeman who was calling. When he had completed his verbal report, the Detective told them somberly that it would have to be their decision whether to follow-up with a visit to the station to make a written and signed statement, as required by procedure. Detective Inspector Jeffries added that in the circumstances, he would be willing to meet them at an alternative location, such as a quiet restaurant – but in the light of past experience, although both Benito and Tomassini remained in prison, he could not guarantee that the threat made in the note could or would not be carried out. Both David and Alessia were visibly tense as he shared the conversation with her. By tacit agreement, the Armstrong family remained at the reception to support the newly married couple until they left for their honeymoon in the Lake District, buoyed by the celebration of their union – then David and Alessia left the hotel with Melody in silently shared shock, returning home together to her garden apartment near Alexandra Park.

Later that evening, David and Alessia talked in their bedroom, unable to sleep. The night felt warm. Oliver's kidnapping and the telephone call with Detective Inspector Jeffries pulled Alessia back to eidetic and distressing memories of her own abductions. David could readily feel her quiet quivering, as he tried to comfort her, even while commenting that the ransom specified was much more than they had jointly been able to set aside for their new home down payment, initial mortgage payment, furniture purchases, and other unavoidable expenses. In response, Alessia remarked that they had both been anxious and concerned about Oliver's autism spectrum disorder – but now that he had suddenly been taken away, leaving his painfully empty crib nearby, together with his forlorn perambulator and playpen downstairs, all she could think of was what a sweet, quiet, and handsome little son he was, and how desperately she wanted him back. David agreed and asked, "So, do you think we should take the Detective Inspector up on his offer to meet at a restaurant, or perhaps at some other discreet location?" Alessia noted that the evidently still active Acerra corporate criminal gang definitely seemed to have police informants, and that they had tried such a meeting before, without retaining the desired confidentiality, leading to an almost disastrous result. She shivered and David held her close, then asked, "What about an unusual location for such a meeting, such as the British Museum, or the National Portrait Gallery?" Alessia nodded slowly, "if Detective Inspector Jeffries and his staff are willing to meet with us at the National Portrait Gallery cafeteria on a weekend, in regular street clothing, that might work – but then again, we don't know how confidential our report would remain within the Department, once filed." At this stage, they were resting in bed with Alessia's head on David's chest. The full moon shone through their window, and the arctic white moonlight spread across them in a benediction that might normally have felt romantic. Crickets chirped nearby. They were startled by a sudden knock on the door, which was opened carefully by Melody, bearing a tray of steaming tea cups with biscuits. "I heard you talking, realized that we were all struggling to rest tonight, and thought to bring you a snack," she said. David and Alessia sat up immediately, pulled a chair and table up to the bed, urging Melody to put her tray down and to be seated. As they all sipped tea, she inquired what they were thinking of doing, in response to Oliver's kidnapping that day and the callous ransom note. She eventually agreed that Alessia's idea as to meeting location and timing might well work, while noting that it remained the case that '*we don't know what we don't know.*' Melody tried to talk about Oliver in a positive manner, observing that his abductor had probably been very disconcerted to realize his disability, and might well end up attempting returning her grandson to his family, regardless of whether any ransom payment was made or not.

After a while, Melody took her tray of emptied cups and saucers back to the kitchen downstairs, and they all retired once more, eventually on this occasion, to restless sleep and exhausting dreams. In the drizzling grey of the next morning, David called Detective Inspector Jeffries again, and ended up agreeing to meet with him in the cafeteria of the National Portrait Gallery on the following Saturday morning, in two days' time. During that time, Melody felt as if she were viewing the world through split screens. She cleaned the rooms of her house obsessively, cooked more extensively than usual in an effort to provide David and Alessia with particularly enjoyable dinners, felt the aching loss of Oliver in her bones – and received regular calls from Danielle, who was thoroughly enjoying her honeymoon with Giancarlo in the Lake District, and wanted to share many of the highlights with her mother. These included long walks in the morning mists before breakfast, a memorable climb all the way up Crinkle Crags, a picnic lunch of fish and chips with rosé wine on the shores of Derwentwater, savory seafood dinners by candlelight at restaurants in Cockermouth and Penrith - and her partially successful efforts to train her unexpectedly reticent husband to become somewhat more adventurous in their lovemaking, while ensuring that they remained in no danger of becoming parents yet. Melody still felt unable to share Oliver's abduction with Danielle, wishing her to remain focused upon her honeymoon, and as his parents had the same concern, there appeared to be no chance that this unwelcome news could come to her daughter's attention.

Melody listened to Danielle's calls encouragingly, hoping that her ebullient spirits and evident enjoyment of married life would not be evanescent, very pleased at their free flow of communication, yet unsure that she really wanted to know all the coupling details now being uncharacteristically shared without reserve.

David and Alessia were soon once again seated with an informally dressed Detective Inspector Jeffries, this time in a quiet corner of the National Portrait Gallery cafeteria, drinking lukewarm Robusta coffee, while David painstakingly wrote a detailed statement concerning the circumstances of Oliver's kidnapping. When in response to a query he added his son's age of almost three years old, Alessia's breath caught in her throat, as she almost sobbed. At a signal from the detective, a plain-clothed colleague waiting nearby came forward to witness David's statement when it was completed, without being provided with an opportunity to read the lines of the yellow legal notebook, then withdrew. When the subsequent discussion turned to details of Oliver's autism spectrum disorder, Alessia excused herself to visit the restroom, where she wept uncontrollably for perhaps ten minutes, before collecting herself, repairing her makeup as best she could, and returning to the cafeteria, where she found David waiting for her alone. He hugged and kissed her and suggested that they take the opportunity to browse some of the historical portraits in the collection for relaxation. They paused before several interesting portraits, such as those of the actress Anouk Aimée, the dancer, Kyra Alanova, Alfred the Great, King of the West Saxons, Anastasia, Grand Duchess of Russia, and the boxer Mohammad Ali, before returning home somberly. That evening, they did their best to demonstrate appreciation for the dinner that Melody had prepared, beginning with a vegetable crabcake salad, followed by a cedar plank-baked salmon with risotto and cheese- coated green beans, and a dessert of cinnamon custard. By way of expressing gratitude, after dinner, David took out his acoustic guitar, sat on the sofa between Alessia and Melody, and played *"Ave Maria"* for them, succeeded by selections from Vivaldi's *"Four Seasons,"* Massenet's haunting *"Méditation of Thais,"* and Debussy's *"Claire De Lune."* Both his mother and his wife placed a hand around his waist as he played, in silent appreciation, shared support and solace, sometimes accompanied by rapt attention as the sonorous chords of his instrument filled the living room. As he set aside the guitar, he hugged them both.

On the fourth working day after Oliver's abduction, Detective Inspector Jeffries telephoned David with an update – that a CCTV recording at an M-5 petrol station had an image of a man, apparently alone with a baby in a front car seat; however, a separate recording of the five-seater vehicle's licence plate had led to a dead end; and that both Benito and Tomassini had been questioned in prison, using a lie detector, without any dependable results. He promised to provide another update as soon as there was further information to report.

That same day, Arkady received a brief call instructing him to *"get rid of the package immediately."* At approximately 6:30 pm the following day, after David and Alessia had returned from work, showered together, and were changing their clothing, a sudden noise just outside the front door caught their attention. David hastened downstairs to investigate, as Alessia was still dressing, and Melody was in the kitchen. A brown paper wrapped parcel of some 3' x 3' x 1' in dimensions with a white ribbon lay on the floor outside, with no discernible label. He hesitated, thinking that it might be an explosive of some kind, then turned it over gingerly, still without encountering any information as to the addressee or the sender. Alessia arrived to join him, agreed on the need for caution, but untied the ribbon and prodded the box gently. David looked at her wryly, "If this were an explosive, I imagine it would have gone off already," then removed the wrapping and opened the box inside – only to gasp in absolute horror and to sit on the floor suddenly, head in hands, as he discovered Oliver's lifeless body inside, his throat sliced open, with rigid limbs and dried bloodstains on his little white embroidered shirt. Melody ran to join them, hearing

Alessia's piercing screams interspersed with shuddering sobs, as she lay face down on the floor. Despite feeling completely shocked and dazed, it was Melody who took charge, lifting the box and bringing it inside to a living room table, then gently persuading each parent to retire to the living room sofa where they had been sitting listening to David's acoustic guitar the night before, and closing the front door, as several alarmed neighbors began to gather outside.

Alessia felt as if she were trying to run from a blazing inferno that was inexorably gaining on her. David was also struggling with a waking nightmare, feeling as if he were attempting vainly to run and hide from an inchoate danger, without success. Melody helped them to get up, and slowly led them, one by one, to their bedroom upstairs, closed the curtains, and encouraged them to support each other in their searing grief. She then stepped outside to explain to the still waiting neighbors that her family had just received some bad news that would be shared with them later.

Afterwards, Melody called the local police station to report what had happened, mentioning Detective Inspector Jeffries' name as the principal officer on the case, and telephoned an undertaker, to initiate arrangements for Oliver's funeral. It was only then that she looked at his little body in the cardboard box that had been covered with brown wrapping paper and wept in an armchair. Meanwhile, David regained some measure of self-control, and looked across the bed at Alessia, who was weeping more quietly now, lying on her back, eyes closed, tears streaming down her face. Her utter desolation spurred his efforts to remove her shoes and outer clothing, then to embrace her gently, rocking her gently in his arms, wordlessly. At some point, he realized that calls needed to be placed to their workplaces with explanations as to their absences that day. He postponed action and hugged Alessia, now finally able to vocalize his intended comforting. When she eventually dozed off, exhausted by the intensity of her grief, David covered her with a silk bedsheet, arose, and went downstairs where he encountered Melody, who seemed to be staring blankly into space. He first covered the body of his murdered son with a blue blanket from his nearby playpen, and kneeling beside his dazed mother, stroked her hands and her hair, until she looked at him and said, "Oliver was just here in that high chair in the dining room a few days ago, when I last gave him crushed pear baby food and milk. Now he's gone..." David told her that at least, Oliver would have had no recognition of what was occurring and that it would all have been over very quickly. Melody sighed deeply, shook her head, and updated her son as to what she had been able to do so far. Her report represented a catalyst for David, who got up, telephoned the department store where he was still completing his month of departure notice, as well as his wife's bank branch, and explained their inability to come to work as best he could. He then called Detective Inspector Jeffries, who had already been alerted as to Oliver's demise, and was ready with sincere if embarrassed condolences, while also reporting that a determined and thorough search for the despicable informant within the force was now under way. David retained sufficient presence of mind to retort that he had understood such a search to have been conducted after his wife's abduction. In response, the detective commented that it had not yet been established that the same criminal gang was responsible and remarked that since his office would need an autopsy report, one of his associates would arrange for this, then contact him later that day. David thanked the detective somewhat curtly and ended the telephone call, now impelled by a measure of cold, bitter anger and utter frustration.

A few days later, Giancarlo was sitting with Danielle on the grass near the shores of Derwentwater, in a more secluded location than before, after completing a picnic luncheon of shepherd's pie and apple cider, followed by ruddy red strawberries. He felt replete, as Danielle's head rested in his lap, and reflected upon their almost completed honeymoon. It was still hard to believe that they were actually married, after such a prolonged 'secret' engagement period, based on her request. He considered himself to be an extraordinarily fortunate man, to have such an accomplished, beautiful, and passionate young lady as his wife, and realized that he was still in the process of attempting to understand many aspects of her evidently quite extrovert personality. Meanwhile, Danielle was relaxing, eyes closed, enjoying the scent of daffodils, peonies and asters, the sturdy, muscular body of her still new husband, and his eagerness to please her, despite his apparent, previously unexpected reticence, where sensual matters were concerned. In the present situation, for instance, she wished that he would open her blouse and caress her already partially aroused breasts without being asked to do so and sighed audibly. She was surprised and pleased when, after looking at her with concern for a few moments, Giancarlo appeared to divine her ardent thoughts, and set out put them into practice, if somewhat clumsily. As one loving caress led to another, Giancarlo soon found himself intensely engaged in making love with his bride on the grass, after hastily glancing around to reassure himself that no one else was nearby. Later, they sat, looking out at the cerulean blue water of the lake, and talked about their plans to accept Melody's invitation to live with her for at least a few months, until they could rent or even purchase a home of their own, in a reprise of the plans previously made by David and Alessia. When Danielle asked whether he wanted to have a Catholic convalidation ceremony anytime soon, he shook his head. Giancarlo commented that he had been learning a few words of Mandarin Chinese from a client and had been particularly struck by the way in which a change in tone made the same word mean different things. He cited the example of '*ai ren*,' which could mean wife or lover, and added that he hoped to have both in her for the rest of his life. When Danielle inquired as to whether he had also learnt the Mandarin Chinese phrase for husband or lover, he shook his head again, and they both chuckled. As they continued gazing at the sunlight breaking through the cumulus clouds above Derwentwater, with lambent reflections on the plashing lake, Danielle was thinking about her first sustainable architecture projects as an employee and reflected that from the drafted form of a building to its implementation, she would be always dealing with diagrams of forces, from the perspective of physics. She sat up, still partially nude, and shared her thought with Giancarlo, adding that the abstract patterns of the physical universe were more concrete than the things we can feel or touch. He nodded, then kissed her yet upright left nipple, commenting that while she did not feel like an abstract pattern to him at all, he understood her point. They laughed readily together and prepared to leave their picnic location as a light drizzle began, with wispy mist rising over the water.

It was not until two days later, after arrival at Melody's house, that Giancarlo and Danielle finally learnt what had happened to Oliver. They were thunderstruck, and initially very angry not to have been told about his abduction before leaving on their honeymoon. Melody reached over to her daughter as they were all seated at the dining table, patted her hand, then got up to hug her. "Dear Danielle and Giancarlo – you both deserve to have had the lovely honeymoon that I've been hearing about, without involvement, before it became unavoidable, in dealing with the very sad events that have now led to the murder of my grandson." As Melody regained her seat, tears trickled down her face, and now it was Danielle's turn to get up and to hug her mother from behind. When Alessia began to weep also, giving way to paroxysms of grief, David turned to her, hugging, and kissing her, and stroking her hair, until she had regained sufficient composure to join her family in completing dinner. During the next few weeks, despite the bleak continuing sadness occasioned, but perhaps also soothed by the elegiac funeral in Highgate at which Oliver's short life was celebrated, Melody felt a measure of fulfilment, as her home was fully occupied by her children and their spouses for the first time. She woke up each morning with a sense of purpose, eager to do all that she could to help them through their days. Melody occupied herself in busily cleaning her home until it sparkled, cooking appetizing meals – now often based upon culinary experiments - in the kitchen, in regular grocery shopping trips, and in pruning her bountiful rose bushes almost all the time, apart from continuing volunteer work at the local nursing home, where she was now regarded as something of a celebrity because of her impactful reading.

It was suddenly time for David and Alessia to move to Hastings and to take up their new employment. Melody did her best to be quietly encouraging, despite her dismayed realization that it would not be too long before Giancarlo and Danielle would also *'spread their wings'* and relocate to a home of their own. On their last day at work in London, Alessia's bank colleagues held a crowded farewell reception in a small, somewhat warm ballroom at a nearby hotel. As family members were included in the invitation, David attended, and was eventually recognized by a few of his former colleagues, including the dour manager who had ended his employment. They both shook hands and pretended to meet for the first time, with Alessia posing in between, and feigning smiles for several photographs. Despite her genuine gratitude for the abundance of good wishes offered to her, Alessia remained deeply disconsolate. While sipping a glass of sparkling Dom Perignon champaign, David and his spouse held each other's hands for mutual support. He stroked her long, brunette hair and told her that she was looking all the more lovely that day – during the current reception, and at an earlier department store luncheon where she'd encountered associates only mentioned by her husband previously - because of the inimitable mixture of abiding sorrow and irrepressible anticipation in her eyes. Alessia responded with her first unalloyed smile since Oliver had been abducted, and commented "who would have thought when we met at the bank only five years ago that we would have fallen so very deeply in love, married despite the difficulties posed by my brothers and parents, and that we would have encountered so much cherished joy and rapture combined with such profound distress and recurrent trauma along the path of our lives?" David answered that he would gladly re-live those years with her again, without any hesitation, because of the treasured joys that she had mentioned. Alessia looked up at him adoringly, tears sparkling again in her grey eyes – but of an entirely different kind – and stroked his right cheek.

When Giancarlo visited Paolo and his elder brother inquired why he had chosen to live with Danielle in her mother's house, rather than in the three-bedroom home in Camden Town where they had all lived since their arrival in London from Reggio di Calabria, Giancarlo smiled, and advised him once again to get married soon. He added that the apartment was looking more and more like a '*bachelor's pad*' now, with clothing scattered in the living room and dishes stacked in the kitchen sink. Paolo laughed, with the rejoinder that he clearly had not been upstairs recently, then added with a twinkle in his eyes, "speaking of clothing in the living room, you never did explain why you left your clothing mostly on the floor, evidently in a rush, that day when Danielle was visiting." Giancarlo responded with the remark that it was a pity Mrs. Armstrong didn't have at least one more daughter so that the Amato and Armstrong families in London could complete the trifecta with three weddings instead of only two. He added one of his trademark jokes, "By the way, what would you say is the height of laziness?" When Paolo shook his head dismissively, Giancarlo continued, "how about dreaming about sleeping?"

More seriously, he remarked that Danielle had been encouraging him to read a range of literature he'd not encountered before, including a wise author, Rabindranath Tagore. One of his interesting sayings was…" *you can't cross the sea merely by standing and staring at the water.*" "So, when are you planning to cease staring at the water?" he asked. Paolo changed the subject, asking when Giancarlo planned to take Danielle to meet their parents, to encounter the reminder that she'd already met their mother, father, and other family members, when they all visited with David and

Alessia. As the brothers were talking, there was a knock on the front door, and Paolo opened it to find the couple under discussion, coming to say goodbye before relocating to their new home in Hastings. When invited in, David remarked upon having learned from Danielle that Giancarlo might be visiting his brother that afternoon, and Alessia asked her siblings when they might be able to come to a '*house warming*' which would almost be on the beach. Everyone laughed, then the mood of the gathering suddenly changed, as Paolo extended his deepest condolences on Oliver's death, then trailed off, realizing how inadequate to the situation the words seemed, and they sat in awkward silence in the living room for a while.

Melody sat in her bedroom room reading "*A Tale of Two Cities*" by Charles Dickens in the mid-morning. She began by thinking that it might be a good choice for her next visit to the nursing home where she continued to volunteer, but the opening sentences speaking of the best and worst of times, infused by wisdom and folly as well as light and darkness, stopped her in her tracks with their evocative paradoxes. In her mind's eyes, her marriage to Joseph was beginning, at least sometimes, to blur with the nuptials of David and Alessia, as well as Danielle and Giancarlo – and she paused to reassure herself that dinner had been cooked and set aside for the latter couple, who should be returning from work that evening. In one of her dressing table drawers, she still had a folder with some of Alessia's paintings, including one of Melody herself as a seated, smiling matron, sunlight streaming through the windows – but also, dark, melancholy landscapes with shadowed cemeteries and oblique tombstones, almost as if her daughter-in- law had had a presentiment concerning Oliver's death. She reminded herself to return these striking watercolors at the next opportunity, when Alessia was visiting with David. During their last visit, she had wondered whether her son might once again become a father soon but thought better of making any inquiries.

Their comments concerning life in Hastings suggested that both were enjoying the new jobs near their home there, as well as the opportunity to walk on the beach regularly. David seemed to be relishing banking as a manager, and Alessia's grey eyes glowed when talking about cognitive behavioral therapy applications. Melody returned to her reading, and paused again, upon encountering the phrase "*recalled to life*," describing Alexandre Manet's release from the Bastille in Paris, after eighteen years in prison. In a sense, life without Joseph had been a sentence of imprisonment, forcing her to discard dreams of rearing their children and of sharing life together, replacing them with the fortitude to bring up David and Danielle on her own. Would it were possible to change the course of their lives somehow, and to avoid that horrible construction site accident that so suddenly took Joseph away from her! But then, as Melody reminded herself, so many other aspects of life would have altered, including her access to the insurance provisions made by Joseph, as well as his employer, enabling her to fund the needs of their children. Life often resembled the chiaroscuro favored by Alessia in her paintings, and also appeared as a palimpsest, with past and present melding into one. Melody recalled an injunction by a recently read author, Paolo Coelho, "*Make peace with your past, so it cannot destroy your present,*" and consciously set out to lose herself in her "Tale of Two Cities," with such success that with the passing hours, she found herself at the end, bursting into empathetic, yet somewhat self-pitying tears while reading the final lines of Sidney Carton..."*It is a far, far better thing that I do than I have ever done; it is a far, far better rest that I go to than I have ever known.*" When Melody finally recovered herself, she realized that Giancarlo and Danielle should be home soon, so prepared to take a rapid shower and to change clothing before setting the table, as usual, to welcome them, while resolving to begin reading the riveting work of Dickens just completed to her audience at her next nursing home class.

David and Alessia had completed furnishing their home in Hastings and were sitting together on their favorite lime green sofa, her head rested in his lap, as they shared comments about their day at work. Alessia kicked off her shoes, stretched out her legs, and told him about her first consultancy presentation to a group of municipal mental health providers concerning cognitive behavioral therapy. As she began, her audience had appeared to be variously doubtful and bored, looking at their phones and whispering to each other, in a way that undermined her own self-confidence in the presentation she was about to make. Alessia reported that she took a deep breath and plunged into her lecture, telling her audience that although their non-verbal communication suggested little interest in the topic, making her disheartened, she had just completed the process of adjusting her own thoughts, so as to influence her own emotions and behavior, and to eliminate dysfunctional assumptions. She went on to tell the story, in vivid detail, of the time when she stood with her family, as a very young girl, outside their home in the very early morning, looking with dread at a neighbor's house blazing. By the time Alessia completed the story, she had the full attention of every member of the audience, as she explained that childhood memories, whether repressed or at least superficially accepted, can influence the way in which people perceive current events, and generate such intense anxiety and negative thoughts that self-fulfilling prophecies might well follow. David himself listened with increasing interest as she recounted having told her group about Oliver's death, if not all of the background details, and her own reactions to the situation as a young mother. By the time that she was explaining to the group best practices in coping with challenges such as dichotomous thinking, over- generalizing, and selective abstractions, by analyzing profoundly negative attitudes and feelings and converting them into ways of driving manageable, short-term goals that could help clients and patients to address specific problems in productive ways, she had them making notes at a rapid pace, while taking account of the citations, and other examples offered. David bent over and congratulated her, kissing her lips tenderly. "I've sometimes thought you might have had a tendency to blame yourself for Oliver's abduction and murder and I'm so relieved that you felt able to speak openly about your reactions with your group," he commented. "During the funeral in the cemetery at Highgate, you were evidently still so deeply stunned that you hardly looked at me, or anyone else. Alessia responded that while she had pulled herself up short, on occasion, when negative thoughts about her responsibility for such terrible events intruded, she had actually been more anxious, recently, about the potential for Benito and Tomassini to reach out again, through a gang member, to attack them in the future. David told Alessia that he agreed they should be alert to any further dangers of this kind – but also felt that the killing of their beloved little son would have caused them to experience such sufficient evil satisfaction and *schadenfreude* as to focus their attention elsewhere, at least, for now.

Alessia used one of her feet to stroke David's left leg and asked him whether his current role of bank manager was helping him to set aside his negative experiences at the Marylebone Village bank branch where they met, and to build a new sense of professional satisfaction. David nodded and remarked that the distance between the lived experience of a bank manager and a teller, even in the same branch, was much more significant than he'd previously thought. He mentioned his full accountability during weekly review meetings at regional headquarters for a set of quantitative targets, such as gross and net profit, and strategic expense reduction as well as strategic revenue enhancement. At the same time, there were so many business environment constraints, including interest rates, the national and local levels of unemployment as well as inflation, electricity, gas, and water costs – and even the alacrity of the local Council, when it came to maintaining the roads in the vicinity of the branch. While recounting the staff workshops on customer service that he'd recently led, Alessia smiled broadly and inquired whether he remembered their own discussions about such workshops at the branch where they met. David sat up and lifted Alessia into his lap, facing him. "Sometimes, I still find myself thinking that all the years we've spent together so far must be a dream. How could that skinny, nervous, introverted young black man ever have attracted the interest of such an alluring young lady from southern Italy, with all the world at her feet?" Alessia held him close and kissed his face repeatedly. "The very first morning I saw you, so fashionably dressed and so clearly determined to do a good job at the bank, I thought that you probably would be a successful manager someday. But it is true that it never occurred to me that we could ever be a couple, or even close friends. For all of my prior adult life, I've thought vaguely about eventually getting married to someone from a family in Reggio di Calabria, who was familiar with our culture, food, society, and customs."

David smiled, took her hand, and kissed it, then massaged her shoulders gently. "So, what exactly changed your mind?" he asked. Alessia buried her face against his chest. "I think there were several significant occasions," she answered – for instance, the day we had a picnic in Hyde Park, when it was so very relaxing to talk with you; then the afternoon when we were sitting on a bench in a little park near the restaurant where you were working, and you kissed me for the first time." David placed his hands under her cream- colored blouse with three large, decorative pink buttons on either side and stroked her back. "I remember those occasions very well," he commented. "I thought that you really seemed to have no idea how attractive you were and was so outraged when you told me how that fellow Benito had captured your hand in a rude manner, during a movie, with Paolo sitting right next to you both." Alessia and David hugged each other tightly. She murmured, "My hero! Sometimes I dream about the time you suddenly appeared with boxes of pizzas in hand, at the door of the room where Tomassini had tied me naked to the bed, when I was feeling so helpless, thinking we'd likely never see each other again..." David smiled. "And I remember my extreme shock, seeing you there, believing you must have been raped – then escaping with you in a bedsheet through the window, down the fire escape, with those fellows shooting at us..." Alessia murmured, "You really were so very brave, coming to rescue me all by yourself, with bare hands!" They continued hugging each other for a while, before retiring to bed.

Melody had recently added some cyclamen with sheer purple petals to her garden, and was admiring the effect, shovel in hand, with watering can nearby, when she felt an unusual sense of fulness and discomfort in her lower abdomen, as well as a slight pain in her back. Later that evening, when she discussed with Danielle what she dismissed as the result of recent stresses, her daughter grew serious and after inquiring whether her legs felt a little swollen, insisted that she make an appointment for a medical check-up at their local National Health Service clinic. Melody demurred at first, but eventually acquiesced, when Danielle demanded that she be allowed to make the appointment for her and go with her to the clinic. After arrival and registration, they both read magazines and newspapers for a long while in her General Practitioner's waiting room but were eventually called in for Melody's consultation. Dr. Creighton was an elderly man with a yellow bow tie and a white coat, who listened to her intently and sympathetically, then took her to his screened examination table, and palpated her groin. He then asked a series of questions concerning Melody's eating, bowel, and bladder habits, and ended up recommending that she see an oncologist.

Danielle seemed to be more worried by the referral than her mother, who continued to insist that she was in generally good health and reminded her daughter that the entire family had been through a great deal in recent years, arguing that there was absolutely nothing to worry about. That evening, however, Danielle insisted upon taking her place in the kitchen, and prepared a meal of spaghetti bolognese for Giancarlo and Melody.

It was only later, at night while attempting to settle down to sleep that Melody began to reflect upon Dr. Creighton's expression as she answered his questions, and to wonder whether she might really require specialist medical attention and diagnosis. She eventually found herself dreaming about Joseph, as she did quite regularly – but on this occasion, they appeared to be searching unsuccessfully for each other within a thorny maze. Melody awoke out of this nightmare with a start and ended up descending to the kitchen to make a hot cup of cocoa, which she sipped in an armchair, while thinking about Giancarlo's recent comment that he was negotiating an advance in compensation from his employer, so Danielle and he could make a down payment on an apartment near London Bridge. She had responded to this news with smiling encouragement, while beating back unarticulated questions as to why her daughter and son-in-law could not make themselves comfortable in her large, three-bedroom home for at least a while longer, and save on all such living costs. The momentary silence of the house seemed to bare its teeth, and then gentle sleep sounds from upstairs attracted her attention, as she completed her still hot beverage and returned to her room.

In the morning, Danielle woke first. She saw tentative fingers of yellow sunshine stretch across the white coverlet on her bed, to reach Giancarlo's half-covered back, and studied her husband as he slept, black hair tousled, breathing deeply, while reaching back to their honeymoon in the Lake District, wondering, not for the first time, how she had ended up with such a charming, vibrant, yet somewhat shy and thoughtful Caucasian man, who also happened to be her brother-in-law, from a southern Italian family. Danielle's mind wandered to some of the shared experiences of David and Alessia, who had sometimes been treated rudely while traveling on the tube or bus, or even while walking, and braced herself against similar experiences. She also retraced her steps, in her mind's eye, to the afternoon spent with Alessia in Alexandra Park, when they were discussing the nature of love. Danielle recalled that Alessia had spoken of mutual understanding, appreciation, and acceptance – she reworded the latter as tolerance – thought about her sister-in-law's vividly evocative description of lovemaking and measured her remarks against her evolving experience with Giancarlo. She didn't always understand him, but certainly accepted all of his aspects in full, tolerated attitudes and behavior that seemed strange, and regularly enjoyed their shared passion, without reserve. As she revisited the comments made by the GP who had examined her mother at the clinic, Danielle felt a twinge of dread, and almost shivered in the warmth of the morning – then arose and went to the kitchen to prepare breakfast. She was anxious about Melody's health and convinced that she had been working too hard at home. Danielle was also concerned about her brother and her sister-in-law, who were both evidently still trying to recover from Oliver's murder, thinking of the times when Alessia sometimes tended to smile in a brittle manner, and to speak more softly than usual, while David's hair was already beginning to show sprinkles of white. She settled down to prepare omelette, toast with cream cheese, and coffee for breakfast, and hugged her mother when she appeared. "You made dinner last night and now you've made breakfast. Do you think that I'm an invalid?" asked Melody irritably. Danielle hastened to reassure her that it was simply her wish to be more helpful, as Giancarlo arrived at the table as well.

Paolo completed a long, warm shower and dressed, feeling vaguely unhappy as he gloomily contemplated his parents' framed wedding photograph on the wall, when he went downstairs. Now that both Alessia and Giancarlo were married and living elsewhere, he felt perennially lonely, missing even his brother's bizarre jokes, and coping with a gnawing regret that his positive intentions to guide his sister's life appropriately had caused her so much cumulative pain and deep distress, now including the malicious murder of his baby nephew. Paolo was certain that Benito and Tomassini were implicated if not incriminated in the latest atrocity against Alessia and her husband. He suddenly realized that their parents had been told of Oliver's birth, but neither informed about his autism spectrum disorder nor his demise. As he ate breakfast alone and prepared to go to work at the bookstore in Tottenham Court Road, his thoughts ran on an elegant young lady in a fashionable blue dress with a silver belt, who had said that she was from Ancona, while talking with the bookshop's owner, who was also an Italian, from Turin. She had asked for Paolo's assistance in finding a book entitled "Letters on Familiar Matters" by Petrarch, as well as Gibbon's "Decline and Fall of the Roman Empire," with a lovely smile that enchanted him, even as he attempted to refocus upon shelving books, telling himself that it was very likely he would never see her again.

But she had returned later in the previous week to browse through assorted novels by Elena Ferrante in the basement of the bookshop. Paolo had been glad to see her, if only briefly, on each occasion, while berating himself for having no idea how to convert their brief conversations into an invitation to go out with him. As she ascended the winding metal stairs to the ground floor, evidently with the intention of leaving, Paolo followed her and asked in desperation, "What made you so interested in the history of the Roman empire?" She countered piquantly, "And there I was thinking that you wanted to bring the works of other potentially interesting Italian authors to my attention!" He stammered, taken aback, and eventually asked her for her name, and why she was so interested in Italian literature and history. In response, she extended her hand, which he took awkwardly, and introduced herself as Isabella Rosetti, then explained that she was a writer. Paolo recovered sufficient confidence to introduce himself in turn, and to inquiry as to some of the books she had published. Isabella laughed, saying "Alas, I am a yet unpublished writer." The attention of Matteo, the bookshop owner, was attracted by her vibrant laughter, as they were talking near the exit, and he called to Paolo, asking him to see him when he had a moment. In the flurry of customers coming in and departing, Paolo felt desperate at the thought of losing the opportunity to see her again. Gathering his courage, he asked how he could contact her so they could talk again. In a quite matter of fact manner, Isabella gave Paolo a business card and said goodbye.

Danielle was working late into the evening on a rendering of a sustainable residence, using a combination of bricks, alloy steel, and wood, having called Giancarlo to explain her plan to complete a project in order to take the next morning off, so she could accompany her mother to her appointment with an oncologist. Her hands skillfully completed the depiction with a few rapid strokes, and after a final review, Danielle filed the document and allowed herself to sit for a few moments, head in her hands, as she worried about Melody's health. At that moment, her mother was setting the dinner table, after arriving from an exhilarating reading to her 'students' from "A Tale of Two Cities," and preparing a meal of spicy curried beef with vegetables and rice. Turning to Giancarlo, who was watching the television news on the living room sofa, she inquired whether he knew how much longer Danielle would take in arriving home. After obligingly calling his wife again, he reported that she should be arriving by taxicab within thirty minutes. Meanwhile, Giancarlo complimented Melody on the aroma wafting from her kitchen, saying that it seemed to be redolent of Jamaica, and tried out one of his trademark jokes. "Did you ever hear the one about a mother who always told her son – '*never do anything that you'll regret later in life?*' He thought it was the most wonderful advice he'd ever received, and had it tattooed on his forehead." To Giancarlo's deep gratification, Melody laughed outright, and told him that he had shared one of the most amusing jokes she'd ever heard.

Since they were benefiting from a long summer evening, Melody decided to prune some of her roses, and was enjoying this activity when she paused, noticing a recurrence of discomfort in her lower abdomen. It was at this point, pruning shears paused in hand, when Danielle arrived, greeted her mother, looked at her expression, and gently led her inside. The next morning, she traveled by taxicab with Melody to St Thomas Hospital at London Bridge, helped her to register in the Urology Department, and again sat with her in a waiting room – on this occasion, there were few magazines or newspapers but an array of charts on the walls, with views of internal human organs. Melody deliberately pushed away her memories of being told where Joseph's body had been taken, following his workplace accident, although they kept returning. After another long wait, mostly in silence, they were ushered in to see the oncologist in residence, who took Melody behind a screen to palpate her abdomen and to ask a series of questions, then established that she was post menopause, before ordering an MRI report, leading to another wait. Danielle began to feel torn between her desire to remain with her mother, and her stated plans to be at work by midday. In the event, the MRI test was completed, and the report made available to her mother's oncologist by 1:00 pm. During a follow-up appointment soon after that time, they were given the confirmed diagnosis of advanced ovarian cancer and engaged in a quite unexpected discussion of whether surgery could do any good, or whether palliative treatment would be the best option. Noticing her daughter's stricken face, Melody pulled herself together, and calmly asked several questions. In the light of the answers provided, she declined surgery in writing, accepted a palliative treatment plan, and after thanking the oncologist, silently led

Danielle out to the taxicab rank in front of the hospital so they could return home.

Today, Melody listens to a recorded musical playlist put together by David, including several of his acoustic guitar presentations that she has heard in person before. It is raining outside, and she is pleased that her flowers, as well as all the plants and trees in the vicinity, are being revitalized. She is looking out through the open door and thinking, as she often does, about the first day when Joseph took her to the beach in Montego Bay, where they ended up spending many hours. Melody remembers swimming with her then future husband most of the way out to the reef and back, followed by coconut water and crackers – perhaps they also enjoyed goat cheese? - for lunch as they sat on the jetty and talked, subconsciously learning that they truly enjoyed each other's company, even as she was telling herself that he probably had several ladies in his life, and was unlikely to seek her out again. A bus passes on the road outside, the noisy torque of its engine increasing as it climbs the hill towards Alexandra Park.

As the sound fades away, Melody returns to that shimmering day at the beach with Joseph, as they swim out together again towards the reef, enjoying the restless blue-green waves, with the sun beginning to set. Since her oncologist had gently explained that her ovarian cancer was so far advanced that her remaining life expectancy ranged from a few months to a year at most, she had been tempted by both David and Danielle's urgings to get a second opinion; but then, found herself feeling '*in her bones*' that the prognosis provided was correct. So, she told her family, now including Alessia and Giancarlo, that she wanted to enjoy the remainder of her days as much as possible, rather than going from clinic to clinic, or hospital to hospital, in search of a perhaps somewhat more encouraging evaluation. To her surprise, Melody felt liberated by this decision. It took several days for her to convince her family that she should continue her nursing home readings, house cleaning and cooking routines, as well as gardening, but they eventually arrived at a reluctant acceptance of her response. Danielle and Giancarlo ceased to mention the need for a new home. David and Alessia visited more frequently from Hastings and spent entire weekends at Melody's home.

During weekdays alone, she listened to music, read even more widely than before, spent more time volunteering at her adopted nursing home, tended her beloved roses, even put in a new bed of yellow chrysanthemum and violet hydrangeas, and regularly walked down *memory lane* in the adored company of Joseph. One of the quotations she had read somewhere, without recalling the author, enjoyed, and adapted, as she was only middle-aged, although much of her hair was already white - was that "*old age provides a breathing space before we die, in which to see why we did what we did.*" Thinking of a recent conversation with Danielle, she wondered whether, had she been born into Hinduism, exactly how the balance of energies she had generated during her life would have impacted her next cycle of existence. Now and then, Melody looked curiously at herself in her bathroom mirror, and recognized her reflection mainly by her eyes.

One weekend afternoon, when both couples were at Melody's home, insisting upon helping her to prepare dinner in the kitchen, and ending up with a mélange of beef soup with dumplings and green bananas, ciambotta or eggplant stew, and risotto with sauteed shrimp, there was a sudden knock on the door. Alessia removed her apron and opened the door to find her brother Paolo, accompanied by a strange young lady in a bright yellow pencil skirt and a cream blouse with pink ruffles. After hugging his sister, Paolo introduced her as the writer, Isabella Rosetti, who immediately turned on him, saying, "How many times have I told you not to introduce me in that way?" Alessia greeted her, saying whatever her profession, she was welcome, and invited them to be seated on the living room sofa – then wondered for a moment whether she might have committed a *faux pas*, in her turn, given her elder brother's long-confirmed single status. Everyone, including Melody, came out to greet them, and invited the guests to dinner, which was almost ready. Alessia and Danielle took turns helping Melody in the kitchen and setting the table, while David and Giancarlo offered them aperitifs, and tacitly agreed to defer any inquiries about Paolo's relationship with Isabella until dinner was served.

However, looking around the living room, she inquired why all the ladies of the house were in the kitchen, and all the gentlemen seated with her friend and herself. An uncomfortable silence ensued for a few seconds, then the query become moot, as a hearty soup appetizer was served. Once they settled down to eat, accompanying the dinner with a Chianti brought by Giancarlo, he toasted the guests, and asked Paolo to explain how he had met Isabella. They looked at each other, and she smilingly remarked that it might be better for her to begin the requested response. "I visited one of my favorite bookstores in Tottenham Court Road one day, looking for some volumes needed for my research, and encountered a tall, striking but very shy man, who set out to help me. He did so, quite effectively, and a few days later, I returned to the shop, hoping to see him again. But Paolo was so tongue-tied that even though he had every opportunity to ask me out, he could not bring himself to do so, until the very last moment as I was leaving...." Paolo took up the story at this point, and commented that he might have a slightly different perspective on their initial meeting, but was delighted to add that when he telephoned Isabella to invite her to a play at the National Theatre, she accepted, and that they had been going out together every weekend, to locations that even included his favorite pub. Isabella picked up the narrative again..."He eventually mustered the courage to kiss me only after imbibing a few pints in that pub. At any rate, we are now enjoying each other's company, and I'm very glad to finally meet Paolo's family. By the way, I'm currently a marketing manager for a publishing house, and when not on the job or with Paolo, spend practically all my time working on my first novel." They all praised the entrees, followed by Alessia's crème brulée. After dinner, David entertained the family for a while with his acoustic guitar, on condition that they all sang along with him, to melodies such as "*Country Roads*." As the evening came to an end, with the departure of Paolo and Isabella, Melody retired to bed early, and was eventually followed by two sets of very concerned couples.

The following day, Melody finally remembered where she had packed away an old photograph album, consisting mainly of black and white landscape photographs that she had taken in the vicinity of Montego Bay. She paused, stunned, to encounter a photo that she had taken of Joseph at the beach, struggling to remember when, and how exactly that day had unfolded. He looked so tall, strong, and proud that she found herself in a reverie, taking her back to their first night and morning together, after their wedding. However, she really could not recall any details of the beach day recorded in her antique album with faded mauve covers. Melody found another photograph, this time depicting them both during their wedding ceremony, and was lost again in seas of wide-ranging thoughts and feelings, like serried waves swelling to the shore. In the photo, she could discern her parents in the background, and could just about recognize herself, in the clearly shy, so very serious young girl in her white wedding veil, looking up with obvious adoration at her husband to be. Melody reflected, in passing, that Joseph had truly introduced her, over time, to so many important ideas – including the caution that a way of seeing was a way of not seeing. She recognized that some of the remaining photographs had been made during their early years in Brixton, one taking her back to the view from her kitchen window, where she had spent so much time and energy in preparing family meals.

Realizing that only a few faded landscape views remained, Melody closed her photograph album and her eyes, sitting quietly for a few moments, and then replaced it exactly where it had been found in her dressing table drawer.

Melody increasingly experienced bloating, enjoying her meals less and less, while sometimes sharing her abnormal discharges and worsening back pains with Danielle. On the other hand, her soul soared in her dreams, which regularly revolved around her early days and years with Joseph as the youthful, vibrant man who had taken her swimming at sunset, while enthralling her with his thoughts, fusing their bodies with incredibly erotic love, and infusing her very soul. As the weeks passed, she found herself perceptibly weaker physically, if energized from time to time by the thought that she might well be eventually reunited with her husband in some other dimension of human experience.

At her request, David took Melody to see a nearby attorney, who helped her to create a witnessed will, leaving her house with its contents to Danielle and Giancarlo, and her savings as well as an investment account to her son. A coruscating kaleidoscope of assorted memories came to her unbidden, now and then - she once again visited David in a neighbor's basement where he was hiding after fleeing from a supermarket, and returning to much earlier years, asked her mother why her red ginger flowers were always dying, after blooming in such bountiful, serried clusters.

As the weeks went by, Melody remained active, but learnt to hide her intense discomfort to avoid stressing her family. She was still reading "A Tale of Two Cities" to her nursing home audience. When her voice faltered from time to time, they attributed this to her consummate skill in evoking the feeling behind the words, and never tired of listening. However, she ventured out to the nursing home less and less often, on the last occasion, only with David's assistance – despite telling him, almost angrily, that she could take a taxi there and then return by herself. One evening, Danielle returned home with Giancarlo after work, to find Melody lying on the kitchen floor, her body rigid, but her face serene, her solitary struggles ended. They lifted her gently to the living room sofa, and after calling David, Danielle perched at one end, hot tears coursing down her face, as she sobbed so uncontrollably that Giancarlo felt helpless to console her. However, when David and Alessia finally arrived, and they all hugged each other, Danielle calmed down as her brother murmured that it would comfort the family to believe that their parents' spirits had reunited and were now once again engaged in their favorite pastime of swimming towards a radiant island sunset. Alessia added that Melody had finally regained a truly peaceful sleep.

www.ingramcontent.com/pod-product-compliance
Lightning Source LLC
Chambersburg PA
CBHW020445130626
46549CB00001B/311
* 9 7 9 8 8 8 9 4 5 0 3 0 6 *